THE ROAD TO RUIN

James Rickards is the *New York Times* bestselling author of *The Death of Money, Currency Wars* and *The New Case for Gold*, which have been translated into fourteen languages. He is the editor of the newsletter *Strategic Intelligence* and is a member of the advisory board of the Centre for Financial Economics at Johns Hopkins University. An adviser on international economics and financial threats to the Department of Defence and the US intelligence community, he served as a facilitator of the first-ever financial war games conducted by the Pentagon. He lives in Connecticut. Follow @JamesGRickards.

ALSO BY JAMES RICKARDS

Currency Wars

The Death of Money

The New Case for Gold

THE ROAD TO RUIN

THE GLOBAL ELITES' SECRET PLAN
FOR THE NEXT FINANCIAL CRISIS

James Rickards

PORTFOLIO
PENGUIN

PORTFOLIO PENGUIN

UK | USA | Canada | Ireland | Australia
India | New Zealand | South Africa

Portfolio Penguin is part of the Penguin Random House group of companies
whose addresses can be found at global.penguinrandomhouse.com

Penguin
Random House
UK

First published in the United States of America by Portfolio/Penguin,
an imprint of Penguin Random House LLC 2016
First published in Great Britain by Portfolio 2016
006

Printed in Great Britain by Clays Ltd, St Ives plc

A CIP catalogue record for this book is available from the British Library

ISBN: 978–0–241–18920–7

www.greenpenguin.co.uk

MIX
Paper from
responsible sources
FSC
www.fsc.org   FSC® C018179

Penguin Random House is committed to a
sustainable future for our business, our readers
and our planet. This book is made from Forest
Stewardship Council® certified paper.

To the memory of John H. Makin,
economist, mentor, and friend. We need him now more than ever.

When he had opened the third seal, I heard the third living creature cry out, "Come forward." And I beheld a black horse, and its rider held a scale in his hand. I heard a voice in the midst of the four living creatures. It said, "A measure of wheat costs a day's pay, and three measures of barley cost a day's pay. But do not damage the oil and the wine."

Revelation 6:5–6

CONTENTS

INTRODUCTION

FELIX SOMARY WAS PERHAPS THE GREATEST ECONOMIST OF THE TWEN-tieth century. He is certainly among the least known.

Somary was born in 1881 in a German-speaking part of what was then the Austro-Hungarian Empire. He studied law and economics at the University of Vienna. There he was a classmate of Joseph Schumpeter's and took his Ph.D. with Carl Menger, the father of Austrian economics.

During the First World War Somary served as a central banker in occupied Belgium, but for most of his career he was a private banker to wealthy individuals and institutions. He moved to Zurich in the 1930s where he lived and worked until his death in 1956. Somary spent most of the Second World War in Washington, D.C., where he served as a Swiss envoy on financial affairs and provided advice on finance to the War Department.

Somary was widely considered the world's greatest expert on currencies. He was frequently called upon by central banks to advise on monetary policy. Unfortunately for those banks, his sound advice was mostly ignored for political reasons.

He was called the Raven of Zurich for his uncanny ability to foresee financial catastrophes when others were complacent. Ravens in Greek mythology are associated with Apollo, god of prophecy. In the Old Testament book of Kings, ravens are commanded by God to minister to the prophet Elijah. Somary was perhaps the greatest economic prophet since antiquity. The English-language translation of Somary's memoir is titled *The Raven of Zurich*.

Somary not only foresaw the First World War, the Great Depression, and the Second World War before others, but he accurately warned about the deflationary and inflationary consequences of those cataclysms. He lived through the demise of the classical gold standard, the currency chaos of the interwar period, and the new Bretton Woods system. He died in 1956 before the Bretton Woods era came to an end.

Somary's success at forecasting extreme events was based on analytic methods similar to ones used in this book. He did not use the same names we use today; complexity theory and behavioral economics were still far in the future when he was engaged with markets. Still, his methods are visible from his writings.

A vivid example is a chapter in his memoir called "The Sanjak Railway," which describes an episode that occurred in 1908 involving Somary's efforts to syndicate a commercial loan. The loan proceeds were to build a railroad from Bosnia to the Greek port city of Salonika, today's Thessaloniki. The railroad itself was an insignificant project. Somary was engaged by backers in Vienna to report on its financial feasibility.

The proposed route crossed an Ottoman province called the Sanjak of Novi Bazar. This route necessitated an application from Vienna to the Sublime Porte for permission.

What happened next shocked Vienna. Foreign ministries from Moscow to Paris protested vehemently. As Somary writes, "The Russian-French alliance had reacted to Austria-Hungary's application for a rail concession with a storm of protest unparalleled in intensity—and had in turn made a political countermove by proposing a railway from the Danube to the Adriatic."

This railroad incident took place before the Balkan Wars of 1912–13, and six years before the outbreak of the First World War. Yet, based on the French-Russian reaction alone, Somary correctly inferred that world war was inevitable. His analysis was that if an insignificant matter excited geopolitical tensions to the boiling point, then larger matters, which inevitably occur, must lead to war.

This inference is a perfect example of Bayesian statistics. Somary, in effect, started with a hypothesis about the probability of world war, which in the absence of any information is weighted fifty-fifty. As incidents like the sanjak railway emerge, they are added to the numerator and denominator of the mathematical form of Bayes' theorem, increasing the odds of war. Contemporary intelligence analysts call these events "indications and warnings." At some point, the strength of the hypothesis makes war seems inevitable. Bayes' theorem allows an analyst to reach that conclusion ahead of the crowd.

The sanjak railway episode echoes rivalries in our own day about natural gas pipelines from the Caspian Sea to Europe, some of which may traverse old Ottoman sanjaks. The players—Turkey, Russia, and Germany—are the same. Where is our new Somary? Who is the new raven?

Somary also used the historical-cultural method favored by Joseph Schumpeter. In 1913, Somary was asked by the seven great powers of the day to reorganize the Chinese monetary system. He declined the role because he felt a more pressing monetary crisis was coming in Europe. A decade ahead of a powerful deflation that held the world in its grip from 1924 to 1939, he wrote:

> Europeans found the Chinese amusing for their rejection of paper money and their practice of weighing metallic currency on scales. People presumed that the Chinese were five generations behind us—in reality they were a generation ahead of Europe. Under the Mongol emperors they had experienced a boom in which paper billions were issued to finance military conquests and vast public works, only to go through the bitter deflationary consequences—and the impression of all this had lasted through many subsequent centuries.

Somary also showed his mastery of behavioral psychology in analyzing an incident from July 1914, in which King George V of England assured the kaiser's brother, who was the king's cousin, that war between England and Germany was impossible:

> Doubtless the King too had spoken in good faith to his cousin, but I was uncertain how much insight the King could have into the situation. I had seen six years before how little informed more capable rulers had been; the information available to insiders, and precisely the most highly placed among them, is all too often misleading. I relied more the on the judgment of *The Times* than of the King. On behalf of those friends whose assets I was managing, I converted bank deposits and securities into gold and invested in Switzerland and Norway. A few days later the war broke out.

Today, the king's mistaken views would be described by behavioral psychologists as cognitive dissonance or confirmation bias. Somary did not use those terms, yet understood that elites live in bubbles beside other elites. They are often the last to know a crisis is imminent.

Somary's memoir was published in German in 1960; the English-language translation only appeared in 1986. Both editions are long out of print; only a few copies are available from specialty booksellers.

One year after the English edition was published, on October 19, 1987, the Dow Jones Industrial Average dropped over 20 percent in a single day, ushering in the modern age of financial complexity and market fragility. One is inclined to believe that had Somary lived longer he would have seen the 1987 crash coming, and more besides.

Using Somary's methods—etiology, psychology, complexity, and history—this book picks up the thread of financial folly where the Raven of Zurich left off.

—

Is economics science? Yes, and there the problems begin. Economics is a science, yet most economists are not scientists. Economists act like politicians, priests, or propagandists. They ignore evidence that does not fit their paradigms. Economists want scientific prestige without the rigor. Today's weak world growth can be traced to this imposture.

Science involves both knowledge and method. Sound method is the way to acquire knowledge. This is done through induction, basically a hunch, or deduction, an inference drawn from data. Either an inductive or deductive approach is used to form a hypothesis: a rigorous guess. The hypothesis is tested by experimentation and observation, which lead to data. The hypothesis either is confirmed by data, in which case the hypothesis becomes more widely accepted, or is invalidated by data, in which case the hypothesis is rejected and replaced by new hypotheses. When a hypothesis survives extensive testing and observation, it may become theory, a conditional form of truth.

Scientific method applies readily to economics. The familiar distinction between hard sciences such as physics and soft sciences such as economics is spurious. Academics today categorize specific branches of science as best suited to explain particular parts of the universe. Astronomy is a sound way to understand galaxies. Biology is a fruitful way to understand cancer. Economics is an excellent way to understand resource allocation and wealth creation. Astronomy, biology, and economics are branches of science applied to distinct areas of knowledge. All are science, and amenable to scientific method.

Still, most academic economists are not scientists; they are dogmatists. They cling to an old version of their science, are not open to new views, and discard data that contradict dogma. This decrepit landscape would be academic but for the fact that economists control powerful positions in central banks and finance ministries. Their use of outdated theory is not merely academic; it destroys the wealth of nations.

This topic bears discussion before the next financial crisis because so much is at stake. The United States' economy has grown, albeit sluggishly, for more than seven years since the last crisis as of this writing. That's a historically long expansion. The time since 2008 roughly tracks the tempo of panics in 1987, 1994, 1998, and 2008. Seven years between crises is not a fixed span. A new crash in the near term is not set in stone. Still, no one should be surprised if it happens.

With a financial system so vulnerable, and policymakers so unprepared, extreme policy measures will be needed when catastrophe strikes. This book is a plea to reimagine the statistical properties of risk, apply new theories, and turn back from the brink before it's too late.

Scientists understand that all theories are contingent; a better explanation than the prevailing view eventually emerges. Newton is not considered wrong because Einstein offered a better explanation of space and celestial motion. Einstein advanced the state of knowledge. Unfortunately economists have shown little willingness to advance the state of their own art. The Austrians, Neo-Keynesians, and monetarists all have their flags firmly planted in the ground. Research consists of endless variations of the same few themes. The intellectual stagnation has lasted seventy years. Ostensible innovation is really imitation of ideas limned by Keynes, Fisher, Hayek, and Schumpeter before the Second World War. These originals were transformative, but the postwar variations are limited, obsolete, and if used doctrinally, dangerous.

The Austrian understanding of the superiority of free markets over central planning is sound. Still, the Austrian school needs updating using new science and twenty-first-century technology. Christopher Columbus was the greatest dead-reckoning navigator ever. Yet no one disputes he would use GPS today. If Friedrich Hayek were alive, he would use new instruments, network theory, and cellular automata to refine his insights. His followers should do no less.

Neo-Keynesian models are the reigning creed. Interestingly, they have little to do with John Maynard Keynes. He was above all a pragmatist; those who follow in his name are anything but. Keynes advocated for gold in 1914, counseled for a higher gold price in 1925, opposed gold in 1931, and offered a modified gold standard in 1944. Keynes had pragmatic reasons for each position.

Churchill once sent a cable to Keynes that read, "Am coming around to your point of view." Keynes replied, "Sorry to hear it. Have started to change my mind." It would be refreshing if today's economists were half so open-minded.

Keynes's insight was that a temporary lack of private aggregate demand can be replaced with government spending until "animal spirits" are revived. Spending works best when a government is not heavily indebted, and when a surplus is available to finance the spending. Today economists such as Paul Krugman and Joseph Stiglitz, using invalid equilibrium models (the economy is not an equilibrium system), propose more deficit spending by deeply indebted countries for indefinite periods to stimulate demand, as if someone with four televisions buying a fifth is the way forward. This is folly.

Monetarists are no better. Milton Friedman's insight was that maximum real growth with price stability is achieved by slow, steady growth in the money supply. Friedman wanted money supply to rise to meet potential growth—a variation of the Irish toast, "May the road rise to meet your feet."

Friedman's adopted formulation, $MV = PQ$ (originally from Fisher and his predecessors), says that money (M) times velocity (V) equals nominal GDP (consisting of real GDP [Q], adjusted for changes in the price level [P]).

Friedman assumed velocity is constant and ideally there should be no inflation or deflation (an implied $P = 1$). Once maximum real growth is estimated (averaging about 3.5 percent per year in a mature economy), the money supply can be smoothly increased to achieve that growth without inflation. While useful for thought experiments, Friedman's theory is useless in practice. In the real world, velocity is not constant, real growth is constrained by structural (i.e., nonmonetary) impediments, and money supply is ill defined. Apart from that, Mrs. Lincoln, how was the play?

Prevailing theory does even more damage when weighing the statistical properties of risk.

The extended balance sheet of too-big-to-fail banks today is approximately one *quadrillion* dollars, or one thousand trillion dollars poised on a thin sliver of capital. How is the risk embedded in this leverage being managed? The prevailing theory is called value at risk, or VaR. This theory assumes that risk in long and short positions is netted, the degree distribution of price movements is normal, extreme events are exceedingly rare, and derivatives can be properly priced using a "risk-free" rate. In fact, when AIG was on the brink of default in 2008, no counterparty cared about its *net* position; AIG was about to default on the *gross* position to each counterparty. Data show that the time series of price moves is distributed along a power curve, not a normal curve. Extreme events are not rare at all; they happen every seven years or so. And the United States, issuer of benchmark "risk-free" bonds, recently suffered a credit downgrade that implied at least a small risk of default. In brief, all four of the assumptions behind VaR are false.

If Neo-Keynesians, monetarists, and VaR practitioners have obsolete tools, why do they cling tenaciously to their models? To answer that question, ask another. Why did medieval believers in a geocentric solar system not question their system when data showed inconsistent planetary motion? Why did they write new equations to explain so-called anomalies instead of scrapping the system? The answers lie in psychology.

Belief systems are comforting. They offer certainty in an uncertain world. For humans, certainty has value even if it is false. Falsity may have long-run consequences, yet comfort helps you make it through the day.

This comfort factor becomes embedded when there is mathematical modeling to support it. Modern financial math is daunting. Ph.D.s who spent years mastering the math have a vested interest in maintaining a façade. The math bolsters their credentials and excludes others less fluent with Ito's calculus.

Financial math is also what practitioners call elegant. If you accept the modern finance paradigm, the math provides a wealth of neat solutions to difficult problems such as options pricing. No one stops to question the paradigm.

This financial façade is reinforced by the tyranny of academic advancement. A young scholar in a highly selective finance program is rightly concerned with fellowships, publication, and faculty appointment. Approaching a sexagenarian thesis adviser with an abstract that refutes what the adviser has held dear for decades is not an astute career move. Most deem it better to bang out the thousandth variation of a dynamic stochastic general equilibrium model using autoregressive conditional heteroscedasticity to explain the impact of quantitative easing on swap spreads. That's the way to get ahead.

Then there is simple inertia, like staying in a warm bed on a cold morning. Academics have their comfort zones too. New knowledge is like a dive in the surf in winter—bracing, exhilarating, but not everyone's cup of tea.

The preference for certainty over uncertainty, the allure of elegant mathematics, the close-minded academic mentality, and inertia are good explanations for why flawed paradigms persist.

If academic reputations were the only stakes, the world could be patient. Good science wins in the end. Still, the stakes are higher. The world's wealth is at risk. When wealth is destroyed, social unrest follows. Investors can no longer indulge policymakers who refuse to seek better solutions for the sake of what is tried and not-so-true.

This book is about what works. Since the 1960s, new branches of science have been revealed. Since the 1980s, cheap computing power has allowed laboratory experimentation on economic hypotheses that cannot be tested in real-world conditions. The rise of team science, long common in medicine, facilitates interdisciplinary discoveries beyond the boundaries of any one area of expertise. Recently, a 250-year-old theorem, scorned for centuries, triumphantly reemerged to solve otherwise unsolvable problems.

The three most important new tools in the finance toolkit are behavioral psychology, complexity theory, and causal inference. These tools can be used separately to solve a particular problem or combined to build more robust models.

All three tools seem more inexact in their predictive power than current models used by central banks. Yet they offer a far better reflection of reality. It is better to be roughly right than exactly wrong.

Behavioral psychology is understood and embraced by economists. The leading theorist in behavioral psychology, Daniel Kahneman, received the Nobel Prize in economics in 2002. The impediment to the use of psychology in economics is not appreciation, it's application. Finance models such as VaR are still based on rational behavior and efficient markets, long after Kahneman and his colleagues proved that human behavior in markets is irrational and inefficient (as economists define these terms).

For example, Kahneman's experiments show that when subjects are given a choice between receiving $3.00 with 100 percent certainty and $4.00 with 80 percent certainty, they greatly favor the first choice. Simple multiplication shows the second choice has a higher expected return than the first, $3.20 compared with $3.00. Still, everyday people prefer the sure thing to the risky choice, which has a higher expected return, but leaves some chance of coming away empty-handed.

Economists were quick to brand the first choice as irrational and the second choice as rational. This led to the claim that investors who favor the first choice were irrational. But are they really?

It is true that if you play this game one hundred times, the choice of $4.00 with an 80 percent probability almost certainly produces more winnings than the $3.00 sure thing. *What if you play the game only once?* The expected return equations are the same. But if you need the money, the $3.00 sure thing has independent value not captured in the equations.

What Kahneman discovered must be combined with evolutionary psychology to redefine rationality. Imagine you are a Cro-Magnon during the last ice age. You leave your shelter and see two paths to hunt game. One path has plentiful game, but large boulders along the way.

The second path has less game, but no obstacles. In modern financial parlance, the first path has a higher expected return.

Yet evolution favors the path with less game. Why? There could be a saber-toothed cat behind one of the boulders on the first path. If there is, you die and your family starves. The path with less game is not irrational when *all* costs are considered. The saber-toothed cat is the missing mammal of modern economics. Academics typically quantify first-order benefits (the game) and ignore second-order costs (the cat). Investors can use this book to see the saber-toothed cats.

The second new tool in the toolkit is complexity theory. The crucial question in economics today is whether capital markets are complex systems. If the answer is yes, then *every* equilibrium model used in financial economics is obsolete.

Physics provides a way to answer the question. A dynamic, complex system is composed of autonomous agents. What are the attributes of autonomous agents in a complex system? Broadly, there are four: *diversity, connectedness, interaction*, and *adaptation*. A system whose agents exhibit these attributes in low measure tends toward stasis. A system whose agents exhibit these attributes in high measure tends toward chaos. A system whose agents have all four traits in Goldilocks measure, not too high and not too low, is a complex dynamic system.

Diversity in capital markets is seen in the behavior of bulls and bears, longs and shorts, fear and greed. Diversity of behavior is the quintessence of markets.

Connectedness in capital markets is also manifest. With the use of Dow Jones, Thomson Reuters, Bloomberg, Fox Business, email, chat, text, Twitter, and telephone, it is difficult to imagine a more densely connected system than capital markets.

Interaction in capital markets is measured by trillions of dollars of stock, bond, currency, commodity, and derivatives transactions executed daily, each of which involves a buyer, seller, broker, or exchange interacting. No other social system comes close to capital markets in interaction measured by transaction volume.

Adaptation is also characteristic of capital markets. A hedge fund that loses money on a position quickly adapts its behavior to get out of the trade or perhaps double down. The fund changes its behavior based on the behavior of others in the market as revealed by market prices.

Capital markets are demonstrably complex systems; capital markets are complex systems nonpareil.

The failing of prevailing risk models is that *complex systems behave in a completely different manner from equilibrium systems.* This is why central bank and Wall Street equilibrium models produce consistently weak results in forecasting and risk management. Every analysis starts with the same data. Yet when you enter that data into a deficient model, you get deficient output. Investors who use complexity theory can leave mainstream analysis behind and get better forecasting results.

The third tool in addition to behavioral psychology and complexity theory is Bayesian statistics, a branch of etiology also referred to as causal inference. Both terms derive from Bayes' theorem, an equation first described by Thomas Bayes and published posthumously in 1763. A version of the theorem was elaborated independently and more formally by the French mathematician Pierre-Simon Laplace in 1774. Laplace continued work on the theorem in subsequent decades. Twentieth-century statisticians have developed more rigorous forms.

Normal science including economics assembles massive data sets and uses deductive methods to derive testable hypotheses from the data. These hypotheses often involve correlations and regressions used to forecast future events deemed likely to resemble past events. Similar methods involve the use of stochastics, or random numbers, to run Monte Carlo simulations, which are high-output versions of coin tosses and dice rolls, to infer the likelihood of future events.

What if there are no data, or little data to start? How do you estimate the likelihood of a secret accord among a small group of central bankers? Bayesian probability provides the means to do just that.

Mainstream economists assume the future resembles the past within certain bounds defined by random distributions. Bayes' theorem stands this view on its head. Bayesian probability posits that certain events are *path dependent*. This means some future events are *not* independent like random coin tosses. They are influenced by what precedes them. Bayes' theorem begins with a sound prior hypothesis formed inductively from a mixture of scarce data, history, and common sense.

Bayesian probability is solid science, not mere guesswork, because the prior hypothesis is tested by subsequent data. New data tend either to confirm or to refute the hypothesis. The ratio of the two types of data is updated continually as new data arrive. Based on the updated ratio, the hypothesis is either discarded (and a new hypothesis formed) or accepted with greater confidence. In brief, Bayes' theorem is how you solve a problem when there is not enough initial data to satisfy the demands of normal statistics.

Economists reject Bayesian probability because of the grubby guesswork in the initial stages. Yet it is used extensively by intelligence agencies around the world. I encountered analysts using Bayesian probability in classified settings at the CIA and Los Alamos National Laboratory. When your task is to forecast the next 9/11 attack, you can't wait for fifty more attacks to build up your data set. You work the problem immediately using whatever data you have.

At the CIA, the potential to apply Bayesian probability to forecasting in capital markets was obvious. Intelligence analysis involves forecasting events based on scarce information. If information were plentiful, you would not need spies. Investors face the same problem in allocating portfolios among asset classes. They lack sufficient information as prescribed by normal statistical methods. By the time they do have enough data to achieve certainty, the opportunity to profit has been lost.

Bayes' theorem is messy, but still it's better than nothing. It's also better than Wall Street regressions that miss the new and unforeseen. This book explains how to use Bayesian probability to achieve better forecasting results than the Federal Reserve or International Monetary Fund.

This book parts ways with the "Big Four" schools—classical, Austrian, Keynesian, and monetarist. Of course, all have much to offer.

Classical economists including Smith, Ricardo, Mill, and Bentham, among others, appeal in part because none of them had Ph.D.s. They were lawyers, writers, and philosophers who thought hard about what works and what does not in the economies of states and societies. They lacked modern computational tools, yet were filled with insights into human nature.

Austrians made invaluable contributions to the study of choice and markets. Yet their emphasis on the explanatory power of money seems narrow. Money matters, but an emphasis on money to the exclusion of psychology is a fatal flaw.

Keynesian and monetarist schools have lately merged into the neoliberal consensus, a nightmarish surf and turf presenting the worst of both.

In this book, I write as a theorist using complexity theory, Bayesian statistics, and behavioral psychology to study economics. That approach is unique and not yet a "school" of economic thought. This book also uses one other device—history. When asked to identify which established school of economic thought I find most useful, my reply is Historical.

Notable writers of the Historical school include the liberal Walter Bagehot, the Communist Karl Marx, and the conservative Austrian-Catholic Joseph A. Schumpeter. Adherence to the Historical school does not make you a liberal, a Communist, or an Austrian. It means you consider economic activity to be culturally derived human activity.

Homo economicus does not exist in the natural world. There are Germans, Russians, Greeks, Americans, and Chinese. There are rich and poor, or what Marx called bourgeoisie and proletarians. There is diversity. Americans are averse to discussion of class, and soft-pedal concepts like bourgeoisie and proletariat. Nevertheless, integration of class culture with economics is revealing.

This book will follow these threads—complexity, behavioral psychology, causal inference, and history—through the dense web of twenty-first-century capital markets into a future unlike anything the world has ever seen.

CHAPTER 1
THIS IS THE END

Nice, nice, very nice—
So many different people
In the same device.

From *Cat's Cradle*, a novel by Kurt Vonnegut, 1963

The Conversation

Aureole is an elegant, high-ceilinged restaurant of sleek modern design on West Forty-second Street in Manhattan. It sits midway between tourist throngs in Times Square and Bryant Park's greenery. The neo-classical New York Public Library, whose entrance is attended by the twin marble lions, Patience and Fortitude, looms nearby.

I was there on a pleasant evening in June 2014 with three companions at a window table. We arrived at Aureole after a short walk from the library lecture hall where I had earlier delivered a talk on international finance.

The library offered free access to the lecture. Free access to any event in New York City guarantees an eclectic audience, more diverse than my typical institutional presentation. One gentleman in attendance wore an orange suit, bow tie, sunglasses, and lime-green derby hat. He was seated in the front row. His appearance did not raise an eyebrow.

New Yorkers are not only bold dressers, they're typically astute. In the question-and-answer session after the lecture, one listener raised his hand and said, "I agree with your warnings about systemic risk, but I'm stuck in a company 401(k). My only options are equities and money market funds. What should I do?" My initial advice was "Quit your job."

Then I said, "Seriously, move from equities to half cash. That leaves you some upside with lower volatility, and you'll have optionality as visibility improves." That was all he could do. As I gave the advice, I realized millions of Americans were stuck in the same stock market trap.

At Aureole, it was time to relax. The crowd was the usual midtown mix of moguls and models. I was with three brilliant women. To my left was Christina Polischuk, retired top adviser to Barclays Global Investors. Barclays was one of the world's largest asset managers before being acquired by BlackRock in 2009. That acquisition put BlackRock in a league of its own, on its way to $5 trillion of assets under management, larger than the GDP of Germany.

Across the table was my daughter, Ali. She had just launched her own business as a digital media consultant after four years advising Hollywood A-list celebrities. I was among her first clients. She brought millennial savvy to my lecture style with good success.

To my right was one of the most powerful, yet private, women in finance; consigliere to BlackRock CEO Larry Fink. She was BlackRock's point person on government efforts to suppress the financial system following the 2008 meltdown. When the government came knocking on BlackRock's door, she answered.

Over a bottle of white Burgundy, we conversed about old times, mutual friends, and the crowd at the lecture. I had addressed the audience on complexity theory and hard data that showed the financial system moving toward collapse. My friend on the right didn't need any lectures on systemic risk; she stood at the crossroads of contagion in her role at BlackRock.

Under Larry Fink's direction, BlackRock emerged over the past twenty-five years as the most powerful force in asset management. Black-

Rock manages separate accounts for the world's largest institutions as well as mutual funds and other investment vehicles for investors of all sizes. It sponsors billions of dollars of exchange-traded funds, ETFs, through its iShares platform.

Acquisitions engineered by Fink including State Street Research, Merrill Lynch Investment Management, and Barclays Global Investors, combined with internal growth and new products, pushed BlackRock to the top of the heap among asset managers. BlackRock's $5 trillion of assets were spread across equities, fixed income, commodities, foreign exchange, and derivatives in markets on five continents. No other asset management firm has its sheer size and breadth. BlackRock was the new financial Leviathan.

Fink is obsessively driven by asset growth, and the financial power that comes with it. He typically rises early, devours news, keeps a grueling schedule punctuated by power lunches and dinners, and is asleep by 10:30 p.m., ready to do it all again the next day. When he's not shuttling between his east side Manhattan apartment and his midtown office, Fink can be found on the global power elite circuit including Davos in January, IMF meetings in April, St. Petersburg, Russia, in June for "white nights," and so on around the calendar and around the globe, meeting with clients, heads of state, central bankers, and other lesser-known yet quietly powerful figures.

Such power does not go unnoticed in Washington. The U.S. government operates like the Black Hand, a Mafia predecessor portrayed in *The Godfather Part II*. If you pay protection money in the form of campaign contributions, make donations to the right foundations, hire the right consultants, lawyers, and lobbyists, and don't oppose the government agenda, you are left alone to operate your business.

If you fail to pay protection, Washington will break your windows as a warning. In twenty-first-century America, government breaks your windows with politically motivated prosecutions on tax, fraud, or antitrust charges. If you still don't fall into line, the government returns to burn down your store.

The Obama administration raised the art of political prosecution to a height not seen since 1934, when the Roosevelt administration sought the indictment of Andrew Mellon, a distinguished former secretary of the treasury. Mellon's only crimes were being rich and a vocal opponent of FDR. He was eventually acquitted of all charges. Still, a political prosecution played well among FDR's left-wing cohort.

Jamie Dimon, CEO of JPMorgan Chase, learned this lesson the hard way when he publicly criticized Obama's bank regulatory policy in 2012. Over the course of the next two years, JPMorgan paid more than $30 billion in fines, penalties, and compliance costs to settle a host of criminal and civil fraud charges brought by the Obama Justice Department and regulatory agencies. The Obama administration knew that attacking institutions was more remunerative than attacking individuals as FDR had done. Under this new Black Hand, stockholders paid the costs, and CEOs got to keep their jobs provided they remained mute.

Fink played the political game more astutely than Dimon. As *Fortune* magazine reported, "Fink . . . is a strong Democrat . . . and has often been rumored as set to take a big administration job, such as Secretary of the Treasury." Fink had so far managed to avoid the attacks that plagued his rivals.

Now Fink confronted a threat greater than targeted prosecutions and West Wing animus. The threat involved the White House, but emanated from the highest levels of the IMF and the G20 club of major economic powers. This threat has an anodyne name intended to confuse nonexperts. The name is G-SIFI, which stands for "globally systemic important financial institution." In plain English, G-SIFI means "too big to fail." If your company is on the G-SIFI list, it will be propped up by governments because a failure topples the global financial system. That list went beyond large national banks into a stratosphere of supersize players who dominated global finance. G-SIFI even went beyond too big to fail. G-SIFI was a list of entities that were too big to leave alone. The G20 and IMF did not just want to watch the G-SIFIs. They wanted to control them.

Each major country has its own sublists of SIFIs, and systemically important banks (SIBs) that are also too big to fail. In the United States, these banks include JPMorgan, Citibank, and some lesser-known entities such as the Bank of New York, the clearing nerve center for the U.S. treasury market.

I knew this background when I sat down to dinner that evening. The latest development was that governments were now moving beyond banks to include nonbank financial companies in their net.

Some nonbank targets were easy prey, including insurance giant AIG, which almost destroyed the financial system in 2008, and General Electric, whose credit operations were unable to roll over their commercial paper in the panic that year. It was the General Electric freeze, more than Wall Street bank failures, that most panicked Ben Bernanke, Federal Reserve chairman at the time. The General Electric credit collapse spread contagion to all of corporate America, which led directly to government guarantees of all bank deposits, money market funds, and corporate commercial paper. The General Electric meltdown was a white-knuckle moment that governments resolved never to repeat.

Once GE and AIG were swept in, the issue was how far to cast the nonbank net. Prudential Insurance was snared next. Governments were moving to control not just banks and large corporations, but the world's biggest asset managers as well. MetLife Insurance was next on the hit list; BlackRock was directly in the crosshairs.

I asked my dinner companion, "How's this whole SIFI thing going? You must have your hands full."

Her reply startled me. "It's worse than you think," she said.

I was aware of the government's efforts to put BlackRock in the nonbank SIFI category. A behind-the-scenes struggle by BlackRock management to avoid the designation had been going on for months. BlackRock's case was straightforward. They argued they were an asset manager, not a bank. Asset managers don't fail; their clients do.

BlackRock insisted size itself was not a problem. The assets under management belonged to the clients, not to BlackRock. In effect, they argued BlackRock was just a hired hand for its institutional clients, and not important in its own right.

Fink argued that systemic risk was in banks, not BlackRock. Banks borrow money on a short-term basis from depositors and other banks, then loan the funds out for a longer term as mortgages or commercial loans. This asset-liability maturity mismatch leaves banks vulnerable if the short-term lenders want their money back in a panic. Long-term assets cannot be liquidated quickly without a fire sale.

Modern financial technology made the problem worse because derivatives allowed the asset-liability mismatch to be more highly leveraged, and spread among more counterparties in hard-to-find ways. When panic strikes, even central banks willing to act as lenders of last resort cannot easily untangle the web of transactions in time to avoid a domino-style crash of one bank after another. All of this was amply demonstrated in the Panic of 2008, and even earlier in the collapse of hedge fund Long-Term Capital Management in 1998.

BlackRock had none of these problems. It was an asset manager, pure and simple. Clients entrusted it with assets to invest. There was no liability on the other side of the balance sheet. BlackRock did not need depositors or money market funds to finance its operations. BlackRock did not act as principal in exotic off-balance-sheet derivatives to leverage its client assets.

A client hired BlackRock, gave it assets under an advisory agreement, and paid a fee for the advice. In theory, the worst that could happen to BlackRock is it might lose clients or receive fewer fees. Its stock price might decline. Still, BlackRock could not suffer a classic run on the bank because it did not rely on short-term funding to conduct its operations, and it was not highly leveraged. BlackRock was different from a bank, and safer.

I said, "Well, I know what the government is doing. They realize you're not a bank and don't have funding risk. They just want information. They want you on the nonbank SIFI list so they can come in, poke around, look at your investments, and report the information to Treasury in a crisis. They'll combine that with information from other sources. The information gives them the big picture if they need to put out a fire. It's a pain, and it's expensive, but you can do it. It's just another compliance cost."

My friend leaned in, lowered her voice, and said, "No, it's not that. We can live with that. They want to tell us we can't sell."

"What?" I replied. I heard her well enough, but the implication of what she said was striking.

"In a crisis, they want to pick up the phone and order us not to sell securities. Just freeze us in place. I was in Washington last week on this and I'm going back next week for more meetings. You know it's not really about us, it's about our clients."

I was shocked. I should not have been. BlackRock was an obvious choke point in the global flow of funds. The fact that regulators might order banks to behave in certain ways was not surprising. Regulators can close banks almost at will. Bank management knows that in a match with regulators, the bank will always lose, so they go along with government orders. But government had no obvious legal leverage over asset managers like BlackRock.

Yet the flow of funds through BlackRock on a daily basis was enormous. BlackRock was a strategic choke point like the Strait of Hormuz. If you stop the flow of oil through the Strait of Hormuz, the global economy grinds to a halt. Likewise, if you stop transactions at Black-Rock, global markets grind to a halt.

In a financial panic, everyone wants his money back. Investors believe stocks, bonds, and money market funds can be turned into money with a few clicks at an online broker. In a panic, that's not necessarily true. At best, values are crashing and "money" disappears before your eyes. At worst, funds suspend redemptions and brokers shut off their systems.

Broadly speaking, there are two ways for policymakers to respond when everyone wants his money back. The first is to make money readily available, printing as much as necessary to satisfy the demand. This is the classic central bank function as the lender of last resort, more aptly called printer of last resort.

The second approach is to just say no; to lock down or freeze the system. A lockdown involves closing banks, shutting exchanges, and ordering asset managers not to sell. In the Panic of 2008, governments pursued the first option. Central banks printed money and passed it around to reliquefy markets and prop up asset prices.

Now it looked like governments were anticipating the next panic by preparing the second approach. In the next panic, government will say, in effect, "No, you can't have your money. The system is closed. Let us sort things out, and we'll get back to you."

Money locked down at BlackRock is not their money, it's their clients'. BlackRock manages funds for the largest institutions in the world such as CIC, the Chinese sovereign wealth fund, and CALPERS, the pension fund for government employees in California. A freeze on BlackRock means you are freezing sales by China, California, and other jurisdictions around the world. The U.S. government has no authority to tell China not to sell securities. But because China entrusts assets to BlackRock, the government would use its power over BlackRock to freeze the Chinese. The Chinese would be the last to know.

By controlling one financial choke point—BlackRock—the U.S. government controls the assets of major investors normally beyond its jurisdiction. Freezing BlackRock was an audacious plan, obviously one the government could not discuss openly. Thanks to my dinner companion, the plan had become crystal clear.

Ice-Nine

In the 1963 dark comedic novel *Cat's Cradle*, author Kurt Vonnegut created a substance he called ice-nine, discovered by a physicist, Dr. Felix Hoenikker. Ice-nine was a polymorph of water, a rearrangement of the molecule H_2O.

Ice-nine had two properties that distinguished it from regular water. The first was a melting point of 114.4°F, which meant ice-nine was frozen at room temperature. The second property was that when a molecule of ice-nine came in contact with a water molecule, the water instantly turned to ice-nine.

Hoenikker placed some ice-nine molecules in sealed vials and gave them to his children before he died. The novel's plot turns on the fact that if the ice-nine is released from the vials, and put in contact with a large body of water, the entire water supply on earth—rivers, lakes, and oceans—would eventually become frozen solid and all life on earth would cease.

This was a doomsday scenario appropriate to the times in which Vonnegut wrote. *Cat's Cradle* was published just after the Cuban Missile Crisis, when the real world came dangerously close to nuclear annihilation, what scientists later called nuclear winter.

Ice-nine is a fine way to describe the power elite response to the next financial crisis. Instead of reliquefying the world, elites will freeze it. The system will be locked down. Of course, ice-nine will be described as temporary the same way President Nixon described the suspension of dollar-to-gold convertibility in 1971 as temporary. Gold convertibility at a fixed parity was never restored. The gold in Fort Knox has been frozen ever since. U.S. government gold is ice-nine.

Ice-nine fits with an understanding of financial markets as complex dynamic systems. An ice-nine molecule does not freeze an entire ocean instantaneously. It freezes only adjacent molecules. Those new ice-nine molecules freeze others in ever-widening circles. The spread of ice-nine would be geometric, not linear. It would work like a nuclear chain reaction, which starts with a single atom being split, and soon splits so many atoms that the energy release is enormous.

Financial panics spread the same way. In the classic 1930s version, they begin with a run on a small-town bank. The panic spreads until it hits Wall Street and starts a stock market crash. In the twenty-first-century version, panic starts in a computer algorithm, which triggers preprogrammed sell orders that cascade into other computers until the system spins out of control. A cascade of selling happened on October 19, 1987, when the Dow Jones Industrial Average fell 22 percent in one day—equivalent to a 4,000-point drop in the index today.

Risk managers and regulators use the word "contagion" to describe the dynamics of financial panic. Contagion is more than a metaphor. Contagious diseases such as Ebola spread in the same exponential way as ice-nine, chain reactions, and financial panics. One Ebola victim may infect two healthy people, then those two newly infected persons each infect two others, and so on. Eventually a pandemic results, and a strict quarantine is needed until a vaccine is found. In *Cat's Cradle*, there was no "vaccine"; ice-nine molecules were quarantined in sealed vials.

In a financial panic, printing money is a vaccine. If the vaccine proves ineffective, the only solution is quarantine. This means closing banks, exchanges, and money market funds, shutting down ATMs, and ordering asset managers not to sell securities. Elites are preparing for a financial ice-nine with no vaccine. They will quarantine your money by locking it inside the financial system until the contagion subsides.

Ice-nine is hiding in plain sight. Those who are not looking for it cannot see it. Once you know ice-nine is there, you see it everywhere. This was the case after my conversation with my insider friend about the BlackRock asset freeze.

The elite ice-nine plan was far more ambitious than the so-called living wills and resolution authority under the 2010 Dodd-Frank legislation. Ice-nine went beyond banks to include insurance companies, industrial companies, and asset managers. It went beyond orderly liquidation to include a freeze on transactions. Ice-nine would be global rather than case-by-case.

The best-known cases of elites' freezing customer funds in recent years were the Cyprus banking crisis in 2012 and the Greek sovereign debt crisis in 2015. These crises had longer-term antecedents, but Cyprus and Greece were where matters came to a head and banks blocked depositors from their own money.

Cyprus was known as a conduit for Russian flight capital, some illegally obtained by Russian oligarchs. In the Cyprus crisis, the two leading banks, Laiki Bank and the Bank of Cyprus, became insolvent. A run on the entire banking system ensued. Cyprus was a Eurozone member and used the euro as its currency. This made the crisis systemic despite the Cypriot economy's small size. A troika consisting of the European Central Bank (ECB), the European Union (EU), and the IMF had fought hard to preserve the euro in the 2011 sovereign debt crises and did not want to see that work undone in Cyprus.

Cyprus did not have the clout to drive a hard bargain. It had to take whatever assistance it could get on whatever terms it could get it. For its part, the troika decided the days of too-big-to-fail banks were over. Cyprus was where they drew the line. Banks were temporarily shut down. ATM machines were taken offline. A mad scramble for cash ensued. Those who could flew to mainland Europe, returning with wads of euros stuffed in their luggage.

Laiki Bank was closed permanently, and Bank of Cyprus was restructured by the government. Bank deposits in Laiki above the insured limit of €100,000 were dumped in a "bad bank" where the prospects of any recovery are uncertain. Smaller deposits were transferred to the Bank of Cyprus. At the Bank of Cyprus, 47.5 percent of the uninsured deposits over €100,000 were converted into equity of the newly recapitalized bank. Precrisis stock- and bondholders took haircuts and received some equity in the bank in exchange for their losses.

The Cyprus model was called a "bail-in." Instead of bailing out depositors, the troika used depositors' money to recapitalize the failed banks. A bail-in reduced rescue costs to the troika, especially Germany.

Investors around the world shrugged and treated Cyprus as a one-off event. Cyprus is poor. Depositors in more advanced countries forgot the incident and adopted an attitude that said, "It can't happen here." They could not have been more wrong. The 2012 Cyprus bail-in was the new template for global bank crises.

A G20 summit of world leaders including President Barack Obama and German chancellor Angela Merkel met in Brisbane, Australia, on

November 15, 2014, shortly after the Cyprus crisis. The meeting's final communiqué includes reference to a new global organization called the Financial Stability Board, or FSB. This is a global financial regulator established by the G20 and not accountable to the citizens of any member country. The communiqué says, "We welcome the Financial Stability Board (FSB) proposal . . . requiring global systemically important banks to hold additional loss absorbing capacity. . . ."

Behind that bland language is a separate twenty-three-page technical report from the FSB that provides the template for future bank crises. The report says bank losses "should be absorbed . . . by unsecured and uninsured creditors." In this context "creditor" means depositor. The report then describes "the powers and tools that authorities should have to achieve this objective. These include *the bail-in power* . . . [and] to write down and convert into equity all or parts of the firm's unsecured and uninsured liabilities . . . to the extent necessary to absorb losses."

What the Brisbane G20 summit showed was that the ice-nine policy as applied to bank depositors was not limited to out-of-the-way places like Cyprus. Ice-nine was the policy of the largest countries in the world, including the United States.

Bank depositors received another harsh lesson in governments' ability to lock down banks during the 2015 Greek debt crisis. Greek sovereign debt was a persistent problem beginning in 2009, and the crisis ran hot and cold over the intervening years. The crisis came to a head on July 12, 2015, when Germany ran out of patience with the Greeks and presented a financial ultimatum at a Brussels summit, to which Greece finally agreed.

The typical Greek citizen may or may not have followed the high-stakes drama in Brussels, yet the fallout was unavoidable. It was unclear if Greek banks would survive or whether depositors would be bailed in under the Brisbane rules. The banks had no choice but to shut down access to cash and credit until their status was clarified.

ATMs stopped providing cash to Greek cardholders (travelers with non-Greek debit cards could get some cash at Athens International

Airport). Greek credit cards were declined by merchants. Greeks drove to neighboring countries and returned with bags full of large-denomination euro notes. The Greek economy reverted to cash-and-carry and quasi-barter almost overnight.

Coming so soon after the Cyprus debacle, the Greek version of ice-nine served as a cautionary tale. Depositors now realized their money in the bank was not money, and not theirs. Their so-called money was ac-tually a bank liability and could be frozen at any time.

The Brisbane G20 ice-nine plan was not limited to bank deposits. That was just a beginning.

On Wednesday, July 23, 2014, the U.S. Securities and Exchange Commission (SEC) approved a new rule on a 3–2 vote that allows money market funds to suspend investor redemptions. The SEC rule pushes ice-nine beyond banking into the world of investments. Now money market funds could act like hedge funds and refuse to return investor money. Fund managers dutifully included glossy flyers in the mail and online notices to investors about this change. No doubt investors threw the flyer in the trash and skipped the notice. But the rule is law, and notice has been given. In the next financial panic, not only will your bank account be bailed in, your money market account will be frozen.

Ice-nine gets worse.

One solution to ice-nine asset freezes is to hold cash and coin. This was quite common prior to 1914, and again in the depths of the Great Depression from 1929 to 1933. In the modern version, cash consists of $100 bills, €500 notes, or SFr1,000 notes from the Swiss National Bank. These are the largest denominations available in hard currency.

Coin could consist of one-ounce gold coins such as American Gold Eagles, Canadian Maple Leafs, or other widely available coins. Coin could also consist of one-ounce American Silver Eagles. Obtaining cash and coin in this fashion allows citizens to survive ice-nine account freezes. Global elites understand this, which is why they have started a war on cash.

Historically, market closures were circumvented by the emergence of cash-and-carry "curb exchanges" where buyers and sellers met in the street to trade paper shares for cash. Regulators will want to suppress twenty-first-century digital curb exchanges to prevent price discovery and maintain the myth of pre-panic prices. Curb exchanges could be conducted online in an eBay-style format with settlement by bitcoin or cash delivered face-to-face. Title to shares can be recorded in a distributed ledger using a blockchain. Eliminating cash helps the suppression of alternative markets, although bitcoin presents new challenges to elite power.

The second reason for eliminating cash is to impose negative interest rates. Central banks are in a losing battle against deflationary trends. One way to defeat deflation is to promote inflation with negative real interest rates.

A negative real rate occurs when the inflation rate is higher than the nominal interest rate on borrowings. If inflation is 4 percent, and the cost of money is 3 percent, the real interest rate is negative 1 percent $(3 - 4 = -1)$. Inflation erodes the dollar's value faster than interest accrues on the loan. The borrower gets to pay back the bank in cheaper dollars. Negative real rates are better than free money because the bank pays the borrower to borrow. Negative real rates are a powerful inducement to borrow, invest, and spend, which feeds inflationary tendencies and offsets deflation.

How do you create negative real interest rates when inflation is near zero? Even a low nominal interest rate of 2 percent produces a positive real interest rate of 1 percent when inflation is only 1 percent $(2 - 1 = 1)$.

The solution is to institute negative interest rates. With negative nominal rates, a negative real rate is always possible, even if inflation is low or negative. For example, if inflation is zero and nominal interest rates are negative 1 percent, then the real interest rate is also negative 1 percent $(-1 - 0 = -1)$.

Negative interest rates are easy to implement inside a digital banking system. The banks program their computers to charge money on your balances instead of paying. If you put $100,000 on deposit and the interest rate is negative 1 percent, then at the end of one year you have $99,000 on deposit. Part of your money disappears.

Savers can fight negative real rates by going to cash. Assume one saver pulls $100,000 out of the bank and stores the cash safely in a non-bank vault. Another saver leaves her money in the bank and "earns" an interest rate of negative 1 percent. At the end of one year, the first saver still has $100,000, the second saver has $99,000. This example shows why negative interest rates work only in a world without cash. Savers must be forced into an all-digital system before negative interest rates are imposed.

For institutions, and corporations, the battle is already lost. It's difficult enough for an individual to obtain $100,000 in cash. It's practically impossible for a corporation to obtain $1 billion in cash. Large depositors have no recourse against negative interest rates unless they invest their cash in stocks and bonds. That's exactly what the elites want them to do.

The elite drumbeat against cash and in favor of negative interest rates is deafening.

On June 5, 2014, Mario Draghi, head of the European Central Bank (ECB), imposed negative interest rates on euro-denominated balances held on deposit at the ECB by national central banks and major commercial banks. Those banks quickly imposed negative interest rates on their own customers. Goldman Sachs, JPMorgan, Bank of New York Mellon, and other banks all took money from clients' accounts under the umbrella of negative interest rates.

On December 8, 2014, *The Wall Street Journal* reported a story with the headline "BANKS URGE CLIENTS TO TAKE CASH ELSEWHERE." The story said large U.S. banks had informed customers "they will begin charging fees on accounts that have been free for big customers." Of course, a fee is the same as a negative interest rate; you have less money in the account over time—a rose by another name.

On January 22, 2015, the Swiss National Bank imposed negative interest rates on Swiss banking system sight deposits in excess of SFr10 million.

On January 29, 2016, the Bank of Japan voted to impose negative interest rates on commercial bank deposits at the central bank in excess of required reserves.

On February 11, 2016, Federal Reserve chair Janet Yellen told a congressional hearing that the U.S. central bank was "taking a look" at negative interest rates. No formal negative rate policy has been implemented in the United States as of this writing.

On February 16, 2016, former secretary of the treasury Larry Summers wrote a *Washington Post* column in which he called for elimination of the U.S. $100 bill.

On May 4, 2016, the European Central Bank announced it would phase out production of the €500 note by the end of 2018. Existing €500 notes would still be legal tender, yet would be in short supply. This ban raised the possibility of buyers' paying a premium in digital money, say €502, for available €500 notes. A premium purchase amounts to a negative interest rate on physical cash, a heretofore unheard-of result.

On August 30, 2016, Kenneth Rogoff, Harvard professor and former chief economist of the IMF, published a manifesto called *The Curse of Cash*, an elite step-by-step plan to eliminate cash entirely.

The war on cash and the rush to negative interest rates are advancing in lockstep, two sides of the same coin.

Before cattle are led to slaughter, they are herded into pens so they can be easily controlled. The same is true for savers. To freeze cash and impose negative interest rates, savers are being herded into digital accounts at a small number of megabanks. Today, the four largest banks in the United States (Citi, JPMorgan, Bank of America, and Wells Fargo) are bigger than they were in 2008, and control a larger percentage of the total assets of the U.S. banking system. These four banks were originally thirty-seven separate banks in 1990, and were still nineteen separate banks in 2000. JPMorgan is a perfect example, having absorbed the assets of Chase Manhattan, Bear Stearns, Chemical Bank, First Chicago,

Bank One, and Washington Mutual, among other predecessors. What was too big to fail in 2008 is bigger today. Depositor savings are now concentrated where regulators can apply ice-nine solutions with a few phone calls. Savers are being prepared for the slaughter.

The ice-nine plan does not stop with savers. Ice-nine also applies to the banks themselves. On November 10, 2014, the Financial Stability Board operating under the auspices of the G20 issued proposals to require the twenty largest globally systemic important banks to issue debt that could be contractually converted to equity in the event of financial distress. Such debt is an automatic ice-nine bail-in for bondholders that requires no additional action by the regulators.

On December 9, 2014, U.S. bank regulators used the provisions of Dodd-Frank to impose stricter capital requirements, called a "capital surcharge," on the eight largest U.S. banks. Until big banks meet the capital surcharge requirement, they are prohibited from paying cash to stockholders in the form of dividends and stock buybacks. This prohibition is ice-nine applied to bank stockholders.

The ice-nine in *Cat's Cradle* threatened every water molecule on earth. The same is true for financial ice-nine. If regulators apply ice-nine to bank deposits, there will be a run on money market funds. If ice-nine is applied to money market funds also, the run will move to bond markets. If any market is left outside the ice-nine net, it will immediately become the object of distress selling when other markets are frozen. In order for the elite ice-nine plan to work, it must be applied to *everything*.

Not even trading contracts can escape ice-nine. Parties to a trade with a failed firm are normally frozen in place if that firm files for bankruptcy. This standstill rule, called an "automatic stay," is designed to avoid a mad scramble for cash and securities that enriches some and disadvantages others. The automatic stay in bankruptcy gives courts time to fashion an equitable asset distribution.

In the 1980s and 1990s, big banks waged a relentless lobbying campaign to change the law so automatic stay provisions did not apply to transactions such as repurchase agreements and derivatives. When firms like Lehman Brothers went bankrupt in 2008, big bank counterparties used their early termination rights to help themselves to whatever collateral was on hand, leaving less sophisticated investors like local towns holding the bag on losses.

On May 3, 2016, the Federal Reserve announced a formal rule-making process to apply a forty-eight-hour version of the automatic stay to the derivatives contracts of U.S. banks and their counterparties. This new rule was the codification of a 2014 agreement among eighteen major global banks, under the umbrella of the International Swaps and Derivatives Association, to give up their early termination rights. The 2014 agreement was the result of pressure applied by the G20's Financial Stability Board in 2011. Importantly, the abandonment of early termination rights extends to the counterparties of the banks such as bond giant PIMCO and wealth managers such as BlackRock. Big banks and institutional investors will now be treated the same as small savers when ice-nine is applied. They will be frozen in place.

The ice-nine solution is not limited to individuals and institutions. It even applies to countries. Nations can freeze investor funds with capital controls. A dollar investor in a nondollar economy relies on the local central bank for dollars if she wants to withdraw her investment. A central bank can impose capital controls and refuse to allow the dollar investor to reconvert local currency and remit the proceeds.

Capital controls were common in the 1960s even in developed economies. Later, these controls largely disappeared from developed economies, and were greatly reduced in emerging markets. The relaxation has been partly at IMF urging, and partly because floating exchange rates make local economies less vulnerable to a run on the bank.

Yet, in an extraordinary speech on May 24, 2016, David Lipton, first deputy managing director of the IMF, laid the foundation for an international ice-nine solution:

The time has come to re-examine our global architecture. . . .
What elements of the architecture are worth revisiting?

We ought to consider whether the short term and volatility of capital flows are problematic. . . . Those flows, because of their reversibility, can be a useful disciplining force for debtors, creating the market incentive for positive reforms. But that reversibility also has costs, when capital flows suddenly stop. We should look again at whether the supervisory frameworks and tax systems of the source countries unduly encourage short-term, debt-creating flows.

I know that . . . it is heretical to say so, but we ought to consider whether a more coordinated approach to capital flow measures and macro prudential policies in the capital destination countries may be warranted.

Cutting through the jargon, this is a call for coordination between capital "source countries" (mainly the United States) and "destination countries" (emerging markets) to change tax and banking rules to discourage short-term debt and encourage equity and long-term bonds instead. In a liquidity crisis, equity and long-term debt are easy to lock down by closing brokers and exchanges. Residual short-term debt can then be locked down with capital controls on countries.

At the other end of the spectrum from big banks, institutional investors, and nations is the humble ATM. Consumers have been lulled into believing cash is readily available by swiping their bank cards at ubiquitous cash machines. Is it really?

ATMs are already programed to limit withdrawals on a daily basis. You may be able to withdraw $800 or even $1,000 in a day. But have you tried to withdraw $5,000? It cannot be done. If the daily limit is $1,000, banks can easily reprogram the machines to drop the limit to $300, enough for gas and groceries. It's even easier to turn off the machines, as happened in Cyprus in 2012 and Greece in 2015.

Getting cash from a bank teller is not a practical alternative to a disabled ATM. For more than modest amounts you will be flagged by a well-trained teller who will summon his supervisor for approval of your withdrawal. The supervisor will recommend that a "Suspicious Activity Report," or SAR, be filed with the U.S. Treasury. SARs were intended to identify money launderers, drug dealers, and terrorists. You are none of the above. The report will be filed anyway. Banks fear regulators more than embarrassed clients. There is no upside for the bank to cut you a break. Your name will end up in a Treasury file next to members of the drug cartels and Al Qaeda.

Even this self-help to acquire cash has limits because bank branches carry relatively small supplies of hundred-dollar bills. If a real run on cash emerged, customers would be turned away sooner than later. The hundred-dollar bill itself is a wasting asset because of inflation.

This overview shows stock exchanges can be closed, ATMs shut down, money market funds frozen, negative interest rates imposed, and cash denied, all within minutes. Your money may be like a jewel in a glass case at Cartier; you can see it but not touch it. Savers do not realize the ice-nine solution is already in place, waiting to be activated with an executive order and a few phone calls.

House Closed

A typical reaction to the ice-nine overview is that it seems extreme. History shows the opposite. Closed markets, closed banks, and confiscation are as American as apple pie. A survey of financial panics in the past 110 years beginning with the Panic of 1907 shows bank and exchange closures with depositor and investor losses are not unusual.

The Panic of 1907 originated in the great San Francisco earthquake and fire of April 18, 1906. Western insurance companies sold assets to pay claims. The selling put pressure on East Coast money centers and reduced liquidity among New York banks. By October 1907, the New York Stock Exchange index had fallen 50 percent from its 1906 high.

On Tuesday, October 14, 1907, a failed attempt to corner the market in United Copper shares using bank loans was revealed. In a tight money environment, the lender bank quickly went insolvent. Then suspicion fell on a larger institution, Knickerbocker Trust, controlled by an associate of the speculators. A classic run on the bank developed. Depositors in New York and around the country lined up to withdraw cash and gold, which was legal tender at the time.

At the height of the panic, on Sunday, November 3, 1907, J. Pierpont Morgan convened a meeting of the leading bankers in his town house on Thirty-sixth Street and Madison Avenue in Manhattan. Morgan famously ordered the town house library doors locked with the bankers inside. Morgan informed the bankers they were not allowed to leave until they worked out a rescue.

Morgan's associates oversaw a process by which bank books were quickly examined. A triage solution was agreed. Banks that were sound were expected to join the rescue fund. Banks that were insolvent were allowed to fail. In between were banks that were technically solvent but temporarily illiquid. They were required to pledge assets for cash in order to meet depositors' withdrawals. At no point was there any thought of bailing out every bank in New York.

It was expected that, in time, the panic would subside, deposits would return, and the pledges could be unwound at a profit to the rescuers. That is exactly what happened. By November 4, the panic subsided. Still, many depositors were wiped out. Importantly, the panic was contained and did not spread to every bank in the city. The process is no different from a quarantine of Ebola victims to stop the spread of the virus to a wider population.

This rescue model used by Morgan was abandoned one hundred years later in the Panic of 2008. With the exception of Lehman Brothers, all major banks were bailed out by the U.S. Treasury and Federal Reserve without discrimination between the solvent and the insolvent.

The Brisbane G20 bail-in template can be seen as a return to the principles of J. P. Morgan. In the next crisis, there will be blood. Insolvent institutions will be permanently closed and losses more widespread.

Seven years after the Panic of 1907 came the Panic of 1914, on the

eve of the First World War. The panic was triggered by an Austrian ultimatum to Serbia on July 23. This new panic was broader and lasted
longer than the Panic of 1907.

European diarists uniformly recall the months before the ultimatum as among the most pleasant in memory. The assassination of Arch-
duke Franz Ferdinand, heir to the Austro-Hungarian Empire, and his
wife Sophie in Sarajevo on June 28, 1914, was at first considered an unfortunate symptom of instability that had plagued the Balkans for years,
not as the casus belli it became.

The Austro-Hungarian general staff led by Count Franz Conrad von
Hötzendorf had been spoiling for a fight with Serbia. They were held
back by Franz Ferdinand's moderating influence on his uncle, the Emperor Franz Josef. The assassination was a double blow to peace—it removed a moderating influence and provided von Hötzendorf with a
reason to crush Serbian ambition in the Balkans. On Friday, July 23,
1914, Austria-Hungary delivered an ultimatum to Serbia. The ultimatum was intended to be unacceptable. While London and Paris basked
in a glorious summer glow, the dogs of war were unleashed.

On July 24, Russia ordered a partial mobilization of land and sea
forces in support of Serbia. On July 25, Serbia accepted some, but not all,
of the terms of the Austro-Hungarian ultimatum and ordered a general
mobilization. In response, Vienna broke off diplomatic relations with
Serbia and ordered its own partial mobilization.

Once market participants saw war was inevitable, they acted in the
same mechanical way as the generals with their mobilization plans and
timetables. The period of the classical gold standard immediately preceding the war, 1870–1914, is best seen as a first age of globalization, a
simulacrum of the second age of globalization that began in 1989 with
the fall of the Berlin Wall. New technologies such as the telephone and
electricity tied diverse financial centers together in a dense web of credit
and counterparty risk. In 1914, global capital markets were no less
densely connected than they are today. With the advent of war, French,
Italian, and German investors all sold stocks in London and demanded

proceeds in gold shipped to them by the fastest available means. Under the rules of the game, gold was the ultimate form of money, and it would be hoarded to fight the war. A global liquidity crisis commenced in lockstep with the political crisis.

The City of London was then the unrivaled financial capital of the world. Selling from the Continent put pressure on London banks to liquidate their own assets to meet claims. What ensued was not a classic run on the bank, but a more complex liquidity crisis. Sterling-denominated trade bills guaranteed by London banks were not rolled over. New bills were not issued. Liquidity dried up in the world's most liquid money market. This liquidity crisis was eerily similar to the collapse of the commercial paper market in the United States in 2008.

Contagion spread to New York. Just as French banks sold London shares to get gold, London investors sold New York stocks for the same reason. The world was in a scramble for specie. Stock markets and money markets were in distress as investors dumped paper assets and demanded gold.

On July 28, 1914, Austria-Hungary declared war on Serbia. By July 30, stock exchanges in Amsterdam, Paris, Madrid, Rome, Berlin, Vienna, and Moscow had closed their doors and all major protagonists with the exception of the United Kingdom officially suspended convertibility of currency to gold. On Friday, July 31, 1914, the City did the unthinkable and closed the London Stock Exchange. A small sign posted on the members' entrance said simply "HOUSE CLOSED."

With London closed, all of the selling pressure in the world was now directed at New York as the last major venue where stocks could be sold for gold. The selling in New York was already intense in the days preceding the London closure. On July 31, 1914, just hours after London closed, and fifteen minutes before the New York opening bell, the New York Stock Exchange closed its doors also. This was partly at the urging of the U.S. secretary of the treasury, William McAdoo. The New York Stock Exchange would remain closed for more than four months until December 12, 1914.

The United States was officially neutral at the start of the First World War and able to trade with all of the combatant nations. While the stock exchange was closed, banks remained open. European parties who sold assets of any kind, including real estate or private equity, could demand conversion of proceeds into gold to be shipped to Hamburg, Genoa, or Rotterdam.

Stocks were still traded through private negotiation on the informal "curb exchange" that emerged on New Street in lower Manhattan in an alley behind the New York Stock Exchange building. On Monday, August 3, 1914, *The New York Times* carried this advertisement: "We are prepared to buy and sell all classes of securities on the following terms and conditions: Bids must be accompanied by cash to cover; offers to sell must be accompanied by the securities properly endorsed." The ad was signed "New York Curb."

Some historians concluded that the New York Stock Exchange was closed because its board thought heavy selling from abroad would cause stock prices to collapse. Research conducted by William L. Silber in his classic book *When Washington Shut Down Wall Street* reveals another more intriguing explanation. Silber shows that U.S. buyers were ready to pounce on bargains offered by desperate European sellers, and stock prices would have stabilized.

According to Silber, the real reason the exchange was shut, and the reason the U.S. Treasury was involved, was not stock prices but gold. European sellers were entitled to convert their sales proceeds into gold at the U.S. subtreasury building located on Wall Street across from the exchange. Treasury was concerned that U.S. banks would quickly run out of gold so it shut down stock trading to hoard the gold. The exchange closure was an early application of the ice-nine approach.

The Great Depression, and the years leading up to the Second World War, brought the most radical ice-nine freezes in the twentieth century. The depression in the United States is conventionally dated from the stock market crash in October 1929. Yet the global depression began even earlier in the United Kingdom, which experienced depressed conditions through the late 1920s. Germany entered a downturn in 1927. In the United States, stocks and industrial output plunged and unemployment soared beginning in 1929. The most acute phase of the depression, including a global banking panic, was concentrated in the years 1931–33.

The European bank panic started in Austria with the failure of Creditanstalt on May 11, 1931. This led quickly to bank runs throughout Europe and the evaporation of commercial credit in London in a dynamic similar to the Panic of 1914. City bankers informed the Bank of England and the U.K. Treasury they would be insolvent in a matter of days if a rescue was not organized by the government.

Unlike 1914 when gold convertibility was nominally maintained, this time the U.K. Treasury broke with the gold standard and devalued sterling. The devaluation eased financial conditions in the United Kingdom and shifted pressure to the United States, which now had the strongest currency in the world. The United States became a magnet for global deflation.

In December 1930, the Bank of United States (a private bank despite its official sounding name), which catered to immigrants and small savers, suffered a bank run and closed its doors. The bank may have been solvent. Prejudice against Jewish and immigrant customers of the bank played a role in the refusal of the large New York Clearing House banks to rescue it.

The clearinghouse believed the damage could be contained to the Bank of United States. They were wrong. Bank runs spread like an out-of-control prairie fire. Parts of the United States literally ran out of money. Communities resorted to barter and use of "wooden nickels" to buy food. More than nine thousand U.S. banks failed during the Great Depression. Many depositors lost their savings when the bank liquidations were completed.

In the winter of 1933, President Hoover sought agreement from President-elect Roosevelt to announce some form of general bank closure or debt relief. Rather than join forces with Hoover, FDR preferred to wait until he was sworn in on March 4, 1933. Panic reached epic proportions. Savers around the country lined up at banks to withdraw funds. They stored cash in coffee cans or under mattresses at home.

Roosevelt acted decisively. Less than thirty-six hours after being sworn in, at 1:00 a.m. on Monday, March 6, 1933, Roosevelt issued Proclamation 2039, which shut every bank in America. FDR gave no indication when they might reopen.

Over the next week, bank regulators purported to examine the books of closed banks and proceeded to reopen banks deemed solvent based on that examination. This process was similar to the "stress tests" conducted by Treasury Secretary Tim Geithner in 2009 in response to another financial panic.

What matters most in such cases is not the actual health of the banks, but the U.S. government's ability to give a "seal of approval" to relieve savers' anxiety. In fact, the banks reopened on March 13, 1933, after a one-week "holiday." Confidence was restored. Customers lined up again—this time not to withdraw cash, but to deposit.

The bank holiday was followed on April 5, 1933, with the notorious Executive Order 6102 requiring with limited exceptions that all gold held by U.S. citizens be surrendered to the U.S. Treasury under pain of imprisonment. FDR also prohibited gold exports. These gold strictures were not removed until President Ford issued Executive Order 11825 on December 31, 1974, which revoked prior executive orders on gold.

In short order, Proclamation 2039 and Executive Order 6102 were used to subject all of America's gold and cash in the bank to an ice-nine lockdown. Executive authority to do this again today exists under current law. Congress cannot stop it.

The global financial system stabilized after 1933, then collapsed again in 1939 with the advent of the Second World War. Warring nations, led by the United Kingdom, once again suspended the convertibility of their currencies to gold and prohibited gold exports. Because gold was money at the time, these prohibitions represented another systemic freeze.

The global financial system started to thaw in anticipation of an

Allied victory in the war. The seminal event was the July 1944 Bretton Woods conference. The conference itself was the end result of two years of intense behind-the-scenes struggles between the United States and United Kingdom, represented by Harry Dexter White and John Maynard Keynes respectively, as vividly described by Benn Steil in his book *The Battle of Bretton Woods*.

An alternative to periodic panic and lockdown is a system that is coherent, controlled, and rigorously rule based. That was the case under the classic Bretton Woods system from 1944 to 1971. During that twenty-seven-year golden age, signatories to the Bretton Woods agreement pegged their currencies to the U.S. dollar at fixed exchange rates. The U.S. dollar was pegged to gold at the fixed rate of $35 per ounce. The dollar-gold peg meant the other currencies, notably pounds sterling, French francs, German marks, and Japanese yen, were indirectly pegged to gold and one another via the dollar. The U.S. dollar was the common denominator of global finance, exactly as White and his boss, Treasury Secretary Henry Morgenthau, intended.

Importantly, there was more to the Bretton Woods system than fixed exchange rates. The system would be administered by the International Monetary Fund, a de facto world central bank. IMF governance was structured in such a way that the United States maintained a veto over all important decisions. Bretton Woods participants were allowed to use capital controls to maintain dollar reserves and limit volatile capital flows in order to support their obligations under the fixed rate system. Capital controls in major Western economies were lifted in stages beginning in 1958. Full convertibility of all major currencies was not achieved until 1964.

Currency pegs to the dollar were not immutable. Members could apply for exchange rate adjustments under IMF supervision. The IMF would first offer to make temporary funding available to the nation whose currency was under stress. The goal was to give that nation time to make structural reforms to improve its balance of trade, and bolster foreign exchange reserves so the peg could be maintained. Once the adjustments were made, and the reserves bolstered, the borrower could repay the IMF and the system continue as before.

In more dire cases, where temporary measures proved insufficient, devaluation was approved. The most high-profile devaluation under Bretton Woods was the 1967 sterling crisis. There the sterling peg was adjusted from $2.80 to $2.40, a 14 percent decline. One peg that could not be adjusted was the dollar-to-gold ratio. Gold was the anchor of the entire system.

The international system of capital controls and fixed exchange rates overseen by the IMF and the United States was complemented by a regime of financial repression. At the end of the Second World War, the U.S. debt-to-GDP ratio stood at 120 percent. Over the next twenty years, the Federal Reserve and U.S. Treasury engineered a monetary regime in which interest rates were kept artificially low and mild inflation was allowed to persist. Neither rates nor inflation surged out of control. The slight excess of inflation over rates from financial repression was barely noticed by the public. Americans enjoyed the postwar prosperity, rising stocks, new amenities, and a congenial culture.

Financial repression is the art of keeping inflation slightly higher than interest rates for an extended period. The old debt burden melts from inflation while new debt creation is constrained by low rates. Just a 1 percent difference between inflation and rates cuts the real value of the debt by 30 percent in twenty years. By 1965, the U.S. debt-to-GDP ratio was down to 40 percent, a striking improvement from 1945.

Diminution in the dollar's value was so slow there seemed no cause for public alarm. It was like watching an ice cube melt. It happens, yet slowly.

There were few financial crises in the tranquil time from 1945 to 1965. Russia and China were not integrated with the global financial system. Africa was barely a blip on the global scale. Emerging Asia had not yet emerged, and India was stagnant. Latin America was subordinate to U.S. hegemony.

As long as oil flowed, only Europe, Japan, and Canada mattered to

U.S. economic interests, and they were locked in to the Bretton Woods system. No ice-nine solution was imposed because it already existed. The Bretton Woods system was a global ice-nine. The United States controlled over half the world's gold, as well as the dollar—the only forms of money that mattered.

The Bretton Woods system began to wobble badly beginning in 1965. The system suffered combined blows from U.S. inflation, sterling devaluation, and a run on U.S. gold. The United States was unwilling to make structural adjustments it required of other nations. In February 1965, French president Charles de Gaulle famously called for the end of dollar hegemony and a return to a true gold standard. De Gaulle's finance minister, Valéry Giscard d'Estaing, called the dollar's role under Bretton Woods "an exorbitant privilege."

The United Kingdom, Japan, and Germany were willing to play along with the pretense that the dollar was as good as gold. The United Kingdom was broke. Germany and Japan relied on the U.S. nuclear umbrella for their national security. None were yet in a strong position to challenge the United States.

The rest of Western Europe, urged on by de Gaulle, took a different view. France, Spain, Switzerland, the Netherlands, and Italy increasingly cashed in their dollar reserves for gold. A full-scale run on Fort Knox ensued.

In the most famous example of an ice-nine solution in the twentieth century, President Nixon closed the gold window on August 15, 1971. It was no longer possible for U.S. trading partners to exchange dollar reserves for gold at a fixed price. Nixon put up a "HOUSE CLOSED" sign for the world to see.

The Money Riots

The period from 1971 to 1980 in international finance is best described as chaotic, not only in a colloquial sense, but in a scientific sense. Equilibrium was perturbed. Values wobbled violently. IMF members tried, and failed, to reestablish fixed exchange rates at new parities along with a new dollar parity to gold.

Monetarists such as Milton Friedman urged the world to abandon gold as a monetary standard. Floating exchange rates became the new normal. Countries could make their goods cheaper by letting their currencies devalue instead of making structural adjustments to improve productivity.

Keynesians embraced the new system because inflation caused by devaluation lowered unit labor costs in real terms. Workers would no longer have to suffer pay cuts. Instead their wages were stolen through inflation in the expectation that they wouldn't notice until it was too late. Monetarists and Keynesians were now united under the banner of money illusion.

In this brave new world of elastic money and zero gold, ice-nine solutions were no longer needed. If panicked savers wanted their money back, there was no need to close the system—you could print money and give it to them.

The ice-nine process had been reversed. With floating exchange rates, an ice age ended, glaciers melted, and the world was awash in a sea of liquidity. This was the financial equivalent of global warming. There was no problem that could not be solved with low rates, easy money, and more credit.

Easy money did not end financial crises; far from it. There was a Latin American debt crisis beginning in 1982, a Mexican peso crisis in 1994, an Asian-Russian financial crisis in 1998, and the 2007–9 global financial crisis. In addition, there were occasional market panics including October 19, 1987, when the Dow Jones Industrial Average fell 22 percent in one day. Other market crashes included the burst dot-com bubble in 2000, and the market break after the 9/11 attacks.

What was new was that none of these crises involved widespread bank defaults or closures. Without a gold standard, money was now elastic. There was no limit to the liquidity central banks could provide through money printing, guarantees, swap lines, and promises of extended ease called forward guidance. Money was free, or nearly free, and available in unlimited quantities.

This new system was not always neat and tidy. Investors suffered losses on the real value of their principal in the 1970s and 1980s. Still, the system itself stayed afloat. The Latin American debt crisis was solved with Brady bonds, named after U.S. treasury secretary Nicholas Brady. Brady bonds used U.S. Treasury notes to partially guarantee repayment on new bonds used to refinance defaulted debt. Treasury Secretary Robert Rubin tapped the Exchange Stabilization Fund (ESF) to provide loans to Mexico in 1994 when Mexico could not roll over its debts to Wall Street. The ESF had been created with profits from FDR's 1933 gold confiscation and still exists as a Treasury slush fund. The ESF was a way to go around Congress, which had refused a Mexican bailout.

The IMF and Federal Reserve rather than the U.S. Treasury provided rescue funds in the 1997–98 crisis. The crisis began with the Thai baht depreciation in July 1997. The IMF gave emergency loans to Korea, Indonesia, and Thailand in the first phase of that global liquidity crunch.

The crisis abated in the winter and spring of 1998, then burst into flames in late summer. Russia defaulted on its debt and devalued the ruble on August 17, 1998. The IMF prepared a financial firewall around Brazil, then seen as the next domino to fall.

The world was shocked to learn the next domino was not a country, but a hedge fund—Long-Term Capital Management. The IMF had no authority to bail out a hedge fund. The task was left to the Federal Reserve Bank of New York, which supervised the banks that stood to fail if LTCM defaulted.

In an intense six-day period, September 23–28, 1998, Wall Street, under the watchful eye of the Fed, cobbled together a $4 billion bailout to stabilize the fund. Once the bailout was closed, Fed chair Alan Greenspan assisted the banks with an interest rate cut at a scheduled Federal Open Market Committee (FOMC) meeting on September 29, 1998.

Still, markets did not stabilize. The newly recapitalized LTCM lost another half-billion dollars in a matter of days. Wall Street bailed out a hedge fund; now who would bail out Wall Street? The Fed intervened again. Greenspan cut rates in a rare unscheduled announcement on October 15, 1998. That was the only occasion in the past twenty-two years as of this writing when the Fed cut rates without a scheduled FOMC meeting.

Markets got the message. The Dow Jones Industrial Average rose 4.2 percent, its third-largest one-day point gain in history. Bond markets normalized. The bleeding at LTCM finally stopped. The Fed's unscheduled rate cut was an early version of a policy European Central Bank (ECB) head Mario Draghi described in June 2012 as "Whatever it takes."

The new practice of papering over recurrent crises peaked in the fall of 2008 when U.S. regulators guaranteed every bank deposit and money market fund in America. The Fed printed trillions of dollars to prop up U.S. banks and arranged tens of trillions of dollars of currency swaps with the ECB. The ECB needed those dollars to prop up the European banks.

Unlimited liquidity worked. The storm passed, markets stabilized, economies grew, albeit slowly, and asset prices reflated. By 2016, the policy of flooding the world with liquidity was widely praised.

Had the ice-nine approach of 1907, 1914, the 1930s, and Bretton Woods been replaced with a monetary warming that now threatened hurricanes? Were there limits on what elastic money could do? In late 2016, the world was on the verge of finding out.

Extraordinary policy measures used in 2008 had mostly not been unwound by 2016. Central bank balance sheets were still bloated. Swap lines from the Fed to the ECB were still in place. Global leverage had increased. Sovereign-debt-to-GDP ratios were higher. Losses loomed in sovereign debt, junk bonds, and emerging markets. Derivatives passed one quadrillion in notional value—more than ten times global GDP.

Global elites gradually realized their monetary ease had simply spawned new bubbles rather than affording a sound footing. The stage was set for another collapse and the elites knew it. Now they doubted their ability to run the same playbook.

The Fed expanded its balance sheet from $800 billion to $4.2 trillion by 2015 to quench the 2008 crisis. What would it do the next time? A comparable percentage increase would leave the balance sheet at $20 trillion, roughly equal to the GDP of the United States.

Other central banks faced the same dilemma. The hope had been that economies would resume self-sustained growth at potential output. Then central banks could withdraw policy support and go to the sidelines. That didn't happen. Instead growth stayed anemic. Markets looked to central banks to keep the game going with easy money. Seven years of complacency had lulled markets to sleep regarding risks of leverage and nontransparency.

In the summer of 2014, elites began to sound the alarm. On June 29, 2014, the Bank for International Settlements (BIS) issued its annual report. It warned that markets were "euphoric" and said, "Time and again . . . seemingly strong balance sheets have turned out to mask unsuspected vulnerabilities."

The BIS report was followed on September 20, 2014, by another warning from the G20 finance ministers meeting in Cairns, Queensland. Their communiqué said, "We are mindful of the potential for a buildup of excessive risk in financial markets, particularly in an environment of low interest rates and low asset price volatility."

Just a few days later, a powerfully connected think tank in Geneva, Switzerland, the International Center for Monetary and Banking Studies (ICMB), issued its annual "Geneva Report" on the world economy.

After years of being reassured by policymakers that the world was deleveraging, ICMB offered this shocking synopsis: "Contrary to widely held beliefs, six years on from the beginning of the financial crisis . . . the global economy is not yet on a deleveraging path. Indeed, the ratio of global total debt . . . over GDP . . . has kept increasing . . . and breaking new highs." The report referred to the impact of excessive debt on the world economy as "poisonous."

Warnings continued. Shortly after the Geneva Report, on October 11, 2014, the IMF added its own alarms. The head of the IMF's powerful policy committee said capital markets are "vulnerable to 'financial Ebolas' that are bound to happen."

Nor could the U.S. government turn a blind eye to the developing storm. The U.S. Treasury's Office of Financial Research in its annual report to Congress issued on December 2, 2014, warned that "financial stability risks have increased. The three most important are excessive risk taking . . . vulnerabilities associated with declining market liquidity, and the migration of financial activities toward opaque and less resilient corners of the financial system."

On December 5, 2014, BIS again warned about financial instability. Claudio Borio, head of the monetary department at BIS, with reference to extreme volatility and the abrupt disappearance of market liquidity, said, "The highly abnormal is becoming uncomfortably normal. . . . There is something vaguely troubling when the unthinkable becomes routine."

These warnings emerged in 2014 as it became clear monetary ease would not restore growth. This first wave of warnings was followed by more explicit warnings in annual reports and meetings for subsequent years. Expansion of leverage, asset values, and derivatives volume continued unabated.

The warnings were not for investors, most of whom are unfamiliar with the agencies involved and the technical jargon used. These warnings were intended for the small number of elite experts who read them. Elites were not warning everyday citizens; they were warning one another.

The BIS, IMF, G20, and other international monetary agencies were issuing warnings to a small group of finance ministers, sovereign wealth funds, banks, and private funds such as BlackRock and Bridgewater. They were given time to adjust their portfolios and avoid losses that would overtake the small investor.

The elites were also laying a foundation so when crisis struck they could credibly say, "I warned you." This despite the fact that most investors scarcely knew of the warnings when they were sounded. This foundation makes it easier to enforce the ice-nine solution. Because investors ignored clear warnings, they would have no one to blame but themselves.

By late 2016, the stage was set. Systemic risk had grown to alarming levels. The symptoms were seen not only in the U.S. financial system, but also in China, Japan, and Europe. The ice-nine apparatus was ready to seize SIFI banks, freeze money market funds, close exchanges, limit cash, and order money managers to suspend redemptions by clients.

In advance of a global freeze, elites had warned certain cronies and insulated themselves from criticism. Only one question remained. Would ice-nine work? There was no doubt about governments' capacity to impose ice-nine. Still, would citizens acquiesce as they had in 1914 and 1933, or would there be a descent to disorder?

If money riots broke out, authorities were prepared for that too.

The United States has been under a state of emergency declared by President Bush in Proclamation 7463 on September 14, 2001. The state of emergency has been renewed annually since 2001 by Presidents Bush and Obama. The state of emergency grants the president extraordinary executive powers, including martial law.

This is not the stuff of conspiracy theorists. States of emergency and similar powers are authorized by acts of Congress and executive orders. These actions have expanded in a steady stream since the Truman administration. Major extensions of these power were ordered by Presidents Kennedy and Reagan to reflect cold war realities.

Emergency powers have been tested continually through exercises in every administration. During one exercise in 1956, President Eisenhower ordered a simulated nuclear attack on the Soviet Union based on the progress of the exercise to that point.

While statutes authorizing martial law were created with nuclear warfare in mind, they are not limited to that circumstance. They can be applied to any emergency situation including money riots in the event of a financial system breakdown and ice-nine asset freeze.

In addition to broad emergency powers applicable to any emergency, dictatorial powers have been given to the president by Congress to respond specifically to financial crises. These powers have been expanded over the decades beginning with the Trading with the Enemy Act of 1917 through the International Emergency Economic Powers Act of 1977 (IEEPA).

The president has authority under IEEPA to freeze or seize assets and institutions if there is a threat to national security with a foreign connection. In globalized markets every financial crisis has a foreign connection. Systemic crises threaten national security if allowed to go unchecked. Therefore the bar to use of IEEPA's confiscatory powers is quite low.

Treasury Secretary Hank Paulson and Fed chairman Ben Bernanke have repeatedly said they lacked authority to seize Lehman Brothers during the Panic of 2008. This is false. There was ample authority under IEEPA. Either Treasury's lawyers didn't think of it or Treasury chose not to use it.

The use of these emergency economic powers and martial law is a more coercive version of the ice-nine plan to freeze accounts in place. Ice-nine is intended to buy time and restore calm while elites work on plans to allocate losses and reliquefy the system with IMF special drawing rights. If events spin out of control faster than elites expect, more radical measures may be needed. Such measures may involve property confiscation. States of emergency and IEEPA enable outright confiscation by the state. If resistance is encountered, martial law powers backed up by heavily militarized local police, the National Guard, and regular military forces will carry out the president's executive orders.

Emergency measures will not be used in a containable financial crisis of the kind we saw in 1998 and 2008. Yet that is not the kind of crisis we are facing. The next financial crisis will be exponentially larger, and impossible to contain without extraordinary measures.

As the next crisis begins, and then worsens, measures described here will be rolled out, one by one. First come asset freezes and exchange closures. Then confiscation backed up with armed force. The question arises—will everyday citizens stand for it?

This question has not arisen in the United States since 1933 when President Franklin Roosevelt confiscated citizens' gold bullion. In the depths of the Great Depression, and a nationwide run on the banks, Americans accepted the gold confiscation as a price they had to pay to restore order. There was great faith in the newly elected Roosevelt, and a sense of purpose in pulling the country away from catastrophe.

Since then, nothing quite so dramatic as gold confiscation has occurred. Market crashes have come and gone. Investor losses have been legion. Still, no widespread seizures have been ordered. The response to crises in the United States has been to cut rates, print money, and reliquefy the system. When necessary, institutions are closed surgically without mass freezes. The ice-nine approach would be new to almost every American alive.

Examples from abroad are less sanguine, and more sanguinary. During the 1997–98 global financial crisis, riots in Indonesia and Korea left many dead. There was literally blood in the streets. Since the 2008 financial crisis, there have been violent protests in Greece, Spain, and Cyprus that have resulted in a few deaths.

Surveys show Americans are far less trusting of government, banks, and media than they have ever been. Political polarization in America has grown to extreme levels. Income inequality has reached levels not seen since 1929. A sense of shared purpose in presidential leadership is gone. In the next crisis, as confiscatory solutions are employed, the popular response is less likely to be passive acceptance and more likely to involve resistance.

Elites are prepared for this also.

Mount Weather, Virginia, and Raven Rock Mountain, Pennsylvania, are two of the most important government sites most Americans have never heard of. In the event of global war, catastrophe, or widespread money riots, U.S. civilian and military leadership will deploy to those locations to continue government operations on an emergency basis.

Mount Weather is located off a state highway in Loudoun County, Virginia, near the Blue Ridge Mountains. Mount Weather is operated by the Department of Homeland Security, and is home base for the FEMA National Radio System. It is known in official circles by its code name, "High Point Special Facility."

Mount Weather contains a network of underground bunkers known as Area B to distinguish it from the aboveground facilities called Area A. During the 9/11 attacks in New York and Washington, the congressional leadership was moved by helicopter from Capitol Hill to Mount Weather's Area B.

Raven Rock Mountain is located in Adams County, Pennsylvania, not far from the Maryland border and the presidential retreat at Camp David. Raven Rock is the main military operations center in the event of nuclear attack or other catastrophe that interferes with normal Pentagon operations. The primary command facility is codenamed Site R, and nicknamed "the Rock."

Raven Rock is the military counterpart to Mount Weather. In the event of a collapse in order, civilian leadership will evacuate to Mount Weather, while military leadership evacuates to Raven Rock. Together, these two facilities, about thirty miles apart and densely connected by secure communications channels, will replace Washington, D.C., as the seat of government power.

The Department of Homeland Security conducts classified exercises to practice the use of Mount Weather. The most recent exercise was called Eagle Horizon 2016, conducted on May 16, 2016. Past versions of Eagle Horizon have included dirty bomb attacks, cyberattacks, and other forms of terrorism. The exact scenario for Eagle Horizon is classified, but could have included a global bank collapse with resulting money riots around the world.

Both Mount Weather and Raven Rock Mountain are operated pursuant to a highly classified plan called the Continuity of Operations

Plan. This is a classified plan for continued operations of the U.S. government during attack, financial collapse, or natural disaster. President George W. Bush activated the Continuity of Operations Plan during the 9/11 attacks, although this was not publicly acknowledged at the time.

This combination of emergency facilities and emergency powers is designed to withstand any military, natural, or financial shock. The United States government is ready for a catastrophe. The American people are not.

A global financial crisis, worse than any before, is imminent for reasons explained in this book. A liquidity injection of the kind seen in 1998 and 2008 will not suffice because central bank balance sheets are stretched. There will be little time to respond. Ice-nine account freezes will be used to buy time while global elites convene an international monetary conference. They will attempt to use special drawing rights (SDRs) issued by the IMF to refloat the system.

SDRs might work. But a more likely outcome is that citizens will see through the sham of resolving a paper money crisis with more paper money. Investors will grow impatient with ice-nine. They will want their money back. The money riots will begin.

Sovereigns don't go down without a fight. The response to money riots will be confiscation and brute force. Governing elites will be safe in their hollowed-out mountain command centers. Private elites will fend for themselves in their yachts, helicopters, and gated communities, which will be converted to armed fortresses.

There will be blood in the streets, not metaphorically, but literally. Neofascism will emerge, order responding to disorder, with liberty lost.

T. S. Eliot had a vision of the modern condition in his 1922 poem *The Waste Land:*

> *Who are those hooded hordes swarming*
> *Over endless plains, stumbling in cracked earth*
> *Ringed by the flat horizon only*
> *What is the city over the mountains*

Cracks and reforms and bursts in the violet air
Falling towers
Jerusalem Athens Alexandria
Vienna London
Unreal

Money riots seem unreal. Yet they come.

CHAPTER 2

ONE MONEY, ONE WORLD, ONE ORDER

Massive progress has been made in the last five years thanks to the crisis. I hope, personally, that it's not going to take another crisis to make yet more progress.

Christine Lagarde, IMF managing director
Davos, Switzerland, January 22, 2015

You never want a serious crisis to go to waste.

Rahm Emanuel, November 21, 2008

SPECTRE IS A FICTIONAL CRIMINAL CONSPIRACY CREATED BY AUTHOR Ian Fleming. The name is an acronym for Special Executive for Counterintelligence, Terrorism, Revenge and Extortion. It first appeared in Fleming's 1961 novel *Thunderball* as the antagonist to his spy-hero James Bond, MI6 agent 007, licensed to kill.

While SPECTRE is criminal, it is organized in ways similar to a modern NGO or the IMF. It is a transnational organization headquartered in Paris. SPECTRE has an executive board of twenty members (the IMF board has twenty-four) with representation from countries around the world; it is not aligned with any one country or ideology. In *Thunderball*, SPECTRE's offices are located behind a front organization that offers assistance to refugees.

The most recent fictional depiction of SPECTRE appears in the eponymous 2015 film featuring Daniel Craig as 007. In the film, the SPECTRE executive board is pictured seated around a large, dark wooden table in a high-ceilinged meeting room in Rome. The board is ethnically and culturally diverse, including women in important leadership roles. The board's agenda includes reports from executives on the performance and profits from distinct business lines. In these reports, the lines between criminal and legitimate enterprises seem to blur seamlessly.

Pondering the operation of today's global monetary elites, the image of SPECTRE leaps irresistibly to mind. Its top-down ontology suits the conspiracy minded. Sometimes life seems to imitate art as in the annual meetings of the elite Bilderberg Group, which are closed, secretive, and in all the best places. But if the Bilderberg Group is real, there is scant evidence for a central committee to subdue humanity. Besides, a top-down process is unneeded to control the world through money. The real process is more subtle.

True elites operate inside spheres of influence. These include finance, media, technology, the military, and politics. Denizens of each sphere have their favorite gathering times and places. Media elites gather each July at the Allen & Company Sun Valley conference in Idaho. Central bankers gather in August at the Jackson Hole, Wyoming, conference sponsored by the Kansas City Federal Reserve. Military and intelligence elites gather at the Munich Security Conference in early February. Thought leaders and public intellectuals can take their pick from among the World Economic Forum in Davos, Switzerland, the Milken Institute Global Conference in Beverly Hills, and the TED (Technology, Entertainment, Design) conference in Vancouver.

These super-elite venues are not run-of-the-mill industry conventions. They are by invitation only, or come with admission and sponsorship conditions that self-select for power elite participation. One encounters heads of state, cabinet officials, CEOs, and billionaires. Hoi polloi need not apply.

The most exclusive gathering, and the one that generates the most conspiracy theories, is the Bilderberg Meeting, held annually since 1954 in various locations. Bilderberg has a core group of about forty regular attendees, and a larger group of about one hundred invitees who vary from year to year depending on topical urgency or political ascendancy. The core group are mostly financial and industrial elites; the broader group leans toward policymakers and public intellectuals.

When I privately briefed the head of Bilderberg in Rockefeller Center a few years ago, he was polite and intensely interested in my views on the euro. I assured him and his associates the euro was here to stay at a time when many economists were shrieking about its imminent demise. At the conclusion of our discussion, he kindly gave me a gift, a Swedish vase designed in a deep blue translucent vortex, which I keep in sight in my writing studio. He did not have horns.

At these and similar gatherings, ideological differences are laid aside. The Sun Valley conference in July 2016 included Fox owner Rupert Murdoch and Brian Roberts, owner of MSNBC. Elite ideology shared by Murdoch and Roberts is more powerful than political shouting matches broadcast for mass consumption. The latter is entertainment. Sun Valley is about power.

The important elite activity at these conferences does not occur at scheduled panels, but at private dinners, and over drinks in suites and secluded bungalows surrounding the main venue. When I appeared at the Milken Institute Global Conference, there were more meaningful conversations in the bar at the Peninsula Hotel, a block away from the main event, than on the stages.

Elite spheres float and overlap like an interactive, three-dimensional Venn diagram. Intersections emerge, blend, and disappear. At interstices are elites who channel power from one sphere to another. Chris Dodd is a good example. As a five-term U.S. senator, and Dodd-Frank sponsor, he is anchored in the political and financial spheres. As head of the Motion Picture Association of America, he is also anchored in the media sphere. When media elites and political elites need to connect, one channel runs through Dodd.

This structure of separate spheres, intersections, and designated channels is how the global power elite rules. This model has greater explanatory power than some imagined close-knit, top-down Committee to Rule the World. Such a committee, if it existed, would be relatively easy to identify, monitor, and expose. In contrast, a floating-spheres model is amorphous, hard to pin down. If an individual member is discredited by scandal or reversal of fortune, she is swiftly sacrificed (with later rehabilitation possible) while the system survives. Media have no interest in elucidating this system; reporters can't imagine it, and media CEOs take part.

Another meme favored by conspiracy mongers is that the global elite is malevolent. A more serious problem than elites' doing evil is they believe they're doing good. This belief insulates elites from self-examination.

While the global elite is amorphous there are individuals, such as George Soros, with across-the-board access in the financial and political worlds who function as supercarriers of the elite program. While Soros is not the unofficial chairman of the power elite (there is no one person in charge), his access to elites everywhere, and his patient embrace of Karl Popper's piecemeal social engineering, make him an exemplar of the elite type. Other paragons of the elite supercarrier include Christine Lagarde, Michael Bloomberg, and Warren Buffett. Presidents and prime ministers are not unimportant, yet they come and go. Elite supercarriers remain influential for decades.

What is the elite agenda? The agenda is unchanging, pursued in centuries past by Caesar and Napoleon, and in the twentieth century by the Rockefeller, Roosevelt, and Bush dynasties. The agenda thrives today in institutions with anodyne names like United Nations and International Monetary Fund. The agenda is simple: world money, world taxation, and world order.

World Money

World money is not a new concept; it has been used throughout history. World money is gold. The elite agenda is to hoard gold and substitute special drawing rights as the currency of world trade and finance.

Other forms of money, including clamshells, feathers, and paper, have been used at certain times and places with tribal consent, or force of law. Any medium can be money based on confidence in its value in some future exchange. Yet gold is the only money good at all times, and all places, and is therefore true world money.

Before the Renaissance, world money existed as precious metal coins or bullion. Caesars and kings hoarded gold, dispensed it to their troops, fought over it, and stole it from one another. Land was another form of wealth since antiquity. Still, land was not money because, unlike gold, it cannot easily be exchanged and has no uniform grade. A century ago, J. Pierpont Morgan summed up the ancient state of affairs in his cryptic remark, "Money is gold, and nothing else."

In the fourteenth century, Florentine bankers (called that because they worked on a bench or *banco* in the piazzas of Florence and other city-states) accepted deposits of gold in exchange for notes, a promise to return the gold on demand. The notes were a more convenient form of exchange than physical gold. Notes could be transported long distances and redeemed for gold at branches of a Florentine family bank in London or Paris. Bank notes were not unsecured liabilities, but rather warehouse receipts on gold.

Renaissance bankers realized they could put the gold in their custody to other uses, including loans to princes. This left more notes issued than physical gold in custody. Bankers relied on the fact that the notes would not all be redeemed at once, and they could recoup gold from princes and other parties in time to meet redemptions. Thus was born "fractional reserve banking," in which physical gold held was a fraction of paper promises made. There has been no end of mischief since.

Despite the advent of banking, notes, and fractional reserves, physical gold retained its core role as world money. Princes and merchants still held gold coins in purses and stored gold in vaults. Gold bullion and paper promises stood side by side.

Silver performed a similar role as seen in the success of the Spanish dollar, an eight-real coin, called in Spanish the *real de a ocho,* or piece of eight. The Spanish dollar contained 0.885 ounces of pure silver. It was a 22-karat coin with a total weight of 0.96 ounces once an alloy was added for durability. The Spanish Empire minted the *real de a ocho* to compete as currency with the Joachimsthalers of the Holy Roman Empire. The Joachimsthaler was a silver coin minted in the St. Joachim Valley (*Thal* in German). The word *Joachimsthaler* was later shortened to *taler,* cognate with the word "dollar" in English.

Both the Spanish piece of eight and the German *taler* were predecessors of the American silver dollar. Spanish dollars were legal tender in the United States until 1857. As late as 1997, the New York Stock Exchange traded shares in units of one-eighth of a dollar, a legacy of the original silver piece of eight.

Similar silver coinage was adopted in Burgundy, the Netherlands (called the *leeuwendaalder* or "lion dollar"), and Mexico in the seventeenth century. Spanish dollars were widely used in world trade. Silver was almost the only commodity accepted by China in exchange for Chinese manufactures until the nineteenth century. China put its own chop on the Spanish coins to make them a circulating currency in China. If gold was the first world money, silver was the first world currency.

Silver's popularity as a monetary standard was based on supply and demand. Gold was always scarce; silver more readily available. Charlemagne invented quantitative easing in the ninth century by substituting silver for gold coinage to increase the money supply in his empire. Spain did the same in the sixteenth century.

Silver has most of gold's attractions. Silver is of uniform grade, malleable, relatively scarce, and pleasing to the eye. After the United States made gold possession a crime in 1933, silver coins circulated freely. The

United States minted 90 percent solid silver coins until 1964. Debasement started in 1965. Depending on the particular coin—dimes, quarters, or half dollars—the silver percentage dropped from 90 percent to 40 percent, and eventually to zero by the early 1970s. Since then, U.S. coins in circulation contain copper and nickel.

From antiquity until the mid-twentieth century, citizens of even modest means might have some gold or silver coins. Today there are no circulating gold or silver coins. Such coins as exist are bullion, kept out of sight.

The disappearance of gold and silver has not obviated world money. Only the form of world money changed. Parallel to the diminution in the role of gold and silver was the rise of bank notes, or fiat currency.

Fiat critics point to August 15, 1971, as the day gold ceased to be money. That day President Richard Nixon temporarily suspended convertibility of foreign dollar holdings into physical gold. That suspension was not by itself dispositive, as France, among others, hoped to return to gold at new parities. The United States technically remained on a gold standard with the dollar devalued from $35.00 per ounce of gold to $38.00 per ounce under the December 18, 1971, Smithsonian Agreement. In October 1973, dollars were devalued again to $42.22 per ounce of gold. These valuations were formalistic because the United States never resumed convertibility after August 1971. On March 19, 1973, most major trading nations moved to floating exchange rates. In June 1974, the IMF formally demonetized gold and adopted a monetary system based on special drawing rights, SDRs. (SDRs created in 1969 were originally linked to gold. By 1973, SDRs were just another form of fiat.) In 1976, the U.S. Congress amended statutes to remove all references to gold or silver as the definition of a dollar.

Yet gold's decline as money is more complicated and interesting than the official chronology suggests. Nixon and the IMF were undertakers throwing the last shovel of dirt on gold's grave. The classical gold standard died on July 28, 1914, with the Austro-Hungarian ultimatum to Serbia and the outbreak of the First World War. The sixty-year period from 1914 to 1974 should be seen as a process of dressing gold's body for burial. This period paved the way for elites to create new forms of world money.

After the Austro-Hungarian ultimatum, events spun out of control. Mobilizations, invasions, and declarations of war came in rapid succession. By August 4, 1914, the United Kingdom, France, and Russia (members of the 1907 Triple Entente) were at war with the so-called Central Alliance of Germany, Austria-Hungary, and the Ottoman Empire. The United States was officially neutral.

The belligerents in 1914 knew gold was a determinant of victory. They immediately suspended redemptions of notes for gold. For the war's duration, their economies would run on nonredeemable paper money, a form of forced borrowing from citizens. The understanding was that after victory, gold convertibility could resume—although this was problematic if you lost. A mad scramble for gold ensued. Citizens were encouraged to turn over the gold they possessed in exchange for war bonds. These measures were not resisted; they were widely accepted. War is existential.

There were two important exceptions to suspension of gold convertibility in 1914—the United States and the United Kingdom—for decidedly different reasons.

In July 1914, London was the world's unquestioned financial capital. The bill on London, a sterling instrument guaranteed by a leading U.K. bank, was the heart of money markets. Sterling bills greased the wheels of world trade. With the war's outbreak, a financial panic emerged and debt moratoria were declared.

The French government sold securities in London for sterling and demanded conversion to gold and shipment to Paris. In order to obtain gold, U.K. banks sold securities in New York and likewise demanded gold for the dollar proceeds. Selling pressure resulted in closure of all major stock exchanges in Europe and New York. Yet demand for gold did not abate.

U.K. Treasury officials and the Bank of England initially leaned toward suspension of gold convertibility. John Maynard Keynes, an adviser to the Treasury at the time, argued persuasively that the United Kingdom should remain on gold. Keynes knew that sound money was the key to military victory. London's ability to finance the war depended on New York's faith in the United Kingdom's credit.

Keynes's vision proved prescient. In October 1915, Jack Morgan, Pierpont's son, managed a $500 million syndicated loan for the United Kingdom and France, equivalent to $11.7 billion in today's dollars. The House of Morgan raised no money for Germany at all.

U.S. banks coped with the gold demand as best they could. The process was complicated by German U-boat attacks in the Atlantic, which made it difficult to ship gold to London. Insurance was impossible to obtain. U-boats also interdicted agricultural exports to the United Kingdom, which the United States needed to earn back the gold owed. In desperation, the Bank of England opened a branch depository in Ottawa, Canada. Gold was shipped from New York to Ottawa by train without risk of German U-boat attack.

The U.S. Treasury intervened with a government-sponsored insurance scheme so transatlantic shipping could resume. Gold flows normalized by November, and the New York Stock Exchange reopened on December 5, 1914.

Despite Keynes's advice, and Morgan's financial acrobatics, gold's continued convertibility in the United Kingdom was mostly for show. U.K. subjects were told it was unpatriotic to hoard gold. They were expected to leave their gold with the banks. Likewise, banks were threatened with possible gold confiscation if they hoarded gold and did not make it available in commerce.

Gold coins were withdrawn from circulation and refined into 400-ounce bars, the London good delivery standard ever since. Banks were first encouraged, then required, to deliver their gold to the Bank of England where it was stored in a central vault.

These gold bullion bars could be privately owned, yet did not circulate as coins once did. Only the wealthy owned them because the

400-ounce size was larger than the more modest amount most could afford.

Few complained about gold's absence due to wartime exigencies. By the end of the war in 1918, habits had changed. The new habit of holding bank notes was ingrained, not just in the United Kingdom, but throughout Europe, and increasingly in the United States. Gold was still privately owned, and notes were backed by gold. Yet a change had occurred. After 1918, physical gold was mostly in the form of bulky bullion bars buried by banks, out of sight and out of mind.

Centralization of gold custody heightened on April 5, 1933, when Franklin Roosevelt issued Executive Order 6102 requiring U.S. citizens to surrender private gold to government fiscal agents under pain of prosecution.

Citizens were not the only ones subjected to FDR's gold sweep. The Gold Reserve Act of 1934, signed into law by President Roosevelt on January 30, 1934, required all monetary gold in the United States, including gold held by the Federal Reserve Banks, to be transferred to the Treasury.

The twelve privately owned regional Federal Reserve Banks located from Boston to San Francisco possessed gold originally contributed by their bank owners after the system was established in 1913. The Gold Reserve Act of 1934 ordered Federal Reserve gold transferred to the U.S. Treasury in exchange for gold certificates, which have appeared on the books of the Federal Reserve ever since.

By 1936, the U.S. Treasury had more gold than it could safely store in existing facilities. The U.S. Bullion Depository at Fort Knox, Kentucky, was opened in 1937 as a secure facility to hold the gold confiscated in 1933 and 1934. Other gold vaults were created at the U.S. Mints, and the military fort at West Point. Gold that was once dispersed in millions of safes and purses from coast to coast now sat in a few vaults protected by the U.S. Army.

In stages between 1914 and 1934, U.S. gold went from private hands, to bank hands, to central banks, to the Treasury. This paralleled the process that took place in the United Kingdom and other developed economies. Governments made gold disappear.

With the outbreak of the Second World War in 1939, gold convertibility, to the extent it remained, was again suspended. Gold shipments between nations mostly ceased.

The only major dealer in official gold during the Second World War was the Bank for International Settlements (BIS) in Basel, Switzerland. BIS did a brisk business as a broker in Nazi gold, including gold taken from Jews and other Holocaust victims. Proceeds were used to help finance the Nazi war effort, killing Americans and their Allies. During the war, BIS was run by an American, Thomas McKittrick. Today BIS remains the single most important agent for gold transfers between sovereign nations and major banks.

By the end of the Second World War, gold had ceased circulating as currency. The Bretton Woods Agreement of July 1944 reintroduced a gold standard, at least for nations, if not citizens. The value of each currency of the forty-four participant nations was pegged to the U.S. dollar at a fixed exchange rate. The dollar was pegged to gold at a value of one thirty-fifth of an ounce. Gold was still world money, yet it wasn't circulating, the dollar was.

Over the next few decades, U.S. trading partners earned dollars selling prosperous postwar Americans everything from transistor radios to Volkswagen Beetles and French wine. These exporting nations converted their dollars into gold. In most cases, the gold didn't go abroad. It stayed in the United States at the Federal Reserve Bank of New York vault on Liberty Street in lower Manhattan. Legal title was changed from United States to Japan as the case might be, yet the gold stayed in place. One exception was France, which demanded and got its gold physically transferred to Paris, where it remains.

By 1968, the Bretton Woods system was breaking down. The equivalent of a run on the bank emerged, except the bank was the gold depository at Fort Knox. Switzerland and Spain joined France in demanding their gold. Nixon shut the gold window to stop the run and preserve what was left of the U.S. gold hoard.

The years 1971 to 1974 were a muddle. Leading economic powers were uncertain whether to return to gold at new parities, keep fixed exchange rates without gold, or move to floating exchange rates.

The decline of Bretton Woods coincided with the height of influence for economist Milton Friedman of the University of Chicago. Friedman built his academic reputation with a monumental study titled *A Monetary History of the United States, 1867–1960*, coauthored with Anna Jacobson Schwartz. Friedman espoused a monetary policy based on the quantity theory of money (a theory articulated earlier by Irving Fisher and others). Friedman's thesis was that the Great Depression was caused by overly tight Fed monetary policy prior to the 1929 stock market crash, and in the years immediately following.

Friedman's solution was elastic money. By that he meant the ability of central banks to create money as needed to counteract effects of recession and temporarily depressed demand for goods and services. Elastic money meant abandonment of gold *and* fixed exchange rates because both regimes put limits on central banks' ability to expand the money supply. Friedman's views were influential in policy responses to the 2008 global financial crisis and its aftermath by Ben Bernanke, and later Janet Yellen.

Friedman's scholarly research and theory of money were impressive. He earned the Nobel Prize in economics in 1976.

Yet Friedman's assumptions were badly flawed. Policy recommendations based on his work proved defective. Friedman believed in efficient markets and rational expectations, two hypotheses since discredited both by data and by advances in behavioral science. In particular, Friedman, and Fisher before him, believed velocity, or turnover, of money was constant. Friedman failed to see that velocity was volatile due to recursive functions in emergent adaptive behavior of market agents. Without stable velocity, the quantity theory of money is useless as a policy tool, although the theory is useful for thought experiments testing outcomes in various states.

It is unfair to blame Friedman for this blind spot. Observed velocity was stable throughout the heart of Friedman's career, 1950–90. It was only with the 1998 global financial crisis that velocity destabilized, a move accelerated by a subsequent crisis in 2008. Yet velocity plunged in the early 1930s also, a fact Friedman must have known. Friedman was too narrow, and ultimately incorrect in attributing the 1930s velocity plunge to gold and fixed exchange rates, which, according to Friedman, limited the Federal Reserve's ability to stimulate with monetary ease.

In Friedman's brave new monetary world, eliminating gold and fixed exchange rates enabled enlightened central bankers to carefully calibrate money supply to target maximum real growth consistent with low inflation. In 1971, Richard Nixon said, "I am now a Keynesian in economics," a variation on Friedman's more famous phrase, "We are all Keynesians now." Nixon could as well have said, "We are all Friedmanites now."

Keynes's impact on fiscal policy, and Friedman's on monetary policy, became a font of hubris in economics. There was no developed country macroeconomic problem that could not be solved with the right application of spending and money printing. Today, Keynes and Friedman hold hands in a hybrid theory called helicopter money.

Friedman's views were decisive in the IMF's decision to demonetize gold, and in unilateral decisions of major economies to abandon fixed exchange rates. By 1974, the last vestiges of the gold standard were gone. Floating exchange rates were the norm. Money was not anchored to gold; money was not even anchored to other money. Money had no anchor; in economists' minds it did not need one.

After 1974, money was what central banks said it was. A de facto dollar standard emerged from 1980 to 2010 at the direction of two Fed chairmen, Paul Volcker and Alan Greenspan, and two treasury secretaries, James Baker and Robert Rubin. U.S. growth in the 1980s and 1990s during Presidents Reagan, Bush 41, and Clinton was robust under this strong dollar standard. By 2010, with the weight of Bush 43 war spending and Obama deficits, the dollar standard dissolved into currency wars that have been raging ever since.

In a brief sixty-year span, from 1914 to 1974, gold progressed from people's money, to bank money, to sovereign money, to no money at all. This last condition is anomalous from the perspective of world history. That fiat money is based in part on Friedman's flawed assumptions should at least give pause.

A seventy-year lacuna for world money is ending. Substitution of fiat for gold since 1974 was always overreliant on academics posing as central bankers, compliant trading partners, and trusting populations. Those three pillars are now fractured. Stagnant growth, asset bubbles, income inequality, financial panics, and currency wars are foreseeable results of the absence of world money. Global elites prefer order.

The next collapse will see world money's reemergence. The elite plan is to rewrite the "rules of the game" of the international monetary system as was done in 1922, 1944, and 1974. The chosen instrument is neither the dollar nor gold, but SDRs.

SDRs were created by the IMF in 1969 to remedy a decline in confidence in the U.S. dollar. Countries that earned dollars from exports were dumping dollars for gold. There was not enough gold to support world trade at the $35 per ounce fixed price. Solutions were to ignore the shortage, revalue gold, or abandon it. Each path was unpalatable to one or more major economic power at the time. A fourth solution was devised: the SDR. The goal was to create a reserve asset that was neither a dollar, nor gold, but a hybrid. The SDR simultaneously alleviated the dollar glut and the gold shortage. The SDR was a paper claim on the IMF's combined resources linked to a fixed gold quantity. The name "paper gold" attached to SDRs from the start.

By 1973, the original SDR link to gold was dissolved. SDRs were now just another form of paper money printed by the IMF. Still, the SDR remained. Some observers believe the SDR is backed by a basket of hard currencies. It is not. The basket is used solely to determine the SDR's foreign exchange value. There is no hard currency backing. SDRs are printed at will by the IMF subject to the concurrence of the IMF's executive board.

SDRs are issued infrequently. There have been only four issuances in the forty-seven years since SDRs were invented. The most recent issuance was in August 2009, near the depths of the global recession that followed the 2008 panic; the last issuance before that was in 1981. By September 30, 2016, SDR204.1 billion were outstanding, equal to about $285 billion at then-current exchange rates.

One interesting property of the SDR is that it solves Triffin's dilemma. This economic conundrum was posed by Belgian economist Robert Triffin in testimony to the U.S. Congress in 1960. Triffin observed that the issuer of a global reserve currency had to run persistent deficits to supply the world with sufficient reserves for normal trade. Yet a nation that runs deficits long enough goes broke. In this context, going broke means trading partners lose confidence in the stable value of the reserve currency and reject it in favor of alternatives. SDRs solve this problem because the issuer, the IMF, is not a country and does not run deficits. There is no confidence boundary on the amount of SDRs issued. The IMF has no trading partners to reject its money. The IMF encompasses all trading partners.

SDRs are not issued in the conduct of normal monetary policy. They are not issued to bail out individual firms or even countries. SDRs exist primarily to provide liquidity from thin air when there is a liquidity crisis or lost confidence in other money forms. SDRs are a world money fire brigade to douse financial infernos.

SDRs are the perfect complement to ice-nine. In the coming collapse, the financial system will first be frozen because central banks are unable to reliquefy the system as in the past. The G20 will convene an emergency meeting, as happened in November 2008, and direct the IMF to reliquefy the system with SDRs. If successful, banks and brokers will gradually reopen. Customers will be allowed to access cash. Transactions in cash and securities will still be denominated in dollars, euros, and yen. Behind this curtain of success, the world will be a different place. The SDR, not the dollar, will be the reference point, or numeraire, for world trade and finance.

Dollars will serve as a local currency not unlike Mexican pesos. All local currency values will be measured in SDRs controlled by the G20. Direction will come collectively from China, the United States, Germany, Russia, and a few other members. This will be a seamless transition that few will understand. Sooner than later, a robust SDR bond market will emerge to absorb global reserves.

This transition has been under way for decades. SDR issuance in 1970-2, 1979-81, and 2009 exemplifies the slow, steady social engineering advocated by Soros and his ilk. On March 25, 2009, Tim Geithner, then U.S. treasury secretary, said he did not oppose expanded SDR use. "We're actually quite open to that" was Geithner's response to a reporter's question about increasing SDR issuance. This remark was not considered radical: just another small step on the slow path to the dollar's demise.

Another step on the road to world money was a November 2015 decision by the IMF executive board to include the Chinese yuan as a reference currency in the SDR basket. The other currencies are dollars, euros, yen, and sterling. This decision was purely political. The yuan did not meet the criteria for a true reserve currency and is unlikely to meet them for at least a decade. A reserve currency requires a deep, liquid sovereign bond market, with hedging instruments, repo financing, settlement and clearing facilities, and a good rule of law. China has none of these. Without bond market infrastructure, reserve holders have little to invest in.

Still, the political symbolism of the IMF's yuan decision is important. The effect is to anoint China as a full member of the international monetary system. Just a few weeks after the IMF decision to include the yuan in the SDR, Paul Ryan, Speaker of the U.S. House of Representatives, slipped a provision into a budget bill that increased China's voting rights at the IMF. This further validated China's membership in the exclusive club of countries that run the world money system.

These triumphs for Chinese power went hand in glove with China's manic efforts to acquire gold since 2006, best understood as an initiation fee for this exclusive club. Publicly U.S. officials and those of the other major economic powers disparage gold. Yet, these powers hoard it as proof against the day confidence in paper money dies. The United States has more than eight thousand tons of gold, the Eurozone has more than ten thousand tons, and the IMF has almost three thousand tons. China's stealth acquisition of four thousand tons, with more on the way, gives China a seat at the table with the other gold and SDR powers.

A curious aspect of the SDR's rise as world money is that individuals can't have any. SDRs are issued by the IMF to its member nations. The IMF also has authority to issue SDRs to multilateral organizations including the United Nations and World Bank. In turn, the UN and World Bank can spend the SDRs on climate change infrastructure and population control. SDR recipients can use them to pay one another or swap them for other hard currencies as needed. Individuals cannot have them—not yet.

In time, a private market for SDRs will develop. Large corporations like GE, IBM, and Volkswagen will issue SDR-denominated bonds. Large banks like Goldman Sachs will make markets in those SDR bonds and write derivative contracts in SDRs for hedging. SDR bank deposits will expand in the same way that eurodollar deposits expanded in the 1960s. Imperceptibly, the dollar will become just another local currency. Important transactions will be counted in SDRs. World money will arrive on tiptoe.

Hedge fund and high-tech billionaires will discover they are billionaires in dollars only. The dollar itself will be devalued against SDRs, controlled by a small clique of countries beyond the reach of the billionaires and their bankers. World money means the dollar is worth what the G20 and IMF decide. Only gold is immune.

World Taxation

For a decade at the start of my career, I was international tax counsel to Citibank, then the world's most powerful private bank. Citibank had branches in more countries than the U.S. Foreign Service had embassies. The bank, under the direction of legendary CEO Walter Wriston, was a bigger platform than the Department of State.

In the early 1980s, my colleagues and I prepared a U.S. income tax return that showed zero liability at a time when Citibank was highly profitable. Wriston objected. He said it was unseemly for the largest bank in the United States to pay no U.S. tax. He instructed us to pay a small amount. "You don't need to pay a lot; just two or three percent. It looks bad if we pay nothing."

We mastered the art of paying *no* taxes, but paying *some* tax was a challenge. There were many levers at our disposal. We used foreign tax credits, investment tax credits, or depreciation on Boeing 747s and the Alaska pipeline, which we legally owned and leased to users.

We also used tax-free municipal bonds and discretionary loan loss reserves to dial down tax liability. The third floor of our corporate headquarters at 399 Park Avenue featured a plastic palm tree in one corner. That symbolized Citibank, Nassau, our zero-tax Bahamas booking center operating at nearby desks. The Cayman Islands and Netherlands Antilles also came in handy.

Our challenge was that Citibank's tax return was a finely tuned machine. Once you moved one lever, another lever might move on its own due to the complex interaction of credits, deductions, and elections in the Internal Revenue Code. We spent an entire year tuning the machine; now we needed to dismantle one small part without ruining the works. We had time and talent to pay the tax. Yet the lesson was not lost on me. For large, complex companies, paying taxes is not a requirement; it's optional.

For developed highly indebted nations, paying their debt is *not* optional. Sovereign debt must be serviced or the global economy is thrown into chaos. Taxes are the primary way that developed economies maintain the façade of solvency. With that façade intact, countries can repay maturing debt with new debt.

This mismatch between a country's need to collect taxes and a company's ability not to pay has led to a shadow struggle between sovereign and corporate power. Sovereign power always wins in the end because countries have decisive tools, including violence. Still, corporate capacity to corrupt a country through lobbying is sufficient in the short run to fend off state power.

In a decentralized system of high-tax developed countries and low-tax haven countries, global corporations easily find ways to avoid taxation. Standard techniques include the transfer of intellectual property like patents and software to tax havens. Once there, intellectual property earns royalties without paying tax to the new host nation.

Another technique is transfer pricing. Corporations in high-tax nations pay inflated costs to their affiliates in low-tax nations. This shifts income to the low-tax nation and creates tax deductions in the high-tax nation. Other more sophisticated techniques include netting centers in high-tax countries where global purchases and sales are booked. Profit and loss from these activities nets out close to zero, which means no tax is due to the host country. Gross profits are spread around to counterparties in low-tax jurisdictions.

Cross-border tax treaties are a fertile area for corporate tax avoidance. Corporate payments as interest, dividends, and royalties move across borders based on the location of payer and payee. Nations impose withholding taxes on these payments because they have no other way to collect taxes from the recipient. The payer is required to withhold the tax; the payee receives its payment net of taxes.

Most developed countries have signed bilateral tax treaties with their trading partners that reduce these withholding taxes, sometimes to zero. The theory is that if the recipient country collects tax, there is no need for the source country to do so as well, because double taxation is mitigated by tax credits. Yet if one hundred countries each sign bilateral tax treaties with one hundred other countries, the result is a dense network of ten thousand treaties with slightly different terms and rates. A ten-thousand-treaty web is a playground for tax lawyers who use back-to-back transactions to claim zero withholding tax on the initial payment, and no income tax in the final host country.

Tax leasing is also an effective tool. Countries have different rules for deciding when a financing transaction is a loan or a lease. Equipment deals can be structured as a loan in one country (to deduct interest) and a lease in another country (to deduct depreciation). The parties double-dip on deductions with one piece of equipment.

The loan-lease double-dip is combined with tax treaty back-to-back structures to obliterate taxes in multiple jurisdictions. As tax counsel to Citibank, I saw triple-dip leases, where a single Boeing 747 was written off in South Africa, the United Kingdom, and Australia at the same time. The separate jurisdictions never knew what hit them.

Other structures are used to convert ordinary income into capital gains that receive favorable tax treatment. Discounts on bond sales disguise hidden interest payments embedded in the discounts. Tax deferral is as powerful as low rates because the real value of money declines in inflation. Deferring a tax liability for ten years reduces the real cost radically by the time the tax is paid.

Derivatives, not clearly addressed in tax treaties, are added to the mix to blow smoke in the eyes of tax authorities. Lobbyists are employed in the main developed countries to ensure that the rules remain unchanged.

Weighing all of the above—property shifting, transfer pricing, netting, tax treaties, leasing, conversion, deferral, and derivatives—it is no surprise that corporate tax collection by individual nations is a sieve. Corporate cash flows through the sieve to the bottom line. Countries are left empty-handed.

Policy elites in the United States, Germany, the United Kingdom, and Japan are well aware of these techniques. These elites attended the same law schools and finance programs as the corporate advisers. The government and corporate elite revolving door results in experts' continually changing sides from tax collector to tax avoider, and back again. It's an elite game.

It may be a game, but the G20 are no longer amused. The weight of sovereign debt, and the incapacity to generate growth, have sent the G20 on a mission to end global tax avoidance. The elite plan is for global taxation through coordinated action and information sharing. Once a developed country tax authority can see all sides of a transaction (instead of just the local piece), the transaction is far easier to attack.

This tax enforcement mission was delegated by the G20 to the G7 (United States, Japan, United Kingdom, France, Germany, Canada, and Italy). The G7 are home to the richest corporations and have the highest tax rates. The G7 have the most to lose from corporate tax avoidance, so they have the highest incentive to stop it.

The G7 use the Organisation for Economic Co-operation and Development (OECD) as their technical secretariat. G20/G7 elites often outsource missions to the IMF, yet sometimes use other multilateral organizations for specialized tasks. The UN is the preferred venue for the climate change agenda. OECD is used for the world tax plan because it represents more advanced economies with the highest incentives to recover lost tax revenue.

The world tax plan is not called the world tax plan. That's too obvious. Technical names are given to these plans to obscure intentions. World money is called the "special drawing right" because that's suitably anodyne. The world tax plan is called BEPS, which stands for Base Erosion and Profit Shifting. If you see reference to "OECD BEPS," just think, "elite world tax plan," and you're on the right track.

Elites make no effort to hide their agenda; they advertise it, yet in opaque jargon on obscure sites that few read, and fewer understand. Here's what the G7 leaders, including Barack Obama and Angela Merkel, said about their world tax plan on May 27, 2016:

> Steady, consistent and concerted implementation of the G20/
> OECD Base Erosion and Profit Shifting (BEPS) package is critical...

to achieve a global level playing field for all engaged in economic activities. We remain committed to lead the process by example. To ensure widespread implementation of the BEPS package, we encourage all relevant and interested countries and jurisdictions to commit to implement the BEPS package and join the new inclusive framework. . . .

We reaffirm G20's call on all relevant countries including all financial centers and jurisdictions to implement . . . defensive measures to be considered against non-cooperative jurisdictions. . . .

We look forward to the initial proposals . . . on ways to improve the implementation of the international standards, including on the availability of beneficial ownership information and its international exchange.

Despite dense jargon, the meaning is clear. The G20 insist on full transaction disclosure on a global basis. They will use the information to enforce tax collections on their own terms. Jurisdictions that refuse to cooperate are subject to "defensive measures." That's a polite way to say they are cut off from international banking channels and their economies destroyed unless they play ball. The invitation to cooperate or be crushed is a Cosa Nostra contrivance in new clothes.

Corporate tax avoidance is a luxury developed economies can no longer afford. Global corporations hold more than $7 trillion of cash, much of it stashed in tax havens, the result of sophisticated tax avoidance. This cash is too tempting a target for government elites to pass up even if their corporate cronies are beneficiaries. A simple 25 percent toll charge on this $7 trillion yields $1.75 trillion in new G7 revenue. The money then goes toward mitigating sovereign debt burdens.

Auditing corporations one at a time, one year at a time, is a fruitless task. Auditors cannot possibly penetrate more than a few avoidance techniques used by corporations. Putting pressure on individual tax havens is a game of whack-a-mole. The list of tax haven jurisdictions is so long—Cayman Islands, Malta, Cyprus, Macao, Isle of Man, British Vir-

gin Islands, and so on and on—that if pressure is applied to one, companies seamlessly move profits to another with a few documents and
keystrokes.

Tax havens will still resist changes to their internal laws. Recently,
tax havens have cooperated with anti–money laundering programs because the cost of turning their backs on dirty business is small in relation
to the benefits of keeping clean businesses such as Apple and Amazon.
Once clean business is besieged for using the zero tax rates legally available, tax havens may push back and side with corporate clients.

The solution in the works for G7 nations is world taxation. This
starts with a centralized tax information database shared by developed
nations. Tax avoidance would be like playing poker with your cards
showing faceup on the table. You could play, but you could never win.

The new world tax system being planned is quite sophisticated. The
problem tax authorities have today is they can see the side of a transaction conducted in their country, yet cannot see the other side because
the counterparty is in another country. Tax authorities can submit
information-sharing requests to other jurisdictions. Still, case-by-case
inquiries are cumbersome and slow. The new world tax system is designed to decrease opacity and ease processing. World taxation is an
automated digital auditor.

Each taxpayer and its affiliates are assigned a unique identification
number. Each transaction type—royalties, interest, dividends, et cetera—
is assigned an identifier. The counterparty to each transaction is identified using its unique code.

All corporate transactions are tagged with these digital identifiers
and submitted to a shared database. This is like a tag-and-release marine
mission aimed at great white sharks. The shark may look fearsome after
release, yet authorities always know where to find it.

The world tax database will be available to all participants in the
system including the G20 nations. The database would be housed on
high-capacity computers using sophisticated algorithms and predictive
analytics. Like the shark, companies could run, but no longer hide.

Once the computers have identified tax games, the G20 will get to work with legal assaults. Transfer prices, asset moves, leases, and tax treaty structures will be challenged using broad antiavoidance statutes. A tax haven that stands in the way will find its international banking connections shut down. This happened to Belize in 2015. International banks were forced by the U.S. Treasury to cut off correspondent relations with Belizean banks. This G20 garrote choked Belizean financial oxygen; its economy crumbled. Soon Belizean banks cooperated with G20 information requests and the financial oxygen was gradually restored. Release of the infamous "Panama Papers," consisting of client records from a law firm that facilitated tax avoidance, is another recent example.

What's wrong with effective tax collection? Why shouldn't corporations and high-net-worth individuals pay their fair share? They should. Yet the notion of "fair share" is debatable, and a moving target. The G20 engaged in nonsustainable borrowing to bail out major banks. That debt must be repaid either through direct taxation or inflation, a hidden tax on savers. G20 governments will not tax at fair rates; rather, they will apply whatever rate is needed to defease the debt. The G20 target rate is considerably higher than the optimal rate from a growth perspective, partly due to past profligacy. Corporations and the wealthy are sitting ducks for sovereign tax targeting.

Sovereigns are insatiable. Once sufficient taxes are secured to sustain short-run debt, history says sovereigns simply spend more on favored interests. Spending is never slashed. Corporations go from sitting ducks to cooked geese. The successful are unceremoniously looted. Sovereign optimization at this stage is to take as much as possible without destroying the corporation.

BEPS is a powerful new tool in the elite tax assault. Even without BEPS, the sovereign war on taxpayers is far along. In 2010, the Foreign Account Tax Compliance Act (FATCA) became law in the United States. It requires banks worldwide to provide information to the U.S. Internal Revenue Service about U.S. taxpayer accounts. Each bank must register with the IRS and obtain a Global Intermediary Identification

Number (GIIN). Foreign banks that fail to do so are subject to formal and informal retaliation, including correspondent account termination by U.S. clearing banks. Inability to clear U.S. dollar payments through correspondents is a death sentence for most banks, so they fall into line with U.S. dictates.

FATCA also allows the U.S. Treasury to enter into agreements with entire countries (called Intergovernmental Agreements, or IGAs), rather than negotiate bank by bank. The IGAs mandate FATCA compliance by every bank in that country. IGAs are implemented coercively. Countries that refuse to sign suffer withholding tax on Treasury interest payments to their residents. Foreign banks put pressure on their own governments to sign IGAs. The United States has globalized its tax compliance to match its globalized tax collections.

The IMF, OECD, and G20 have all endorsed these efforts and have added their own calls for international information collection and information sharing. The G20 final communiqué from the November 2014 meeting in Brisbane, Australia, included technical papers describing an implementation program for data collection.

Prominent economists including Nobelist Joseph Stiglitz and Thomas Piketty have joined the chorus calling for global taxation. In particular, Piketty advanced the thesis that high tax rates are not an impediment to growth. His thesis is riddled with flaws, but attracted a following among global elites nonetheless. Piketty recognizes that high tax rates will not achieve his redistribution goals if collections are thwarted by tax avoidance. He complements his high-tax theories with calls for global taxation so his proposed taxes are actually collected.

The global tax dragnet is not limited to income taxes. Other transaction taxes, including excise, sales, and value-added taxes (VATs), are attractive to sovereigns because they are collected at source on gross amounts, and are not complicated by calculations for deductions. VAT can be avoided by booking purchases in tax havens, so VAT is also ripe for G7 information sharing to attack transfer pricing.

In a recent conversation with an influential international tax lawyer, she told me the U.S. Treasury had "given up" trying to reform the income tax due to its complexities, and the difficulties of advancing reform through Congress. Instead, Treasury and tax writing committees in Congress were focused behind the scenes on imposing VAT, referred to in the United States as a "national sales tax." Japan increased its VAT by 60 percent in April 2014. These trends are part of a global effort to shift from taxes on net amounts, like the income tax, to taxes on gross amounts, which are easier to compute and collect.

The fusion of global information sharing, global enforcement, and global taxation of gross receipts enables developed economies to extract the maximum amount of wealth from productive sectors to sustain nonproductive elites. This continues until the social system collapses, the common fate of civilizations that reach a late stage of prelatic parasitism.

Progressives who view corporations as undesirable autonomous actors should be careful what they wish for. Economists agree that corporations do not bear the true costs of taxation. Corporations are mere agents for a vast network of customers, suppliers, investors, and employees. The global tax assault on corporations is an assault on private capital. Nor is this assault limited to corporations; they are merely the most prominent targets. The techniques applied by the G20 to companies can be applied to individuals as well.

The G20, led by the United States, acting through agents at the IMF and OECD, are well along the path of near perfect information collection and sharing. When these data are processed with the most powerful computers using advanced data mining algorithms, the result is a quantum leap in government's ability to extract wealth from the private sector—corporate and individual. Exigencies of servicing sovereign debt accelerate this process. The prodigality of public spending drives tax rates higher in a ratchet of higher spending, higher rates, higher collections, more enforcement, and more debt to the point of collapse.

World taxation is here, very thinly veiled. Soon the veil will part, and wealth extraction will begin. There will be nowhere to hide, and no way to stop the machine.

World Order

New World Order is not new. Civilizations have devised forms of world order for millennia because the alternative to order is chaos. Order rarely includes liberty or justice. Order mainly ends disorder, and mitigates violence. That is how order achieves legitimacy. The next world order is emerging.

What is new is that world order is no longer circumscribed by a defined "world" such as in the Roman or Chinese empires. The next world order will encompass the globe and all of its civilizations at once.

The Roman world order embodied Europe south of the Danube, and west of the Rhine, and most of modern-day Turkey, North Africa, and the Levant. It was based on conquest, civic duty, military service, and perfunctory worship of state-approved gods. Like any world order, Rome had an expert bureaucracy and efficient tax collection. Rome typically found it unnecessary to destroy what it encountered. If kingdoms and cultures on Rome's periphery were willing to subscribe to Roman order, they were free to keep most local customs and religions. Treaties of friendship and commerce proposed by Roman embassies, involving tribute, peace, and exclusive trading rights, were enough to keep Roman legions at bay. It was a carrot-and-stick approach. Commerce was the carrot, and legions were the stick. This world order was Rome's greatest export.

The fall of Rome was followed in Western Europe by the Dark Ages, during which civilization's unifying institution was the Catholic Church. Yet the Church's reach was attenuated and fell short of a world order. The emergence of Charlemagne's empire in the ninth century AD, called the Carolingian Renaissance, was a partly successful new world order. Charlemagne combined military force and religion with expanded emphasis on education, literacy, and monetary reform to achieve a unified order that included the western half of the former Roman Empire, and territories in northern and central Europe that had never been conquered by Rome. This new world order was briefly successful, yet lasted less than seventy-five years after Charlemagne's death in 814 before disintegrating into disorder again.

After the end of this first renaissance, Europe continued as a patchwork of warring feudal kingdoms and princely states until the Renaissance of the fourteenth through sixteenth centuries. The Holy Roman Empire was mostly a façade except for the half century from 1506 to 1556 when the Burgundian, Habsburg, and Holy Roman crowns were combined with new world conquests during Charles V's reign.

Charles V's legacy proved no more durable than Charlemagne's. The emperor abdicated his thrones. His domains reverted to separate kingdoms. Now traditional warfare over land, titles, and wealth had the added element of deep religious division between Catholic princes and those supporting Protestant devotions.

The late-sixteenth-century religious wars culminated in the Thirty Years' War of the early seventeenth century. From 1618 to 1648, Europe devoured itself in its first demonstration of total war since antiquity. Civilian populations were starved and slaughtered and cities destroyed in ways not seen since the pagans. What ended the desolation was the Peace of Westphalia, from which emerged the modern state system of sovereignty and diplomacy we have had ever since.

Under the Westphalian system, states existed within recognized borders. Each state's sovereignty was recognized by others. Principles of noninterference were agreed. Religious differences between states were tolerated. States might be monarchies or republics. Permanent state interest, or *raison d'état,* was the organizing principle of international relations. War was not eliminated, yet it was mitigated by diplomacy and balance-of-power politics. The object of the balance of power was to prevent one state from becoming so powerful it could conquer others and destroy world order.

Throughout the eighteenth and nineteenth centuries, France was the threat against which the balance of power was maintained. By the late nineteenth and early twentieth centuries, Germany and Russia became the primary threats. Great Britain, and later the United States, served as principal counterweights first to French, and then to German and Russian power.

The Westphalian system collapsed utterly in the horrors of the First and Second World Wars. The interwar period, 1919–39, saw efforts to build another world order based on multilateral organizations like the League of Nations. These efforts failed due to the legacy of a vindictive 1919 Treaty of Versailles. That treaty made Germany revanchist, and revenge inevitable.

After the Second World War, another world order emerged: the bi-polar world of U.S. and Russian hegemony over their respective empires. The United States acted through alliances such as NATO supported by gold, nuclear weapons, and sea power. Russia acted through a land-based empire, the Union of Soviet Socialist Republics, and proxy states including Cuba, North Korea, and North Vietnam.

This postwar condominium included elements of the Westphalian system such as statehood, sovereignty, and diplomacy, now supplemented with more robust versions of the failed multilateral institutions of the interwar period. The United Nations, International Monetary Fund, World Bank, and later the G20 were a new multilateral metastructure imposed on the state system to maintain peace, promote growth, and instill monetary stability.

This overview is intentionally Occidental. Elsewhere Mongols, China, and Islam developed their own world orders. The Mongol Empire, which included China at its height, lasted through the thirteenth and four-teenth centuries. The Mongols amassed the largest coterminous empire ever before dissolving into smaller khanates and local cultures. China's world order was based on the emperor's divinity, and a closed culture that excluded foreign influence as barbaric. Islamic caliphates were based on submission to Allah's will revealed through the prophet Muhammad and recorded in the Koran. Unlike China, Islam did not wall itself off from the world; it conquered with great success. By the eighth century, the Umayyad Caliphate stretched from Spain to the Indus River, while Islam itself eventually spread farther, from East Africa to Indonesia and beyond.

Despite the longevity and geographic reach of China and Islam, these world orders did not survive beyond the early twentieth century due to their technological backwardness, Western imperialism, and the advent of total war. The last major Islamic caliphate, the Ottoman Empire, finally collapsed in 1922 in the aftermath of the First World War. Ottoman remnants were carved up by European diplomats, first by the secret Sykes-Picot Agreement of 1916, and later by the 1919 Versailles Treaty. Chinese imperial order collapsed in 1912 with the fall of the Qing dynasty followed by a failed republic, warlordism, Japanese invasion, and Communist revolution. With no robust alternatives to face the West, China and Islam became marginal to the modified Westphalian bipolar world that emerged after 1945. For the first time in history, a world order existed that encompassed the world.

Henry Kissinger offers a brilliant overview of this process in his book *World Order*. Kissinger's sweep is so extensive, he may be said to have identified an impulse toward order that pervades international relations, and stands opposed to the disorder of war and devastation caused by figures as diverse as Napoleon and Hitler. In the simplest terms, conquerors cause disorder while people and most rulers prefer order. The antipode to disorder is order in some form, be it empire like the Roman or Carolingian, or the Westphalian state system.

Order does not presuppose democracy. Order is a condition compatible with diverse value systems. Democracy and liberty are desirable, and combine well with capitalist economic modes. Yet these values are not universally prized. Interestingly, the failed world orders of China and Islam have reemerged in the twenty-first century, the former as a centralized Communist bureaucracy, and the latter in a radical form as a decentralized reign of terror. Neither China nor Islam promotes democracy or liberty. Liberal values will have to make their way in the world, if they can, through culture and education, without necessary assistance from a new world order.

Disorder has always manifested itself kinetically. The costs of disorder are counted in death and destruction. Through the replacement of bronze by steel, the invention of sail and stirrup, and the succession from sword to guns, one constant in the struggle between order and disorder has been its physical form. Wealth, a key complement to warfare, also existed in physical form as precious metals, jewels, fine art, livestock, or land in possession.

Yet contests among states and nonstate actors are increasingly conducted in digital realms. Obvious examples are computer system hacks by state cyberbrigades and criminal gangs. The line between enlisted cyberwarriors and criminals can be blurred to forestall retaliation. Distributed denial of service is the mildest attack mode. More serious are penetrations that take control of critical infrastructure in dams and power grids so floods and blackouts can commence on cue.

Most threatening are sleeper attack viruses planted deep in stock exchange operating systems awaiting activation as part of a larger attack. Such sleeper viruses also serve as a deterrent to attack by the nation hosting an infected system. One such attack virus, planted by Russian military intelligence, was discovered inside the operating system of the NASDAQ stock market in 2010. The virus was disabled. No one knows how many undiscovered digital viruses are lying in wait.

Viruses can erase customer accounts without trace. Used offensively, these viruses can create an uncontrolled flood of sell orders on widely held stocks such as Apple or Amazon.

Military doctrine calls for attacks to conjoin with force multipliers. An attacker will wait for a day when stocks are already down 5 percent, say 900 points on the Dow Jones Industrial Average, then launch an attack to amplify the downward momentum. The result could be a single-day

5,000-point Dow decline and an emergency New York Stock Exchange closing. This near instantaneous lost wealth does more damage to civilian morale than conventional bombardment.

Digital threats have not displaced physical violence. Recent events in Ukraine, Syria, and Libya show that physical destruction and horrific violence remain as means to achieve political or religious goals. Kissinger's admonition to use diplomacy, and only rarely resort to warfare from necessity, is still relevant.

Yet virtual warfare, especially in financial space, has moved from fantasy to sophisticated reality with stunning speed.

What are the prospects for order and disorder, war and peace, in a digital age?

In the elite view, the new reality demands a new world order that is postsovereign and postnational. This order regards sovereignty and the balance of power—the classic Westphalian framework—as obsolete. As the new world order emerges, new financial arrangements and new governance structures are needed to support it. This new world order provides a framework within which world money and world taxation can be implemented.

Climate change is a convenient horse for elites to ride in the implementation of a new world order. Debating the science of climate change is beside the point. There are heated views on both sides; some science is settled, some not. Global elites treat the debate as settled to mask a larger project. For elites, a global problem once defined conjures a global solution. Climate change is the perfect platform for implementing a hidden agenda of world money and world taxation.

Climate change initiatives are centered in the United Nations, particularly the UN Framework Convention on Climate Change and protocols emerging from the convention. Taken in isolation, climate change seems to have little to do with world money. In fact, the two are closely linked in the new world order.

Every G20 leaders' summit communiqué since the series started in November 2008 makes reference to climate change. Every IMF semiannual meeting, and numerous statements by the IMF managing director, reference climate change and the need to address it on a global basis.

The United Nations launched a project to capture the financial system and redirect capital toward what it defines as sustainable development. In October 2015, the UN issued a 112-page report titled "The Financial System We Need." One report recommendation includes advice on "Harnessing the Public Balance Sheet."

On April 25, 2016, UN project adviser Andrew Sheng laid bare the elite world money plan in an article he coauthored entitled "How to Finance Global Reflation." The article states:

> Investment in global public goods—namely, the infrastructure needed to meet the needs of the developing world and to mitigate climate change—could spur global reflation. An estimated $6 trillion in infrastructure investment will be needed annually over the next 15 years just to address global warming. . . .
>
> With the US, the issuer of the world's preeminent reserve currency, unwilling or unable to provide the liquidity needed to close the infrastructure investment gap, a new supplementary reserve currency should be instituted—one whose issuer does not have to confront the Triffin dilemma. This leaves one option: the International Monetary Fund's Special Drawing Right. . . .
>
> An incremental expansion of the SDR's role in the new global financial architecture, aimed at making the monetary-policy transmission mechanism more effective, can be achieved without major disagreement. This is because, conceptually, an increase in SDRs is equivalent to an increase in the global central bank balance sheet (quantitative easing). . . .
>
> Consider a scenario in which member central banks increase their SDR allocation in the IMF by, say, $1 trillion. A five-times leverage would enable the IMF to increase either lending to member countries or investments in infrastructure via multilateral

development banks by at least $5 trillion. Moreover, multilateral development banks could leverage their equity by borrowing in capital markets. . . .

The IMF and the major central banks should take advantage of this newfound knowledge, and provide equity and liquidity against long-term lending for infrastructure investments. . . .

The linkages among climate change, SDRs, the IMF, World Bank, and the need for global coordination could not be more explicit.

The transition to this new world order based on digital wealth and world money rather than Westphalian sovereignty has some rough edges. Important states like Russia and Iran are actively hostile to the West. Tensions are rising between the United States and China. Rogue states like North Korea, and failed states like Venezuela, remain exceptions to the elite plan.

U.S. digital dollar dominance enables unacceptable U.S. hegemony from the perspective of these confrontational and rogue nations. Led by China, emerging economies are building alternative digital payments systems to avoid dependency on the United States. They are also acquiring physical possession of thousands of tons of gold—a nondigital asset that the United States cannot hack or freeze. These rival gold hoards are less than 10,000 tons today; not yet a match for the 22,000 tons of gold held collectively by the United States, Europe, and the IMF. Gold will continue its move from West to East in coming years to even the scales.

A bipolar financial world may emerge in which Asia, Africa, and South America, led by China and Russia, supported by Iran and Turkey, use one digital payments system, while the United States, Europe, and former Commonwealth nations use another. Each system will be backed by about 20,000 tons of gold, an eerie echo of struggles for missile parity in the cold war, and even older struggles for a balance of power.

Yet this is not the most likely scenario because of its potential for disorder. The Chinese want to join the Western club on equal terms, not destroy it. A more likely scenario is the application of a technique called the shock doctrine. The United States, caught up in the next financial panic, no longer able to defend the dollar's privileged position, will rapidly turn to a reformed IMF with greater voice for China. This new IMF, under G20 direction, will reliquefy a world in panic with massive SDR printing. Climate change priorities will speedily be implemented. Global tax schemes to finance climate infrastructure solutions will be imposed. Information sharing and global cooperation will leave corporations and wealthy individuals without shelter. Coordinated action in the form of global wealth extraction will displace the former practice of sovereign economic competition. Global power elites will share the spoils.

The elite agenda is settled. Elites now await a new shock.

The Shock Doctrine

Naomi Klein's 2007 book, *The Shock Doctrine*, popularized a technique elites use to advance hidden agendas. Elites formulate plans for the world order they wish to see. They wait for an exogenous shock, a natural disaster or financial crisis, then use fear created by shock to advance their vision. New policy is presented to mitigate the fear. The policy is a way to advance the plan for world order. The idea is simple, yet applying shock doctrine involves decades of persistent effort. Shocks come randomly; the elite plan never goes away.

Klein revealed this process from an outsider's perspective. Still, the ultimate insider, President Obama's first chief of staff, Rahm Emanuel, acknowledged the shock doctrine when he said, "You never want a serious crisis to go to waste." This was in reaction to the 2008 financial panic.

President Obama and Emanuel used the 2008 crisis to push through an $813 billion "stimulus" spending package signed into law on February 17, 2009. This was a textbook case of shock doctrine. The program provided no stimulus; the recovery since 2009 is the weakest in U.S. history. The spending program did provide a grab bag of goodies for favored constituents including teachers, unions, and government workers. These constituents had waited eight years, the length of the Bush administration, for their handouts. When it comes to the shock doctrine, patience pays.

Another highly consequential example of the shock doctrine was enactment of the USA Patriot Act on October 26, 2001, in the aftermath of the 9/11 attacks. The Patriot Act contained needed improvements in information sharing among the FBI, CIA, and grand juries. Some surveillance standard easing was urgent at the time.

Still, the Patriot Act was also the codification of a surveillance state wish list percolating below the policy surface for some time. Patriot Act provisions advanced by the U.S. Treasury to block bank mergers and require asset forfeitures had less to do with Al Qaeda and more to do with the Treasury's ongoing war on cash. These provisions were taken down from the shelf where Treasury keeps its wish list, and added to the expanded powers under the act. The Patriot Act is now an overly broad and permanent menace used for state surveillance of political enemies. Under the shock doctrine, all Treasury needed was a shock, which 9/11 provided.

The new world order is tailor-made for application of the shock doctrine. As with all applications of the shock doctrine, elements of the desired end already exist, waiting to expand and be made permanent in response to a new shock. The IMF is a world central bank in all but name. The SDR is world money in a form that everyday citizens cannot comprehend. The G20 is a de facto board of governors for this new order. The elimination and criminalization of cash, even when held by innocent parties, ensures that there are no alternatives to digital payments. Virtual wealth can be tracked, taxed, and turned off based on compliant behavior as defined by global elites. The system is primed for a shock doctrine use case.

The shock doctrine is a ratchet; it turns in one direction, then locks in place. It can turn again in the same direction, but can never be reversed. Policies enacted under the shock doctrine remain long after the emergency that enabled them. The trend is persistently toward more state power, more taxation, and less liberty.

Shock doctrine is an ideal tool for what philosopher Karl Popper called piecemeal engineering. George Soros is Popper's principal champion today. Soros's principal instrument for social engineering, the Open Society Foundations, is named in honor of Popper's best-known book, *The Open Society and Its Enemies.*

Elites are aware that their views are not widely accepted in democratic societies. Elites realize their programs must be implemented in small stages over decades to avoid backlash. Shock doctrine is punctuation to otherwise anti-elite sentiment. When shocks strike, the elites move immediately to implement a new stage of their program. The critical task is to act quickly before the shock fades. The ratchet ensures that elite gains are not soon surrendered. The process goes into remission until the next shock.

Thus the global elite's true typology: a structure of floating, intersecting spheres. Communication courses through conferences and supercarriers who channel concepts between spheres. Content comes from public intellectuals. Their glue is like-mindedness. Their strength is patience. Their method is piecemeal social engineering. Their scalpel is the shock doctrine. Their final success is ensured by the ratchet. This is all employed in obeisance to the agenda: one money, one world, one order.

CHAPTER 3
DESERT CITY OF THE MIND

Keynes asked me what I was advising my clients.

"To insulate themselves as much as possible from the coming crisis and to avoid the markets," I replied.

Keynes took the opposite view. "We will not have any more crashes in our time," he insisted. . . . "And where is the crash coming from in any case?"

"The crash will come from the gap between appearances and reality. I have never seen such stormy weather gathering," I said.

1927 conversation with Keynes recounted
by Felix Somary in *The Raven of Zurich* (1986)

NO KEY UNLOCKS THE MYSTERIES OF CAPITAL MARKETS WITH MORE ease than complexity theory. That theory formally dates from the 1960s, but observation of complex dynamics is as old as humanity. An ancient astronomer seeing a supernova in the night sky was watching complexity in action. Never was complexity put to more urgent use than in Los Alamos, New Mexico, in the mid-1940s.

Los Alamos

The drive from downtown Santa Fe to Los Alamos National Laboratory is desolate and beautiful. The road winds through the desert at a slight incline due to the difference in elevation between the lab and the city. Today the divided highway is improved, a far cry from dangerous dirt roads traversed by the first scientists at Los Alamos who worked on the Manhattan Project in late 1942. The surrounding country is fractured into mesas and canyons, pink desert on top, dark corners below.

What is odd about the drive is the scarcity of day-trippers, RVs, boat trailers, and typical fellow travelers on America's roads. At a certain juncture, the road goes to only one place—to the laboratory itself—and there is no reason to be on that road unless you are cleared to enter one of the most secure places on the planet.

Los Alamos National Laboratory, LANL, is one among seventeen specially designated national laboratories that perform the most advanced research and development in nanotechnology, materials, supercomputing, magnetics, renewable energy, and pure science. Los Alamos is one of only three national laboratories that specialize in nuclear weapons, along with Sandia, in Albuquerque, New Mexico, and Lawrence Livermore, in Livermore, California.

The work of the national laboratories is complemented by a network of private laboratories, mostly associated with elite universities that perform classified research under government contracts and operate under the same strict security protocols. These protocols include secure perimeters, restricted access, and top-secret security clearances for those with access to the most sensitive information. The best known of these private laboratories is the Applied Physics Laboratory at The Johns Hopkins University. The Jet Propulsion Laboratory near Los Angeles is a hybrid public-private model funded by NASA and operated by the California Institute of Technology.

Together these private and public labs comprise a research archipelago stretching from coast to coast that keeps the United States ahead of the Russians, Chinese, and other rivals in the systems essential to defense, space, and national security. They give America its edge in world affairs.

LANL is the crown jewel in this constellation. It is not the oldest, yet in the decades since its creation it has performed the most crucial tasks.

Beginning in 1942, the lab was one of several Manhattan Project locales that developed and built the atomic bomb, which brought an early end to the Second World War and saved perhaps a million lives on both the Allied and Japanese sides.

In the years following the first atomic bombs, Los Alamos was a crucial component in the ensuing arms race against Russian, then later Chinese, nuclear weapons programs.

Nuclear bomb making technology advanced rapidly from the relatively crude fission weapons of 1945 to thermonuclear weapons designed in the 1950s and 1960s. These newer bombs used fission to cause a secondary fusion implosion, releasing far greater energy and achieving a new order of destruction.

These advances in technology and destructive force were not ends in themselves. They were guided by new nuclear war fighting doctrines developed first at RAND Corporation, and later expanded at Harvard University and other elite schools. The doctrine, called Mutual Assured Destruction, or MAD, was the product of game theory in which participants based their actions on expected reactions of other participants who, in turn, acted based on expected reactions of the initial actor, and so on recursively until a behavioral equilibrium was reached.

What RAND Corporation discovered is that winning a nuclear arms race was destabilizing and likely to result in nuclear war. If either the United States or Russia built enough nuclear weapons to destroy the other in a first strike, with no chance of a retaliatory second strike by the victim, the superior power's motivation was to launch the first strike and win the war. Waiting until an inferior adversary achieved decisive first-strike capability seemed less attractive than striking first.

One solution was for each side to build *more* weapons. If an opponent attacked, a substantial number of the victim's weapons would survive the first strike. This provided a sufficient second-strike capability, enough to destroy the attacker. Cold warriors referred to this model as "two scorpions in a bottle." Either scorpion could deliver a fatal sting to the other. The victim would have just enough strength left to reflexively strike back at the attacker before dying. Both would die. The hope was that national leaders would act more rationally than scorpions and avoid striking in the first place. A rough equilibrium or "balance of terror" worked out in those early theoretical efforts prevails to this day.

While the worst days of the nuclear arms race may be past, the threat of nuclear war has not disappeared. LANL remains at the center of nuclear weapons technology and testing.

The laboratory is one of the most secure sites on earth. It is perched atop a mesa with surrounding five-hundred-foot cliffs enveloped by multiple security perimeters. The airspace is restricted, although there is a landing strip nearby for approved flights. Those arriving by vehicle must pass through military checkpoints and show the appropriate badges indicating security clearance or prescreened resident or worker status. An intruder attempting to arrive on foot would have to cross miles of desert, descend canyons around the mesa, climb the mesa walls, and penetrate a secure perimeter. Motion, noise, and infrared sensors and a heavily armed security force ensure that no uninvited visitors make it that far.

On April 8, 2009, I was in a U.S. government jitney with physicists and national security experts invited to attend classified briefings on new initiatives at LANL. The laboratory, and the government city around it, were visible in the distance as we approached on the access road from Santa Fe. Desert heat gave it a glimmering look. The city stood out in its isolation. My companions and I were not visiting Los Alamos that day to study nuclear weapons. Instead, we sought solutions to the quandary of systemic financial collapse.

Capital and Complexity

The systems dynamics of an atomic chain reaction and a stock market meltdown are similar. Each exemplifies complexity in action. There is a straight path from Los Alamos to Wall Street. Few have walked that path, as evidenced by the continued dominance of obsolete equilibrium models in central bank policymaking and private risk management.

Modern complexity theory began in 1960 with the work of Edward Lorenz, an MIT mathematician and meteorologist. Lorenz was modeling atmospheric flows and discovered that minute changes in initial conditions resulted in wildly different outcomes in flow. In a seminal 1963 paper, Lorenz described his results:

> Two states differing by imperceptible amounts may eventually evolve into two considerably different states. If, then, there is any error whatever in observing the present state—and in any real system such errors seem inevitable—an acceptable prediction of an instantaneous state in the distant future may well be impossible. . . . [P]rediction of the sufficiently distant future is impossible by any [known] method, unless the present conditions are known exactly. In view of the inevitable inaccuracy and incompleteness of . . . observations, precise very-long-range forecasting would seem to be nonexistent.

Lorenz was writing about the atmosphere, yet his conclusions apply broadly to complex systems. Lorenz's research is the source of the famous butterfly effect in which a hurricane is caused by a butterfly's wings flapping thousands of miles away. The butterfly effect is good science. The difficulty is that not every butterfly causes a hurricane, and not every hurricane is caused by butterflies. Still, it's useful to know that hurricanes emerge unexpectedly for unforeseen reasons. The same is true of market meltdowns.

Merely because the precise origin of a *particular* hurricane is not forecast far in advance does not mean the likelihood of hurricanes hitting Miami can safely be ignored. Hurricanes in Miami are a near certainty; precautions are always in order. Likewise, the fact that *particular* market panics cannot be predicted to the day does not mean robust insights into the magnitude and frequency of panics cannot be derived. They can. Regulators who dismiss these insights ignore hurricane warnings while residing in soon-to-be-inundated low-lying bungalows.

Complexity and the related field of chaos theory are two branches of the broader sciences of nonlinear mathematics and critical state systems analysis. Los Alamos has been on the cutting edge of these fields from its start. Significant breakthroughs in the 1970s were computational and built on earlier theoretical work from the 1940s and 1950s by iconic figures such as John von Neumann and Stanislaw Ulam.

Theoretical constructs were harnessed to massive computing power to simulate phenomena such as hydrodynamic turbulence. Seeing a fast-flowing stream at sunset is an aesthetic experience; poets try to capture its noetic beauty. Still, an effort to write equations that precisely model the ebb and flow, twist and turn, of every molecule of H_2O in the stream, not just at a point in time, but dynamically through time, presents a challenge. Describing a turbulent flow of water mathematically is one of the most daunting dynamics systems problems known. Los Alamos set out to solve precisely these types of challenges.

The number of complex systems best comprehended using nonlinear and critical state models is vast. Climate, biology, solar flares, forest fires, traffic jams, and other natural and man-made behaviors can all be described using complexity theory. Lorenz's observation that long-run forecasting in nonlinear systems is impossible given minute differences in initial conditions did not mean that no valuable information is derived from the models.

Applied complexity theory is interdisciplinary. Complex systems all have behaviors in common, yet have dynamics unique to each domain. A team out to crack the code in applied complexity theory would include physicists, mathematicians, computer modelers, and subject matter experts from the field being addressed. Biologists, climatologists, hydrologists, psychologists, and other domain experts work together with complexity theorists to model particular systems.

Financial experts are new kids on the block when it comes to this kind of team science. My visit to Los Alamos was part of an effort to bridge the gap between complexity science and capital markets. LANL developed a mathematical methods toolkit that could be applied to various problem sets with modifications specific to each problem. These tools were devised as part of LANL's core mission in nuclear weaponry. My role was to learn how to use these tools on Wall Street.

One of the most important problems addressed at the lab is the readiness and capability of the U.S. nuclear arsenal. Nuclear weapons are designed and engineered to exacting specifications. Yet even the most careful engineering requires testing to identify flaws and suggest improvements.

Conventional weapons frequently fail to detonate. Yet they can easily be replaced as needed, and there are few practical constraints on testing. But belief by an adversary that U.S. nuclear weapons are duds has far more serious consequences. If an enemy thought the U.S. nuclear arsenal was unreliable, they might be tempted to try a first strike. The belief is highly destabilizing. The United States and the world require a high degree of assurance that U.S. nuclear weapons will work as expected in order to maintain the balance of terror and deter nuclear war. The last time the United States tested a nuclear weapon by detonation was September 23, 1992, almost a quarter century ago. How does the United States test its nuclear weapons, especially new smaller designs, without detonations?

The solution used by LANL is to detonate conventional explosives arrayed to simulate some of the implosion dynamics of nuclear weapons, while testing new atomic fusion dynamics at subcritical levels. So-called hydronuclear tests of less than 0.1 tons yield are used. Designs are also tested in computer simulations combining data from past explosions with new data from recent experimental and theoretical advances. These simulations are run on the fastest and most powerful supercomputers in the world. In effect, nuclear weapons are being detonated in supercomputers.

Models used to conduct these tests are among the most complex ever devised. My mission was to see how this modeling and computing power could be applied to another kind of explosion—stock market crashes.

A starting place for this work is to use Bayesian statistics, based on Bayes' theorem, also referred to as causal inference. Bayes' theorem is most useful when data are scarce or a problem is fuzzy and not amenable to conventional data-rich statistical methods involving regressions and covariance. Bayesian methods are used at the CIA and other intelligence agencies to solve problems when information is limited.

After 9/11, the CIA was faced with the problem of predicting the next spectacular terrorist attack. There had been only one such attack on U.S. soil in history. Intelligence analysts did not have the luxury of waiting for ten attacks and thirty thousand dead to look for a robust statistical pattern. We went to war with the data we had.

Bayes' theorem allows you to devise a hypothesis (or several) as a starting place and then fill in the blanks as you go along. Bayes' theorem was formerly called inverse probability because it works backward with new data to update a preexisting conclusion. Bayesian methods are not perfect, but they can allow an analyst to make strong inferences while conventional statisticians are still waiting for more data.

Bayes' theorem in a simplified mathematical modern form states:

$$P(A|B) = \frac{P(B|A)P(A)}{P(B)}$$

where P(A) is the probability of observing event A, without regard to event B

P(B) is the probability of observing event B, without regard to event A

P(A|B) is the conditional probability of observing event A given that event B is true

P(B|A) is the conditional probability of observing event B given that event A is true

In plain English, the formula says that by updating an initial understanding with unbiased new information, you improve your understanding.

In mathematical form, Bayes is used to forecast the likelihood of event A occurring. Event A could be anything from a critical state nuclear chain reaction to an interest rate increase by a central bank. The equation's left side is an initial estimate of the probability of an event occurring on its own without regard to other events, based on a mix of data, history, intuition, and inference. New information goes into the equation's right side. The likelihood of the new information appearing if the initial estimate is or is not true is computed separately. Then the probability of the initial estimate is updated as new information arrives. This process is repeated as often as new data arrives. Over time, the initial estimate gets stronger or weaker. Finally, a robust initial estimate can be used as a basis for decision making in the absence of better information.

The essence of Bayes' theorem is that a chain of events has memory. A new event is not disconnected from prior events like a roll of the dice; it is conditional upon the prior event. Wall Street and central bank models rely on events' being discrete. Each coin toss or roll of the dice has an independent probability free from the prior toss or roll. That is how coin tosses work, yet it's not how the real world works. A nuclear explosion is not unrelated to an earlier neutron release. A market meltdown is not unrelated to earlier excess credit creation. This is why central bank forecasting is abysmal, and why bankers never see panics in advance. Banks are using obsolete non-Bayesian models.

The Bayesian models we discussed at LANL were the most advanced anywhere. Still, they were not conceptually different from basic Bayes. The main advance was construction of a cascade of separate hypotheses, each with its own Bayes equation inside. The cascade was structured from top to bottom like a waterfall. Each hypothesis was contained in its own cell. The cellular array looked like a mosaic when presented graphically.

The top tier of hypothesis cells included those first in a sequence, and usually those with the highest initial probabilities. Below were other cells, later in the sequence, with lower initial probabilities. In a simulation, the top-tier output trickled down as input to middle and lower tiers. Based on that input, lower tiers were updated with new probabilities. Some downstream paths were truncated as their updated odds fell. Other paths were highlighted as their updated odds rose.

The mosaic might contain millions of cells. As cells were abandoned or highlighted, an image emerged from the mosaic not visible at the start. This emergence had a mystical quality to it, the way a hurricane emerges in mid-ocean on a sunny day for no apparent reason. Still, it was hard science. The supercomputer was detonating a nuclear weapon in digital space, yet the earth did not tremble.

The key to a robust Bayesian model mosaic is proper conception of the upstream cells that start the chain reaction. If a top cell is wrongly conceived, remaining output is largely worthless. The art is to get a postulate right and let probable paths progress from there.

As I sat there watching physicists demonstrate Bayesian technique for nuclear weapons testing, my mind turned to applications in capital markets. In fact, there are many.

Complexity theory is a branch of physics. Bayes' theorem is applied mathematics. Complexity and Bayes fit together hand in glove for solving capital markets problems. Capital markets are complex systems nonpareil. Market participants must forecast continually to optimize trading strategies and asset allocations. Forecasting capital markets is treacherous because they do not behave according to the Markovian stochastics widely used on Wall Street. A Markov chain has no memory; capital markets do. Capital markets produce surprises, no different from the butterfly effect identified by Lorenz in 1960. Since 2009 I have achieved superior results using complexity and Bayes to navigate the uncharted waters of systemic risk.

A simple application of Bayes' theorem can provide insights into otherwise secret understandings. A good example is the Shanghai Accord. This was the understanding reached among the United States,

China, Japan, and the Eurozone on the sidelines of the G20 meeting of finance ministers and central banks in Shanghai on February 26, 2016. Those four G20 members comprise two-thirds of global GDP and make up a de facto G4 inside the G20.

The problem confronted by the G4 in Shanghai was that growth in China and the United States was slowing dangerously, and global growth was weakened by that slowdown. Structural reforms were stalled by political gridlock. Fiscal policy was constrained by already excessive debt. Monetary policy was increasingly ineffective, even counterproductive. With structural reform, fiscal stimulus, and monetary ease off the table, the only stimulus channel left was a return to the currency wars.

A cheaper yuan gives a temporary lift to China even if it comes at the expense of its trading partners. China devalued unilaterally in August and December 2015. Both times U.S. stock markets crashed in the aftermath. The G4 needed to find a way to cheapen the yuan without destabilizing the U.S. stock market.

The solution was to maintain the peg between the yuan and the dollar, then devalue the dollar. The yuan gets cheaper relative to the euro and yen, while the yuan-dollar peg is unchanged.

This meant that Japan and Europe would suffer a stronger currency and a trade disadvantage. That's how currency wars work. For every winner, in this case China and the United States, there are losers, in this case Japan and Europe. A cheap yen had prevailed since 2013, and a cheap euro since 2014. Japan failed to make needed structural reforms. Now it was out of time. A new cheap-yuan, cheap-dollar phase was about to commence. The world's two largest economies—China and the United States—needed help. This was the essence of the Shanghai Accord.

The challenge for analysts is that initially there was not a shred of evidence to prove the accord. The G4 meeting was conducted in secret and no explicit press releases or other information was shared. Analysts scoffed at the idea of a Shanghai Accord. Prominent foreign exchange expert Marc Chandler of Brown Brothers Harriman, writing about the Shanghai Accord, said, "Conspiracy theories have run amok."

Bayes' theorem allows an analyst to do better than conspiracy theories. A geopolitical action like the Shanghai Accord with scarce hard data to confirm it is the type of event Bayes' theorem is designed to validate. The process is like a detective solving a crime with no witnesses. You collect evidence and interview suspects until you have a solid case.

To illustrate, consider ten discrete events in a row. Each event has a binary outcome: two possible results that tend to prove or disprove a starting hypothesis. Consider the binary outcomes as "heads or tails."

These binary outcome events have two types. The first type is *random*. This is like tossing a coin. You could get heads or tails with equal probability, yet you never know in advance which it will be. The outcome of each coin toss is independent of prior tosses. The second type is *path dependent*. This means each event depends on prior events or relates to a single determining event.

If the Shanghai Accord hypothesis is true, relevant events would be path dependent. Central bank decisions would all be affected by the secret deal. Policy would not be a random coin toss. Events would be affected to some extent by the secret understanding.

The next step is to look at actions by central banks and consider what outcomes one would expect to observe if the Shanghai Accord hypothesis is or is not true.

If one tosses coins, what are the odds of ten heads in a row? Each coin toss has a 50 percent chance of being heads, and no coin toss is affected by another. The odds of ten heads in a row are roughly one in one thousand. (Mathematically this is expressed as $(1/2)^{10}$. This can be put as: $0.5 \times 0.5 \times 0.5 \times 0.5 \times 0.5 \times 0.5 \times 0.5 \times 0.5 \times 0.5 \times 0.5 = 0.0009765625 \approx 0.001$.)

One chance in a thousand is not impossible. If a daily possibility, it occurs about once every three years. Still, the odds against it are extremely high. No investor would base a trading decision on a sequence of ten heads in a row even though it cannot be ruled out.

Now, consider ten critical events that actually happened between

February 26 and April 15, 2016. Each event had a binary outcome in advance. Call those that confirm the Shanghai Accord heads, and those that refute the Shanghai Accord tails. Reserve judgment for now on whether these events are random or path dependent.

Here are the events:

- February 26, 2016: Before the G20 meeting is quite over, Fed governor Lael Brainard gives a speech in New York and says, "It is natural to consider whether coordination can improve outcomes . . . cooperation can be quite helpful." Heads.
- February 27, 2016: At the conclusion of the Shanghai G20 meeting, U.S. treasury secretary Jack Lew says, "We'll keep each other informed . . . we'll avoid surprising each other." Heads.
- February 27, 2016: Also at the Shanghai G20 meeting, IMF managing director Christine Lagarde says, "There was in the room a renewed sense of urgency, and a renewed sense for collective action." Heads.
- March 10, 2016: The ECB *tightens* policy relative to expectations by announcing that it has no plans for further easing. Heads.
- March 15, 2016: The Bank of Japan *tightens* policy relative to expectations by not expanding its program of quantitative and qualitative easing. Heads.
- March 16, 2016: The Federal Reserve *eases* policy relative to expectations by striking a dovish tone in its press conference. Heads.
- March 29, 2016: Federal Reserve chair Janet Yellen makes her new dovish policy explicit with a speech at the Economic Club of New York. Heads.
- April 13, 2016: Luc Everaert, the IMF's mission chief for Japan, with reference to market intervention to weaken the yen says, "There is no good reason for Japan to intervene at this point." Heads.
- April 14, 2016: Christine Lagarde warns Japan that the IMF's conditions for foreign exchange intervention to weaken the yen have not been met. Lagarde also says she is "quite pleased" the Fed moved to

a dovish stance based on "the international status of the economy." Heads.

- April 15, 2016: An unnamed ECB official tells Reuters, "There was an in-principle agreement about exchange rates expressed at the G20 communiqué." Heads.

There are additional data points, yet this list is sufficient to draw conclusions.

What does the sequence above represent? Did one randomly toss coins and observe ten heads in a row with 1,000-to-1 odds against? Or did one see *exactly* what would be expected if the Shanghai Accord were true?

It is highly probable that this sequence is *not* random, but path dependent. These later events all depend on one initial event—the secret Shanghai Accord.

Importantly, it was not necessary to wait until April 15, 2016, the end of this time line, to draw conclusions. The hypothesis was formed on February 26 based on official remarks at the close of the G20 meeting and Brainard's speech. Subsequent data validated the hypothesis, but were not needed to create it. The hypothesis simply got stronger as time elapsed based on conditional probabilities.

By using Bayes' theorem, an investor could pursue winning strategies— long euro, long yen, long gold, short dollar—with confidence, while Wall Street was still bemoaning "conspiracy theories." It's a matter of taking the math from New Mexico to the marketplace.

Complexity

Bayesian technique is not a science in itself, it's an applied mathematical tool with robust predictive properties. The prime science of capital markets is complexity theory.

Capital markets are complex systems, yet complexity is little understood and even less used in financial economics. From the 1998 global liquidity crisis, to the 2000 tech bubble collapse, to the 2008 panic, policymakers have led the world into one crash after another. Their failure to use complexity theory explains why.

The case for complexity theory is straightforward. It's not difficult to grasp. Investors must grasp it now if they wish to preserve wealth. The next panic will be too late. The ice-nine solution will lock down wealth and make it impossible to take defensive measures.

Complex systems have existed since the beginning of time. The creation of the universe in the Big Bang more than 13 billion years ago instantaneously led to complex dynamics in stars, gases, galaxies, and finally planets. What is new is our understanding of complexity as a formal science. That understanding is traced to the 1960 Lorenz experiments.

The timing of Lorenz's breakthrough was not a coincidence. Prior to 1960, large-scale computing power was available to relatively few scientists, and was mostly applied to traditional problems in physics and operations research. Personal computers were still decades away. Yet by 1960, time-sharing on mainframe computers was available to researchers in more diverse fields, including Lorenz's field, meteorology.

Without computing power, complex dynamic system paths were impossible to observe in graphical form. Humans could see complex system outcomes in tsunamis, fires, and floods. Still, they could not see the dynamics. Computers changed that.

To see what complexity is, it's useful to know what it is not. Many systems are complicated, yet not necessarily complex. A handmade Swiss watch is complicated, but does not produce the highly unexpected behavior associated with complex systems.

Everyday phenomena such as a coin toss, a roll of the dice, or the spin of a roulette wheel are not complex phenomena. Such random processes are highly predictable. You don't know if the next coin toss is heads or tails. You do know if you toss a coin a thousand times, you are certain to get about five hundred heads and five hundred tails. The odds of getting nine hundred heads and one hundred tails are so infinitesimal as to be effectively zero.

Also, random processes such as coin tosses and throws of dice have no memory. This means that a prior coin toss has no impact whatsoever on the next one. Some gamblers who see three heads in a row assume the odds are good the next toss is tails. This is called the *gambler's fallacy* because it rests on a false assumption. The odds on each coin toss are always fifty-fifty. This is why a thousand tosses produce about five hundred heads and five hundred tails even if smaller samples produce an occasional run of heads or tails. When a short-run skew develops, you can be certain that future coin tosses will move the overall distribution back toward fifty-fifty, a phenomenon known as *mean reversion*.

Complex systems in contrast are highly unpredictable. A complex system can produce unexpected results seemingly from nowhere. In capital markets, phenomena such as market crashes, panics, and sequential bank failures are examples of complexity in action.

What is complexity? How can investors use an understanding of complexity to preserve wealth?

Complex systems are everywhere; they are not confined to laboratories or subatomic structures. If you drive a certain road every day that is uncrowded, then one day run into a traffic jam for no apparent reason, you have encountered complexity in action. Deciding if your favorite restaurant will be too crowded on a Friday night or whether the stock market is a bubble is an exercise in solving complex problems. Complexity is ubiquitous.

Complex systems are natural, man-made, or combinations of the two. A hurricane is a natural complex system. A stock market is a man-made complex system. A nuclear explosion is a combination because the natural complexity of uranium atoms is engineered by scientists to the supercritical state that releases a bomb's destructive power.

Complexity theory begins with two tools. The first is the *agent*. An agent is simply an actor in a system. An agent can be a human in the case of capital markets or an atom in the case of a bomb. The agent is the irreducible unit generating behavior behind complex dynamics.

The second tool is *feedback*. This means that initial behavior produces output that affects subsequent behavior. This is why complex systems are said to have memory. When agents act in complex systems they observe prior acts that condition what they do next. Another name for the same idea is *adaptive behavior*. An agent adapts her next move based on what she has learned from prior moves in the system.

Random systems such as coin tosses, dice, or roulette wheels do not contain feedback loops. A coin does not adapt its behavior. In complex systems, behavior adapts all the time. Adaptation is one reason complexity produces surprising results.

Feedback is endogenous or exogenous. *Endogenous* feedback is internal to an agent, a matter of learning from mistakes. A cat that jumps on a hot stove learns not to do it again. *Exogenous* feedback is external to an agent. For a stock trader, it's a matter of watching the behavior of others distilled through market prices. Markets may be going up, down, or nowhere, yet one observes this behavior before making the next move.

Agents and feedback are the building blocks of complex systems. What else is needed? It helps if the agents are *diverse*. If the agents are identical, feedback is weak because one agent's behavior reinforces others' behavior rather than changing it. In stock markets, diverse agents exist as bulls and bears, longs and shorts, rich and poor, old and young. Diversity of agents in capital markets is strong.

Another requirement is that agents *communicate* and *interact* in some way. Diverse agents do not give rise to complex behavior if agents cannot connect. Fifty cavemen sitting in fifty caves may have diverse views about the best way to hunt for food. Still, if they don't leave their caves and communicate, diversity doesn't matter. It's only when cavemen leave their caves, gather around a fire, and start to share ideas that complex behavior emerges.

As diverse agents interact, adaptation begins. Once cavemen start to compare notes around the fire, some change their hunting method based on others' success. Cavemen who don't adapt may starve. A society of more efficient hunters starts to emerge. This is bad news for the mastodon, but good news for the cavemen.

Instead of cavemen, imagine a much larger group of stock traders hunting for the best trades. They have diverse opinions. They communicate on Bloomberg, Reuters, email, and the Web. Interaction is measured in trillions of dollars of daily trading volume. If a portfolio is losing money, the adviser needs to adapt quickly. You learn from others; others learn from you. Those who don't adapt lose clients, or lose their jobs. They are soon out of the game. In short, capital markets exhibit *all* the characteristics of complex systems in a strong form.

These building blocks of complex systems are easy to understand. You need autonomous agents with diverse qualities. The agents need communication channels to interact. The interaction produces new information that feeds back to the agents. Then agents adapt their behavior to improve outcomes in the future.

Complex models do not resemble stochastic models used by central bankers. They do resemble the real world.

Feedback

Complexity in capital markets can be limned in social terms. Is there hard empirical evidence to support the view that capital markets are complex systems? Are there repeatable experiments that prove the point in accord with formal scientific method? The answer to both is yes.

Adaptive behavior arises in many socially based complex systems such as markets, traffic flows, and dating. The source of adaptation comes from competition for scarce resources. If valuable resources are available in unlimited quantities, one does not need survival strategies or adaptive behavior. You just take what you want. Scarcity is what causes individuals to adopt strategies to secure their share of the resources. This problem of allocating scarce resources is the foundation of economic science.

In capital markets, the scarce resource is wealth. In traffic, the scarce resource is a fast lane or a parking space. In dating, the scarce resource is the ideal mate. When competing for scarce resources, you need to make smart choices that increase your chances of winning a highly competitive game. If your trades are losing money, you can't find a parking space, or you can't get a date, it pays to look around and see what the winners are doing. This is adaptive behavior.

One example is Warren Buffett, a winner when it comes to wealth. The SEC requires a quarterly portfolio disclosure by Buffett's company, Berkshire Hathaway. When investors get a look at what Warren Buffett is doing, they copy his trades in the hope of becoming winners too.

This behavior results in the formation of a *crowd* whose behavior reinforces others' behavior in the same crowd. The problem over time is that the winning strategy gets too crowded and no longer works. The first hipster to find a newly opened bar in Brooklyn with great live music may enjoy a few blissful weekends there. Eventually word gets around, the bar becomes crowded, and the hipster has to fight to get a drink. The winning strategy of hanging out in a cool bar becomes a losing strategy of standing-room only. The hipster moves on. So does Buffett.

This adaptive behavior displays feedback and memory. If you recall the bar as cool and uncrowded, you'll go back. If you recall the bar as crowded and noisy, you might not (although some like noisy crowded bars).

To analyze crowds, physicists posit the formation of *anticrowds*. An anticrowd attracts followers that do the opposite of the original crowd. Such crowd-anticrowd behavior exhibits lots of memory and feedback. What separates the crowd and anticrowd are their expectations.

Using the bar example, it's the case that some nights the bar is crowded and some nights there are empty tables. You just don't know in advance. Agents make a forecast based on the best information available. Information might include social media updates from friends at the bar. Real-time information accelerates an agent's reaction function, but it doesn't negate it.

People considering going to the bar, or investors deciding whether to buy a particular stock, fall into three groups for forecasting purposes. The crowd believes the future will resemble the past. The anticrowd believes the future will not resemble the past. The third group does not have a forecast, but mentally tosses a coin and acts based on the random outcome.

Having a model forecast is no guarantee of success. Memory might tell you the bar was crowded last weekend, so you decide to stay home this weekend because you assume the bar will be crowded again. This model says the future will resemble the past. If enough people have the same model and stay home, the bar will actually be uncrowded this weekend. Memory makes you lose out on an enjoyable evening of live music.

Conversely, the anticrowd remembers the bar was too crowded last weekend and decides people will go somewhere else next time. In their model, the future does not resemble the past. They decide to try the bar again next weekend. If they're lucky, they'll get a good table.

Still, if the anticrowd gets too big, the bar may end up overcrowded again. Then some anticrowd members may join the crowd and stay home. The bar might have empty tables next time, and so on.

On rare occasions, the random group might all choose the same course of action (like tossing five heads in a row) and cause crowd members to join the anticrowd, and vice versa, as adaptive behavior takes hold. This random behavior is a catalyst for shifts between crowd and anticrowd allegiance—a snowflake that starts an avalanche.

Scientists have conducted experiments using these same crowd-anticrowd dynamics. A group of individuals begin with a preference in their forecasting model. Through experience and feedback they *self-organize* into crowds, anticrowds, and random actors. The crowd and anticrowd attract the vast majority of participants in roughly equal numbers, while the random actors represent a small minority. This illustrates one of complexity's most powerful traits: *emergence*. Well-defined opposing groups emerge without force or prearrangement from an undifferentiated mass through the workings of feedback and memory.

Emergent behavior is well documented in complexity science. It makes intuitive sense also. A Wall Street cliché says, "For every buyer, there's a seller." In a bull market, buyers are a crowd who believe the future resembles the past. Sellers are the anticrowd who believe that the future will be different. With both in equal proportions the markets can function. What about the small minority of coin tossers? Their individual behavior is random. Do they cause markets as a whole to be random? Or do they cause bulls to become bears, and vice versa, producing non-random persistence?

Research conducted by physicists Neil Johnson, Pak Ming Hui, and Paul Jefferies using financial market data shows the price movement pattern in markets does not correspond to the so-called *random walk* model that is the foundation of modern financial economics. Instead, behavior corresponds to predictions of complexity theorists using principles of feedback and adaptive behavior.

Behavior in financial markets can be broken down into binary choices, expressed as "either/or" or "yes/no" answers to a series of questions. Will you trade stocks today? Will you consider IBM shares? Will you buy or sell? Will you transact in large or small size? And so on. Each of these questions has a yes or no answer. In binary code, yes can be expressed as the digit 1. No can be expressed as the digit 0. Answers to a series of these questions can be expressed as a string of 1s and 0s such as 0011010011. These strings can be computer coded and analyzed for patterns in large data sets and long time series. The answers are highly revealing about how markets actually work.

The random walk model, associated with Princeton professor Burton G. Malkiel, says these decisions resemble a drunk walking down the street. Each step is uncertain. It could be forward or backward. The drunk doesn't know himself. Each step is random, unaffected by the one before. There is no memory, there is no feedback.

The random walk model and the crowd-anticrowd model should produce completely different patterns of 1s and 0s because the random walk has no memory and the crowd does. Patterns produced by each model are quantified, and the model projections compared to experimental data.

Neil Johnson and other physicists do this by beginning with a thought experiment. Imagine the market as a person walking from a fixed point for a certain time period. The walker can move forward or backward the same way the market goes up or down. You want to calculate the distance covered. The purpose is to see if markets are a *random walk* or something else.

For convenience, scientists give the starting place a value of 10. Every step forward adds 1 to this position. Every step backward subtracts 1. From a starting place of 10, if you took two steps forward and one backward, your ending position is 11 ($10 + 1 + 1 - 1 = 11$). This forward/backward value is the same binary output as the yes/no investor choices described above and allows for binary coding and analysis.

This binary walking pattern from a starting position of 10 means that after 9 steps, the walker will either be at position 19 ($10 + 9 = 19$) or position 1 ($10 - 9 = 1$), or somewhere between 1 and 19 depending on the pattern of the walk.

For example, if you start at position 10 and take 9 steps forward you end up in position 19. From that starting position, the new position after each step presents this pattern: 10 11 12 13 14 15 16 17 18 19. This does not appear to be random; the path appears directional. Scientists call this pattern highly *ordered*.

To generalize this experiment for all types of walks, scientists create a measure that describes distance as a function of time. This function is expressed as t^a where t equals the number of moves, a is an exponent, and t^a equals the distance traveled. Both t and t^a can be observed empirically in experiments. The exponent a is derived from results for t and t^a.

In our ordered example, $t = 9$, the number of moves, and $t^a = 9$ because that was the distance traveled. Therefore, $a = 1$ in this example; an exponent 1 applied to a number equals that number. In this highly ordered case, $9 = 9^1$; the number of steps taken equals total distance traveled.

What happens when steps are truly random? In that case, the total distance traveled would rarely equal the total steps taken because some steps would be backward, some forward, and they would cancel each other out. The steps taken are greater than the distance traveled, which means that $t > t^a$. If that is true, then $a < 1$, because a fractional exponent is required for t to be greater than t^a.

For the random walker, many sequences are possible because there are numerous possible combinations of forward and backward movement when taking nine steps. Each step taken by the random walker is like a coin toss that can come up heads or tails. For analytic purposes, say that heads = 1, tails = 0, and each 1 is a step forward, and each 0 is a step back from a prior position.

As an experiment, I tossed a coin nine times and got the following sequence: 110001001, a total of 4 heads and 5 tails. Starting from position 10, and following the walk represented by these random coin tosses, the position sequence is: 11 12 11 10 9 10 9 8 9. In this random walk, the walker moved 1 position (10 − 9 = 1) in 9 steps. This random sequence is referred to by scientists as *disordered* because the sequence does not show strong persistence in one direction or the other.

If this experiment was repeated 1,000 times, easily done on a computer, the average distance from the starting place produced by the random walk of 9 steps would be approximately 3, which is the square root of 9. The distance of $3 = t^a$ in our model. If $t = 9$ (the total steps taken), and $t^a \approx 3$ (total positions moved as shown by the random walk output), then $a \approx 0.5$. The total movement in the 9-step random walk is $3 = 9^{0.5}$.

In a highly *ordered* walk $a = 1.0$. In a random or *disordered* walk $a = 0.5$. What type of walk do actual markets take? Stated formally, what is the value of a based on actual market price movements?

One characteristic of complex systems is they are *neither* highly ordered nor random. Complex systems oscillate between order and disorder. This oscillation comes from agents' deciding to quit the crowd and join the anticrowd or vice versa. A complex system that begins with random behavior can become ordered through feedback and adaptive behavior. Likewise, a highly ordered system can fall into disorder.

Complex systems move back and forth, exactly as markets move from bull to bear phases as investor sentiment moves from fear to greed. Adaptation produces patterns more persistent than a random walk, tending toward order. Still, the system does not become completely ordered because of the crowd-anticrowd dynamic. In other words, the value of exponent a in a complex system should be somewhere between 0.5 and 1.0.

Empirical research on stock markets around the world over extended time periods shows the value of a in real markets is approximately 0.7. This empirical result falls between 0.5 and 1.0, somewhere between random and ordered, exactly what complexity theory predicts. This is strong evidence that capital markets are complex systems.

Not only do capital markets fit a descriptive definition of complex systems based on diversity, communication, interaction, and adaptive behavior, but empirical evidence shows that actual behavior in markets corresponds to the predictive output of a theoretical model. This is science at its best.

The implications of this conclusion are troubling. Professor Neil Johnson puts the matter starkly:

> The standard model that most of the finance world uses to calculate how markets move is not accurate.... Financial markets are Complex Systems and they cannot be described accurately by anything other than a theory of Complex Systems. Standard finance theory may therefore appear to work for a while but it will eventually fail, for example in moments where strong movements appear in the market as a result of crowd behavior. And this is far from being a minor flaw since it is precisely these moments when your money is most at risk.

A grasp of complexity theory is a powerful tool for assessing risk in capital markets. We see how diverse groups of agents can self-organize into a crowd and anticrowd that produce a reasonably stable, yet not random, market. There is persistence, but not complete order.

Panic arises when the crowd and anti-crowd act as one. A completely ordered market system is one in which there are *all* sellers and *no* buyers. Such a market would instantaneously collapse and prices would go to zero. How likely is this? In natural complex systems, collapse happens with some frequency.

The New Madrid Seismic Zone in Missouri and surrounding states has been relatively stable for more than two hundred years. Yet in 1811–12, New Madrid produced four of the largest earthquakes in recorded North American history, estimated at magnitude 7.0 M_w or greater (M_w connotes moment magnitude scale, successor to the Richter scale). Seismologists predict the next New Madrid earthquake could be magnitude 7.7 M_w, about the same as the 1906 San Francisco earthquake. These estimates include 86,000 casualties and two million people seeking shelter. Seismic faults are complex systems; so are stock markets.

The fact that complex systems oscillate between randomness and order does not mean these systems are stable or self-equilibrating. Complex systems go through phase transitions into chaos or collapse with surprising ease. The types of Bayesian simulations conducted at Los Alamos help the analyst to envision a range of outcomes in complex systems, including the financial equivalent of a thermonuclear bomb.

The financial outcomes considered in this book have happened before. Investors may lose money in a market crash, yet markets do tend to bounce back over time. Some crashes are excellent buying opportunities for those on the sidelines with cash who find bargains amid the rubble. Even those who suffer market losses can recoup if they hold their positions instead of selling into the panic. Most markets gain value over time. The lucky few who sell out at tops, and buy after crashes, outperform market averages.

Likewise, the failure of prominent banks seems to be a problem society has learned to manage. Stock investors in failed firms may suffer losses, yet depositors and account holders are routinely bailed out by deposit insurance and government guarantees. Even stock losses are manageable if they are part of larger diversified portfolios. After the crashes in 1987, 1998, 2000, and 2008, the market bounced back and rose to new highs. Why should investors be concerned about collapse?

The archetype for collapse in a complex system is not New Madrid or San Francisco. The archetype is Krakatoa. In 1883, the island of Krakatoa in the Sunda Strait between Sumatra and Java exploded with a force thirteen thousand times greater than the Hiroshima bomb. The force was ten times greater than the Castle Bravo bomb test on Bikini Atoll in 1954. It was four times greater than the largest nuclear explosion ever, the fifty-megaton Tsar Bomba test by the USSR in 1961.

After the 1883 Krakatoa explosion, there was nothing left of Krakatoa. The cause for investor concern is that certain systemic collapses are so large the system does not bounce back. The system ceases to exist.

CHAPTER 4
FORESHOCK: 1998

I have reflected a long time on the Long-Term Capital Management crisis. The thing that struck me most was the story of LTCM . . . is a very modern crisis, but the way it was resolved was almost identical to the way that crises always used to be resolved. The central bank was brought in and banged a few heads together. There was an argument about whether they should have done it, but in the end, that was how it was resolved.

Stanley Fischer, vice chairman of the Federal Reserve Board

God gave Noah the rainbow sign, no more water but fire next time.

"Oh Mary Don't You Weep," gospel song

Money Machine

The 2008 financial panic inspired a legion of books and movies, including a memorable narrative, *Too Big to Fail*, by Andrew Ross Sorkin. By all accounts, the financial system suffered a heart attack that year. The medical metaphor is not a stretch. The world financial system really did have a heart attack, and the patient nearly died. The Fed was a doctor with a defibrillator. What struck me most about 2008 was I had seen this movie before.

Exactly ten years earlier, almost to the day, the financial system suffered its first global heart attack. Fed doctors saved the patient that time too. Yet after 1998 the patient returned to cigars, heavy drinking, and no exercise. A second heart attack was just a matter of time.

If a market diagnostician in 1998 had studied the symptoms and course of that panic, the 2008 debacle could have been avoided. Nothing of the kind occurred. The lessons of 1998 were not learned. Dysfunctional market behavior resumed on an even larger scale with the blessing of banks and regulators.

The 1998 panic, catalyzed by Russian default and the collapse of hedge fund Long-Term Capital Management, seems small in hindsight. Many have not heard of it. Compared with the 2008 panic, the late summer of 1998 seems distant, inconsequential.

Superficially, the problems in 1998 seemed to go away. A few banks, notably UBS, took large write-downs. Some bank executives got fired. Alan Greenspan cut interest rates twice—once at a scheduled Federal Reserve meeting on September 29, 1998, and again at a rare unscheduled meeting on October 15, 1998. The second rate cut did the trick. It told markets the Fed was watching and would do whatever it took to restore calm.

Normality returned. Credit spreads that widened beyond belief began to converge. The stock market shrugged off the LTCM panic and resumed one of the greatest rallies in history. The Dow Jones Industrial Average soared from 7,632.53 on October 1, 1998, to 11,497.12 on December 31, 1999; a 51 percent gain in fifteen months. After LTCM left the headlines, it was as if nothing had happened.

Yet something did happen that had never happened before. Major stock and bond markets around the world were hours away from collapse. The biggest banks were set to fall like dominoes starting with the perennial weak link Lehman. Investors stood to lose more in relative terms than they did in 2008. This was not reported at the time despite intense media focus on LTCM and its reclusive founder, John Meriwether. Only a few insiders at LTCM, the Fed, Treasury, and foreign finance ministries saw the whole picture and understood its significance. Elites foamed the runways and brought LTCM in for a safe landing despite four engines in flames. Global investors were inside the plane with seat belts fastened and no exit. What seems in hindsight like a non-event was a near miss of potentially catastrophic proportions.

The insiders who saved the system were quite prominent at the time. Some became more famous, or infamous, in later years. Peter Fisher led the emergency response by the Fed; he later became vice chairman of mega–wealth manager BlackRock. The bridge-playing Jimmy Cayne, head of Bear Stearns, was LTCM's broker. He had the best information of any outsider on LTCM's market risks. In typical Wall Street style, Cayne refused to share the information with other bank CEOs and nearly wrecked the rescue.

Jon Corzine, head of Goldman Sachs, was a leader in the LTCM rescue along with the CEOs of Citi, JPMorgan, and Merrill Lynch. Corzine, a close friend of Meriwether's, was distracted during the bailout because his own trades were losing billions. Corzine's debacle at MF Global in 2011, ending in bankruptcy, came as no surprise to those who watched his reckless gambles at Goldman.

At the height of the 1998 panic, Goldman pirated LTCM's derivatives positions and used the information to cover their own trades and front-run competitors. Goldman also tried to wreck the LTCM bailout deal at the eleventh hour by front-running the Federal Reserve with a competing offer signed by Corzine, Warren Buffett, and AIG head Hank Greenberg. AIG met its own demise in a government bailout in 2008. Cayne and Corzine were among the heads of the "fourteen families," the fourteen Wall Street banks that participated in the LTCM bailout.

The LTCM rescue would not have succeeded without discreet intervention by legendary bank crisis maestro Bill Rhodes, who finessed foreign bankers and finance ministers for loan waivers while the fourteen families squabbled among themselves. Unknown to outsiders, LTCM had arranged almost $1 billion of credit on an unsecured basis from a nineteen-bank international syndicate. To complete the rescue, waivers were needed from those banks in addition to getting the fourteen families to infuse new cash. Rhodes got those waivers.

LTCM's story was told in detail not long after the fact in an excellent book by Roger Lowenstein, *When Genius Failed*. The reason to revisit the story now is to show how the 2008 panic was foretold by 1998's events. Circumstances were different in 1998 and 2008, yet the dynamics were the same. Disturbingly, the next panic is now foretold by both 1998 and 2008. No lessons were learned. Elites simply expanded the bailout each time. Except next time the panic will be too large, and the bailout too small to stop it.

Ingredients like overleverage, derivatives, and reliance on obsolete risk models were identical in 1998 and 2008. The 2008 collapse could have been avoided if the lessons of LTCM were learned and applied. Instead, Wall Street and Washington turned a blind eye to what occurred in 1998. Policymakers including Fed chair Alan Greenspan and Treasury Secretary Larry Summers persisted with their belief in flawed risk models. Rather than learn lessons, Greenspan and Summers doubled down by supporting Glass-Steagall repeal and derivatives deregulation that made the 2008 collapse inevitable.

Today, we see lessons being ignored again. Wall Street is back to business as usual, relying on misleading models such as value at risk. The next catastrophe will be exponentially larger than the last two. The next time the world will not bounce back.

The Experts

I joined LTCM in February 1994 and reported to the firm's founder, legendary bond trader John Meriwether, known as "JM." I came on board before the fund opened for business, and remained through the collapse, rescue, and unwind until August 1999. The founding partners included two future Nobelists and other fathers of modern finance. There was never as great a collection of financial talent in one place, including universities and think tanks, as there was at LTCM.

LTCM's birth resulted from the near death of Salomon Brothers in 1991. The Salomon name is obscure today, yet in the 1980s, Salomon was synonymous with huge bond bets and complex trading strategies, many invented by Meriwether. In August 1990 and May 1991, a Meriwether subordinate, Paul Mozer, illegally cornered the market in two-year Treasury notes, and lied to the Federal Reserve about his trades. Mozer confessed his crimes to Meriwether, who immediately reported them to the CEO, John Gutfreund, and the president and general counsel of Salomon. Those three officials bungled the internal investigation and never reported the crimes to the government in a timely way.

The scandal reached a critical state on August 18, 1991, when the Treasury Department banned Salomon from bidding in Treasury securities auctions. Salomon's biggest investor, Warren Buffett, knew this was a death sentence and that Salomon would have to file for bankruptcy, wiping out his investment. Yet Buffett was worried about more than his investment. Coming so soon after the 1990 bankruptcy of Wall Street giant Drexel Burnham, Buffett believed another bond dealer default might destabilize the global financial system. A Drexel-Salomon one-two punch might be more than markets could bear.

Buffett called Treasury Secretary Nicholas F. Brady and got Treasury to partially rescind the auction bidding ban four hours later. In exchange, Buffett agreed to clean house, put up new money, and assume operating control of Salomon until the firm stabilized.

Gutfreund resigned under pressure along with president Tom Strauss and general counsel Don Feuerstein. Meriwether's case was more difficult because he reported the wrongdoing internally. Still, he was vice chairman of Salomon, and in the hue and cry the Fed felt all top management needed to leave. Meriwether was allowed to resign; his career on Wall Street was over. JM found himself "on the beach," in Wall Street parlance.

Meriwether set out to build a new firm, a hedge fund not regulated by the Fed or SEC. This allowed him to pursue his complex trading strategies in secrecy, without scrutiny by the government, media, or banks. He systematically recruited former colleagues at Salomon and new faces from academia. The firm was called Long-Term Capital Management. A coming-out announcement for LTCM appeared in *The New York Times* on September 5, 1993, under the headline "JOHN MERIWETHER RIDES AGAIN."

LTCM was based in Greenwich, Connecticut. In addition to Meriwether, the LTCM partners included two future Nobel Prize winners, Myron Scholes and Robert C. Merton, and a former vice chairman of the Federal Reserve Board, David Mullins Jr. Yet the talent went far beyond headline names like Scholes, Merton, and Mullins. Less well known, yet equally accomplished, was Alberto Giovannini, the Italian economist who led the technical design team that created the euro. Another key figure was Greg "The Hawk" Hawkins, from the finance faculty at Berkeley, where he was a colleague of Janet Yellen's. Among the younger talents was Matt Zames, now next in line to be CEO of JPMorgan on Jamie Dimon's departure.

The LTCM spider web went past the partners to include the fund's financial backers. One major investor was the Italian Treasury. This connection was crucial because LTCM was the world's largest trader in Italian government debt. Another investor was the Kuomintang, Chiang Kai-shek's Nationalist Chinese Army, later a political party that dominated Taiwan for decades.

Some of the world's largest banks including Japan's Sumitomo Bank, Germany's Deutsche Bank, and Switzerland's UBS made large investments euphemistically called "strategic relationships." This meant a two-way information flow between LTCM's traders and the banks' top management would be maintained. In the global financial web, LTCM was now near the center.

What united this talent was a rock-solid belief in the tenets of modern finance: efficient markets, mean reversion, rational expectations, and normal distribution of risk. In practical terms, this meant that if two instruments had substantially the same credit risk and cash flow present values, they should trade at similar prices. Markets were scrutinized using sophisticated modeling and massive computing power to spot situations where a price relationship was misaligned.

For example, a U.S. Treasury five-year note issued three years ago has two years left to maturity. Treasury also issues new two-year notes. An old five-year note with two years to maturity and a new two-year note with the same maturity should trade at prices that produce nearly identical yields to maturity for the two notes. There was no material difference between the notes because they were issued by the same government, and matured at the same time.

At times, this yield equivalence did not hold true. Two Treasury notes might trade at different yields for reasons unrelated to credit or cash flow. The reasons for divergent prices included institutional liquidity preferences. Some investors wanted only new or so-called on-the-run notes, and avoided old off-the-run notes. They would implement this preference at government debt auctions by selling their off-the-run notes, using proceeds to buy on-the-run notes. Investor liquidity preference temporarily depressed the price of old notes and placed a premium on new ones.

To devotees of efficient markets, liquidity preference made no sense because the two notes were identical from a credit and cash flow perspective. LTCM considered a pricing difference in this situation an anomaly, and exploited it by buying the old note and selling the new note short. In effect, LTCM took the other side of the trade from the investor. By buying the "cheap" note and selling the "rich" one, LTCM owned the spread between the two notes.

In time, markets would normalize. The new note became "old" in the marketplace. The spread between the two notes converged. LTCM would unwind the trade by selling its long position, covering its short position, and pocketing the spread as profit. Because the notes represented the same risk, and because LTCM had offsetting long and short positions, this strategy was regarded as practically risk free. Profit was just a matter of exploiting investors' irrational liquidity preference.

There were infinite variations on this risk-free arbitrage. Price differences arose in situations that did not involve auctions of new debt. Securities might be taxed differently, and an arbitrage might arise from the tax accounting. Differences might arise between bonds in two different currencies. Pricing adjustments would be made for the currency risk, which could be hedged in a different trade. Yet whenever some difference arose, LTCM's computers were waiting to buy the cheap bond and short the expensive bond. Then LTCM could sit back, wait until the spread converged, and pocket a risk-free profit. LTCM would be rational whenever markets were irrational.

One problem with this strategy was that profits on each trade were steady, yet small. Market forces tended to keep spreads from getting too far out of line. LTCM solved this problem with leverage. Profit on one trade might be small, say 2 percent on an annualized basis. Yet if the trade was leveraged 20-to-1, the 2 percent return became a 40 percent return.

LTCM was not a bank, although it acted like one. How could a hedge fund borrow enough money to achieve 20–1 leverage? Money was borrowed through repurchase agreements, or "repo." In a repo, a bond purchased from one dealer is pledged to another dealer to raise cash to buy more bonds. The result is an inverted pyramid of bonds, pledges, and loans poised on a thin sliver of cash.

Another leverage technique was to hide trades off-balance-sheet using swaps. Swaps are contracts that have the economics of bond trades without actual bonds. Swap counterparties specify a fixed rate, maturity, and currency that synthetically replicate desired cash flows without buying bonds. Swap leverage was higher than with repo because swaps were off-balance-sheet from the bank counterparty perspective. Capital requirements for the banks were lower with swaps than repos. If the off-balance-sheet swaps were accounted for the same as repos, the real leverage at LTCM was not 20-to-1, but 300-to-1. LTCM's swap agreements eventually exceeded $1 trillion.

These arbitrage and leverage strategies worked. Returns to investors were 20 percent in 1994, 43 percent in 1995, 41 percent in 1996, and 17 percent in 1997. In four years, LTCM had almost tripled investors' money.

This occurred by doing supposedly risk-free trades. From the outside, it looked as if LTCM had invented a perpetual motion money machine. High profits, and high fees charged by LTCM, meant the LTCM partners personally made hundreds of millions of dollars. Outsiders did not know that by 1997, the biggest investors in LTCM were the fund's partners themselves.

This was a heady time. Professors and policymakers visited to see what the mystery was about. These office tours were awkward because there wasn't much to see. The panoramic Greenwich Harbor views were beautiful, but strangely quiet. In contrast to hectic shouting in Wall Street dealing rooms, LTCM was mostly silent; the computers did the work. LTCM's trading style meant that once a trade was on the books, it might remain there for months or years as spreads slowly converged and risk-free profits rolled in. The partners debated strategies in meetings that were more like academic seminars than the knife fights that go on in some banks. When the weather was nice, Meriwether and his partners were as likely to be on the links at nearby Winged Foot Country Club as on the trading floor. There was no reason not to golf; the computers were in control.

JM's public persona was the bold, brash, Wall Street "master of the universe," as portrayed in two iconic books, Tom Wolfe's 1987 novel, *Bonfire of the Vanities*, and Michael Lewis's 1989 comic memoir, *Liar's Poker*. Wolfe told the story of larger-than-life bond trader Sherman McCoy, who held a position similar to Meriwether's at Salomon Brothers. The comparison was impossible to miss. Lewis told a real-life anecdote about a million-dollar bet made on the Salomon trading floor between Meriwether and Gutfreund on a single liar's poker hand, a legend that dogged JM.

In fact, JM was soft-spoken and somewhat shy. He was gregarious with friends on a golf course or racetrack, yet shunned the media and the social circuit that are the usual accompaniments of success in the hedge fund world. JM was a Thoroughbred racing enthusiast and owned several horses. Among his few outside activities was membership on the board of the New York Racing Association, operator of the three largest racetracks in New York including Belmont Park, home of the Belmont Stakes, last leg of the Triple Crown. A day at the races was a typical team-building excursion for LTCM staff.

Thoroughbreds, golf courses, and Greenwich calm were at odds with a perception that LTCM must be a frantic beehive of testosterone-laced shouting and sharp elbows. It wasn't. Models and computers were producing the profits. Partners were pilots of an aircraft with automatic navigation. You might intervene now and then to deal with unexpected bad weather, but otherwise you let the autopilot guide the plane to its final destination. Provided the autopilot was properly programmed, all was well.

Every big bank in the world wanted a piece of the action. Foreign banks lined up to become investors. They wanted the same strategic relationship that early bank investors enjoyed. Others wanted to be swap counterparties. Banks could book LTCM trades, then lay off the risk in the marketplace, making their own risk-free profits. Often this risk was laid off with banks that had other swaps with LTCM. It was a merry-go-round of risk passed around and around, ending up in the same place—the banks. It seemed the carousel music would never stop.

LTCM's financial technology was not limited to the fixed income arbitrage Meriwether invented in the 1980s. New structures were discovered. LTCM coinvented the sovereign credit default swap market in 1994 around the same time as a better-known initiative by JPMorgan bankers on a lost weekend in Miami, as recounted in Gillian Tett's brilliant book *Fool's Gold*.

LTCM was the largest holder of Italian government debt, part of a complex arbitrage involving Italian interest rates, different debt classes, and Italian withholding taxes on interest paid to foreign investors. LTCM could hedge interest rates, foreign exchange, and tax risk. One risk the fund could not hedge was default by the Italian government. That risk was tiny, yet not zero. The bond position was so large that even a trivial risk produced a huge expected loss when analyzed statistically.

LTCM needed to make Italian default risk disappear. We needed insurance that did not exist at the time, so we created it.

An LTCM trader, Arjun Krishnamachar, and I teamed up to invent this new insurance. We found a willing counterparty in the Milan branch of Japanese banking giant Sumitomo. The branch had assets in Italy and was willing to take on Italian liabilities for a price. Arjun's job was to devise formulas to price the insurance. My job as chief counsel was to write a contract that defined events of default. This was long before the industry standardized default swap terms. We started with a blank sheet of paper.

Obviously if the government didn't pay you, that was an event of default. That was an easy one. But there are numerous ways for governments to renege on obligations to bondholders, including capital controls, withholding taxes, asset freezes, and hyperinflation. We had to think of them all; otherwise the insurance might not pay off when needed. That was like buying hurricane insurance that covered wind damage, but not floods. We wanted to make sure we were covered against floods. The sovereign credit default swap was our first innovation. It was not the last.

Avarice

After initial success and billions of dollars in profits, greed came to call. The search was on for new ways to make money using leverage and derivatives.

The partners expanded into stock market arbitrage on mergers and takeovers. So-called merger arb involved the spread between the price at which one company offered to buy another, and the current price of the target company stock.

If company A offered to buy company B for $25 per share, payable in company A stock, and company B's stock traded at $21 per share, it was a simple matter to short company A and buy company B. In that case you captured a $4 per share spread. You unwound the trade by delivering your B stock at closing, receiving the A stock in exchange, then covering the short position in A shares, pocketing a $4 per share profit.

The risk in such trades is that the deal falls through, and company B stock drops back to a lower level. The LTCM partners understood this. They reasoned that statistically most deals go through, and profits on the winners offset losses on occasional failed deals. The key was to make huge profits on winners, and the key to that was off-balance-sheet leverage.

LTCM did not trade actual takeover stocks. LTCM partners knew little about the stock market; for them it was all about the math. Buying and selling shares in takeover deals is expensive because of commissions and margin interest on short positions. LTCM used an equity basket swap arranged by its prime broker, Bear Stearns. In an equity basket swap, a limit is placed on the basket's size. In the case of the LTCM–Bear Stearns equity swap, the basket held $15 billion in equities. LTCM put items in the basket or took them out with a phone call to the Bear Stearns swap desk. The swap gave LTCM the same profit or loss as owning actual shares without the expense or capital requirements of ownership.

Old-school arbitrageurs were mystified by LTCM's trading in their market. They had spent decades developing analytic models for assessing if a deal would go through or not. They bought and sold actual stocks and paid high financing costs to do so. Busted deals were their worst nightmare. LTCM knew almost nothing about stocks and was indifferent to the occasional busted deal. LTCM's edge was high leverage and statistical odds, just another mathematical game.

The partners pursued this strategy in the era's biggest takeover deals, including Lockheed-Boeing, MCI-WorldCom, and Citicorp-Travelers. LTCM put long and short stock picks in the swap basket, then Bear Stearns did real stock trades to cover its basket exposure. LTCM and Bear Stearns were both hedged. Bear Stearns got cheap financing because it was a dealer. LTCM got cheap financing because it used an off-balance-sheet swap. Everyone was a winner, everyone was hedged. So it seemed.

In 1996, near the height of LTCM's profits and praise, JPMorgan offered to buy a 50 percent interest in LTCM for $5 billion, a reasonable price considering the management company was making more than $300 million per year in management fees alone. JPMorgan also calculated its ownership position would give it preferred status as an investor, and the opportunity to reap proprietary trading profits.

This offer was rejected. In the words of one LTCM partner, "If we're worth so much money, why would we sell?" This rejection was hubris. If the partners had sold, LTCM would have been part of JPMorgan when the 1998 crisis hit. JPMorgan would have saved LTCM to protect its own reputation. At the time, Bank of America owned D. E. Shaw, another hedge fund that lost billions in 1998. Bank of America quietly propped up D. E. Shaw in the panic. Today D. E. Shaw thrives as a $37 billion asset manager and technology firm. Shaw had a big brother. LTCM did not.

Style drift into merger arb and rejection of JPMorgan's 1996 buyout offer were the first nails in LTCM's coffin. The last nail came in 1997, just prior to the collapse, when the partners embarked on a plan to buy out their original investors. They would own the management company, and the fund itself. This plan was a portal to dynastic wealth.

By September 1997, LTCM's fund capital approached $7 billion, a huge leap from the $1 billion we started with in 1994. Still, investment returns were declining. LTCM's large size in favored trades meant diminishing marginal returns, as those trades grew even larger. Banks were copying LTCM's strategies, making those trades less profitable for all participants. LTCM's partners realized if they pushed out their original investors, they would own a larger piece of the pie and could capture more profits for themselves. To enrich themselves they would leave their original backers out in the cold.

The partners' plan had two parts. The first part was simply to give back money to the outsiders through a forced redemption. This was done as of December 31, 1997, with a $3 billion all-cash distribution. The redemption reduced LTCM's capital to about $4 billion. LTCM partners personally owned about $2.6 billion of that capital with the remainder in third-party hands.

The second part of the plan, led by Myron Scholes, involved an ingenious options strategy to control another $1 billion of the fund's capital. LTCM persuaded UBS to sell the partners a seven-year, $1 billion at-the-money call option on their own fund. This option allowed the partners at any time from 1997 until 2004 to pay $1 billion to buy that amount of the fund plus performance on $1 billion from the day the option was sold. This effectively made the partners owners of the future performance on $1 billion of fund capital.

UBS charged the partners about $300 million for this option based on Scholes's own options pricing formula. UBS hedged the option with a $1 billion investment in the fund. As LTCM made money, UBS would owe more to the partners under the option while profits on the LTCM investment would compensate for that obligation. UBS was hedged on the option and could pocket the $300 million premium.

The new UBS investment was used to finance part of the 1997 distribution to the outside investors. When the dust settled in early 1998, the fund had $4 billion, which was owned $2.6 billion by the partners, $1 billion by UBS, and $400 million by a few foreign banks as strategic relationships. Because the partners effectively owned the UBS investment through the options structure, their real economic ownership was $3.6 billion, or 90 percent of the fund. LTCM was morphing from a hedge fund to a multifamily office with no outside investors at all.

What was curious about the $1 billion option sold by UBS was that it hedged only future profits. UBS did not hedge future losses. It never occurred to anyone that LTCM could lose money. UBS thought it had insured an unsinkable vessel even as it set sail on the *Titanic*.

Vortex

The early months of 1998 were quiet in capital markets. LTCM's profits were small but steady. The fund was on track for a good, if not spectacular year.

The year before, a financial crisis had emerged in Asia in July 1997, starting with devaluation of the Thai baht. Devaluation caused massive capital flight by hot money that chased the carry trade there. In the mid-1990s, investors borrowed cheap dollars, converted to baht, and invested in high-yield Thai development projects in resorts and other real estate. Conversion of dollars to baht was considered low risk because the Thai central bank maintained a fixed exchange rate to the dollar and the baht was freely convertible. Unexpectedly on July 2, 1997, Thailand broke the peg to the dollar. Immediately the baht dropped 20 percent. Lenders suffered colossal losses. Thailand turned to the IMF for technical assistance. Foreign investors dumped local investments and pulled their money out of Thailand. A global panic arose.

The turmoil next hit Indonesia and Korea, which had pursued policies similar to Thailand's. On August 14, Indonesia broke the rupiah's peg to the dollar. The rupiah went into free fall. Panic spread to the streets. Money riots erupted. Police responded with force, and some rioters were killed. The IMF imposed austerity measures that made matters worse.

Global investors no longer trusted emerging market exchange rate policies. They wanted their money back. Dread spread to developed economies. On October 27, 1997, the Dow Jones Industrial Average fell 554 points, its biggest one-day point loss ever. The word "contagion" was widely used in financial circles for the first time since the new age of globalization began in 1989.

The International Monetary Fund acted as a first responder to put out financial fires. The IMF provided cash to Korea, Indonesia, and Thailand to reinforce their reserve positions. In exchange, the IMF imposed harsh conditionality including budget cuts, tax increases, devaluations, and other draconian steps designed to save banks and bond-holders at the expense of everyday citizens. Despite misery, the IMF's castor oil approach worked. By January 1998, events seemed under control. The IMF fireman put out the Asian fire.

From the serenity of Greenwich, LTCM's partners viewed these events not with alarm but with curiosity. If markets collapsed so suddenly, there must be cheap assets around that the computers could locate. Meriwether asked his analysts to find Indonesian corporate debt to buy on the cheap. There was blood in the streets, but for the partners and computers in Greenwich, Indonesia was just another trade.

April 1998 was a losing month for LTCM; the partners were not sure why. Markets seemed quiet. But below the surface the earth had started to shake.

On April 6, 1998, Travelers Group and Citicorp, parent of Citibank, announced a $140 billion merger, the largest in history. Travelers was controlled by legendary Wall Street denizen Sandy Weill. The merger was the capstone of Weill's comeback after he was pushed out of American Express in 1985. The year before the Citicorp deal, on September 24, 1997, Weill and Travelers announced plans to purchase Salomon Brothers from Warren Buffett. This marked Buffett's exit from his Salomon rescue in 1991. Unbeknown to us at the time, the admixture of Weill's Salomon and Citicorp deals doomed LTCM.

Salomon was Meriwether's alma mater. Unsurprisingly, a new cadre of Salomon traders trained by Meriwether were mimicking his trades. These spread trades were volatile. Spreads could widen before they converged. In that case, mark-to-market losses appeared on the books. These losses never troubled the quants because they were sure the spreads would converge again once markets settled down. Trading losses were sometimes viewed favorably because they offered a chance to buy more at a better price, like doubling down after a losing bet in roulette. The difference was the quants believed they had house odds, not gambler's odds. The traders were betting on a sure thing; it was just a matter of time before they won big. They just had to keep doubling down.

Weill despised the double-down mentality, and the volatility that came with it. His technique was to build financial empires by buying targets using his own stock as currency. Weill wanted Travelers' stock price as high as possible to buy Citicorp with minimal dilution of his position in Travelers. Stock markets punish stocks with volatile earnings by discounting their price. Weill ordered traders at Salomon to close out their spread positions to reduce volatility in Travelers' earnings. Traders resented this order, but had no choice.

An unwind meant traders sold spreads instead of buying them. This pushed spreads out further, causing losses at firms like LTCM and Goldman with similar trades. At first, LTCM partners thought this looked like more of a good thing. They added to their positions at attractive valuations. Still, the spreads widened. Weill's order to close out positions was a snowflake; an avalanche awaited.

Market calm returned in June. I took advantage of the quiet to join an Alaskan expedition to climb Denali, the tallest mountain in North America, more than twenty thousand feet high. The 1998 season was one of the worst ever on Denali. Bad weather led to fatalities, including a friend, guide Chris Hooyman, blown off a ridgeline by a 100-mile-per-hour gust as he unclipped his harness to rescue a struggling client. A British special forces team training at nineteen thousand feet was rescued after suffering injuries in one of the highest helicopter rescues ever attempted. Several Korean climbers were killed falling three thousand feet down a steep couloir nicknamed Orient Express. I was fortunate to have an excellent climb with legendary guide Dave Hahn, who arrived in Alaska from Nepal after summiting Mount Everest. I had no idea my dangerous season on Denali was just a warm-up for what awaited on my return.

In August, bond spreads widened again, and losses began to mount at LTCM. Still, 1998 was shaping up as a so-so year for the fund with gains in the single digits instead of the higher returns we were used to—a bad year but not a disaster. In mid-August, I went on vacation with my family on North Carolina's Outer Banks. The other partners were on vacation too, mostly at golf resorts around the world. The Hawk was in Saratoga for the Thoroughbred racing season. Markets were choppy. Still, it was steady-as-she-goes at LTCM—golf, Thoroughbreds, and cocktails at sunset.

Then came the earthquake.

On Monday, August 17, 1998, Russia defaulted on its internal and external debt and devalued the ruble against the dollar. Defaulting on external dollar-denominated debt and devaluing the ruble was shock enough. Still, there seemed no reason to default on internal debt because it was denominated in rubles, which Russia could print. The internal debt default was senseless, yet it happened.

The global financial crisis returned with a vengeance, although it had never really gone away; the virus was merely dormant for a time. Contagion spread from Asia to Russia. Investors studying Russia's inexplicable moves decided anything was possible. Brazil was fingered as the next domino to fall. Suddenly everyone wanted her money back. Stocks went into free fall, liquidity was king, nothing else mattered.

On the morning of Friday, August 21, the phone rang at my vacation home on the Outer Banks. The caller was Jim McEntee, an LTCM partner, and the only one with an old-school trader's temperament. McEntee did not have a Ph.D.; he had worked his way up from the back office at Chase to found his own investment bank, which he later sold to HSBC. He had an uncanny feel for markets you could not put into an equation. He said, "Jim, we lost $500 million yesterday; the partners are meeting Sunday. You should get back for this." I did. We packed the car and drove nine hours to Connecticut. The next six weeks were like one long day of damage control.

LTCM had 106 trading strategies involving stocks, bonds, currencies, and derivatives in twenty countries around the world. From the outside, the trades seemed diversified. French equity baskets had low correlation with Japanese government bonds. Dutch mortgages had low correlation with Boeing's takeover of Lockheed. The partners knew they could lose money on a given trade. Yet the overall book was carefully constructed to add profit potential without adding correlation. Trades were designed to produce composite profits based on relative value spreads, even if spreads widened in one particular trade.

This diversification was a mirage. It existed only in calm markets when investors had time to uncover value and cause spreads to converge. However, there was a hidden thread running through all 106 strategies, what Scholes later called "conditional correlation." All of the trades rested on providing liquidity to a counterparty who wanted it at the time. LTCM was a buyer of risk others wanted to sell. *Suddenly everyone wanted to sell everything.* Investors did not care about relative value; they wanted absolute value in the form of cash. LTCM's solution to this was a capital cushion so it could ride out temporary liquidity demands. The $4 billion of capital was supposed to be enough. Now it appeared LTCM had constructed a ten-foot seawall to stop a fifty-foot tsunami. After losing $500 million in one day, the $4 billion would not last long.

LTCM's first response was to raise new private capital. The estimate was that $1 billion was enough to cover losses and restore confidence. Time was short. The partners knew what was lost, but banks and regulators did not. Hedge funds, including LTCM, typically report results monthly; the daily internal update was not public. The next investor report would reflect the losses in a closing valuation on August 31. We had one week to raise $1 billion in cash before the world discovered what had happened.

August is the worst month to get anything done—let alone raise $1 billion. The rich and powerful are on vacation on yachts and in villas in exclusive locales. Still, the LTCM partners had the best financial connections in the world. Calls went out to George Soros, Prince Alwaleed bin Talal, and Warren Buffett. I call these three the "usual suspects." They always get the urgent phone calls; they don't always invest.

Buffett turned us down after a polite meeting in Omaha with LTCM partner Eric Rosenfeld. Buffett is notoriously wary of derivatives, what he later called "financial weapons of mass destruction." No amount of valuation math from a Harvard professor was going to change that.

Soros and Prince Alwaleed also said no. Their reasons were subtle. A bad situation can always get worse. If LTCM was holding spread trades with embedded gains, those potential gains would only increase as spreads widened. Why throw a lifeline to a drowning man when you can wait for him to drown and collect the life insurance? Soros could afford to wait; desperate sellers only get more desperate.

By August 31, losses at LTCM were $2 billion, 50 percent of our original capital. It seemed surreal that we were still standing, still meeting margin calls, and still operating every day. The reason was our contracts did not give counterparties a way out. LTCM consistently refused to sign termination clauses with subjective criteria such as "material adverse change." We insisted on a numeric trigger of $500 million of remaining capital for an early termination of contract. At that level, counterparties could cancel trades and take collateral. This made sense in 1994 when capital was $1 billion; the $500 million trigger equaled a 50 percent decline. Once capital reached $4 billion, the same numeric trigger represented an almost 90 percent decline. At that point, collapse is unstoppable; a 10 percent cushion won't save you. Banks realized to their horror that they were locked into seat belts on the same flaming plane as the LTCM partners. We would all crash together.

Then a new panic hit the banks. What if losses from LTCM caused one of the banks to fail? What if your bank was also exposed to that failing bank? Who were the weak hands, and how would the panic end? Now the banks not only feared LTCM, they started to fear one another.

On September 2, we announced August results to our investors. I wrote the investor letter, and located Meriwether in our private gym locker room to ask him to sign it. He looked like a man about to sign his own death warrant. I knew the letter would leak immediately. In 1998, we still used fax machines. I had about forty letters to send. The first fax recipients leaked the letter to Bloomberg before the last fax was sent.

CNBC also picked up the story. The panic was no longer about Russia or Brazil; it was about LTCM. We were the eye of the storm.

The fund continued to bleed in early September. We carried on with our capital-raising strategy; only now the target was $2 billion. Having failed with our private network, we hired Goldman Sachs as bankers. They arrived as a deal team in our Greenwich offices. I approached Goldman's lawyer and asked him to sign a customary nondisclosure agreement. He burst out laughing and said, "We're not signing anything." I had no leverage, but I knew where things stood. I had been on Wall Street long enough to know predatory behavior was the rule, not the exception.

A senior Goldman executive downloaded our derivatives positions to a CD-ROM and handed the disc to a junior banker who walked outside to a limo and proceeded straight to Goldman's headquarters near Wall Street. Goldman traders stayed up all night using the LTCM data to front-run their clients in markets around the world. Goldman, led by Jon Corzine, was in similar spread trades as LTCM, and was losing billions itself. With the LTCM data, Goldman unwound trades like a precision guided missile instead of a machine gun firing indiscriminately. Ultimately Goldman failed to raise money for LTCM, but it was mission accomplished in terms of gaining inside information. If Goldman could not save the system, it would at least save itself.

By September 17, the death watch had begun. LTCM still had cash and capital, but no hope of recovery despite wishful thinking by certain partners. A discreet phone call was placed to the Federal Reserve Bank of New York. There was no request for a bailout, no expectation of one. It was inconceivable to us that the Fed would bail out a hedge fund. We simply wanted the Fed to know the situation. It seemed bizarre that Goldman had our information and the Fed did not. So we invited the Fed in.

On Sunday, September 20, a Fed and Treasury delegation arrived in our Greenwich offices led by Peter Fisher, head of open market operations at the New York Fed. Fisher was accompanied by his close associate Dino Kos and Gary Gensler, then deputy assistant secretary of the treasury and protégé of Treasury Secretary Bob Rubin. Fisher, Kos, and Gensler sat down with Meriwether and me in the partners' conference room. For the next five hours we went through LTCM's positions line by line, trade by trade, counterparty by counterparty. When we were done, Fisher's face was white. He remarked, "We knew you guys could shut down the bond markets, but we had no idea you would shut down stock markets too." He was reacting to the $15 billion in takeover deal stocks on our books. If LTCM defaulted, Bear Stearns's hedged stock positions would instantaneously become net long, as the short to LTCM would disappear. Bear would then dump $15 billion in stocks into a falling market to balance its own books. Market contagion and panic from such selling was inevitable.

Fisher organized a breakfast in New York the next morning, September 21, with the heads of JPMorgan, Goldman, Citibank, and Merrill Lynch. The group knew that when LTCM failed, the same disappearing hedge that Bear Stearns faced would emerge at every big bank in every market in the world. This is how net risk in calm markets morphs into gross risk when markets are in distress. The conclusion was inescapable: LTCM was too big to fail. The bailout began, but Wall Street was not really bailing out LTCM; it was bailing out itself.

By Wednesday, September 23, the group expanded to include other major Wall Street firms. That evening we received a term sheet from what was now called the Consortium. Their deal provided a $4 billion cash injection, shared among sixteen banks, divided $250 million per bank. There was also a ray of hope. The Consortium would keep the LTCM team intact to unwind the trades, as if we had built a nuclear reactor and were the only ones who knew how to work the control rods without a meltdown. This was largely true.

The Consortium was willing to value the fund at $400 million. This meant we could keep ten cents on the dollar of the $4 billion we held just six weeks before. Ten cents on the dollar was generous because we were days away from zero. Still, for some partners who saw their net worth drop from $300 million to $30 million, the trauma was intolerable. Over the next few days, we had occasion to call ambulances for partners suffering from stress. Some signed the deal agreements through tears. The situation had the elements of Shakespearean tragedy without the blood.

The deal was well on its way to a soft landing when Goldman pulled the pin on another grenade. Even as it participated in the Consortium from the New York Fed's tenth-floor conference room, Goldman secretly engineered a rival bid in league with Hank Greenberg of AIG and Warren Buffett. Goldman and AIG persuaded Buffett they had the derivatives expertise to unwind LTCM's trades. Buffett would reap the unwind profits without getting his hands dirty. The gang of three—AIG, Goldman, and Buffett—had one condition: everyone at LTCM was to be fired immediately. They wanted sole control of the trades and the embedded future profits. With this secret bid Goldman was no longer front-running LTCM, it was front-running the Fed.

A term sheet signed by Jon Corzine, Hank Greenberg, and Warren Buffett came off the fax machine in the Greenwich office. Meriwether handed the fax to me still warm from the machine. "What should we do with this?" he asked. I knew we were fiduciaries for the fund and had to consider all offers; we could not pick and choose based on personal preferences. Getting fired was irrelevant from a fiduciary perspective. I told JM I would handle it.

I called a senior partner at Sullivan & Cromwell, the white-shoe law firm that represented the bidders. I said, "Look, you want to buy the fund, but the fund is owned by feeder funds." A feeder fund is a legal entity that takes money from investors and funnels it to the main fund. They are organized in tax havens so foreign investors are not taxed on profits in their home countries. "I'd have to arrange votes of the feeder fund investors. We don't have time for that. But there's another way. You could invest in a new feeder and it could buy control of the fund. You could amend the partnership agreement, and cash out the feeders, then you'd own the whole fund." The Sullivan & Cromwell partner said he would call me back.

In the next hour he frantically tried to reach Buffett, who was on a fishing trip with Bill Gates in a remote part of Alaska. They had no cell phone service, and satellite phones were not working either. The Sullivan & Cromwell partner called me back and said, "I can't reach Buffett, and I have no authority to alter the terms of the deal." I said, "Let me be clear. I'm not saying 'no' to your deal; I'm saying it's not feasible—it can't be done the way you want." The lawyer said, "I can't change the proposal." I said, "Okay, then there's nothing done," and hung up. Goldman's gambit was foiled for want of a phone. It was back to the Consortium.

On September 24, we were making steady progress with the Consortium. Still, I should have known better than to underestimate greed on Wall Street. My phone rang—it was Warren Spector, one of the top officials at Bear Stearns. He wasted no time. "We're going to put you into default. I'm on my way to the Fed to tell them. We're pulling out of the Consortium. I'm just calling to tell you first." Bear was pulling its ace from the house of cards, letting the whole house hit the ground.

Bear was uniquely positioned. As LTCM's prime broker, it held $500 million of cash collateral from the fund at all times. Other banks received mark-to-market collateral, but this just kept you even, it did not put you ahead. Bear's collateral was free and clear. It was willing to seize it to protect itself. This would hang the rest of Wall Street out to dry. Bear's brokerage contract with LTCM contained subjective language. Despite ambiguity, Spector now jumped on the contract to call a default.

I had seconds to save our deal with the Consortium and to save global markets. I said, "Warren, maybe you're right, maybe you can do this. But maybe not. If you put us in default, I'll wake up tomorrow with one asset: a $4 billion lawsuit against Bear for breach of contract. That's the amount of embedded arbitrage profit that will be lost if we fail. The rest of Wall Street will join the lawsuit. I can't stop you, but you'd better hope you're right because you're betting your firm." I knew Spector was one of Bear's largest stockholders. My tactic was to target his wealth; Bear's stock would suffer if our lawsuit succeeded. Personal wealth is the only language Wall Street understands. Spector blinked.

Bear Stearns did not call a default, but it refused to join the Consortium. This was not forgotten on Wall Street. Ten years later when Bear Stearns failed, no tears were shed. As far as Wall Street was concerned, Bear's 2008 collapse was payback for its 1998 stab in the back.

From September 25 to September 27, we worked nonstop to document a deal. Early on September 28, markets held their breath. Either LTCM would be saved, or a global panic would ensue. In the midtown deal rooms at rescue law firm Skadden Arps, there were last-minute dramatics. Lehman pleaded with the Consortium for relief because it was near bankruptcy itself. Lehman reduced its pledge from $250 million to $100 million. Goldman and JPMorgan ponied up the difference. The money moved, the deal was done.

The next morning, September 29, was my birthday. I had barely spoken to my family or friends for six weeks. At LTCM, we had worked around the clock, first trying to save the fund, then trying to save the world. My wife secretly organized an email effort among everyone I knew to send me birthday wishes. I went to my office, still numb from the trauma that ended the night before. I opened my computer. I had forgotten it was my birthday. My in-box exploded with greetings. I looked at the screen and cried.

Lessons (Not) Learned

The lessons of LTCM's rescue were clear. Derivatives density and opacity meant neither regulators nor banks knew where risk lay. Derivatives allowed massive leverage because the collateral required was minute relative to their gross value. For LTCM, leverage was infinite because the fund refused to post initial margin; it only offered variation margin on profit or loss after the trade was entered.

Yet there was a deeper peril than obvious leverage and transparency issues. The great menace, one Wall Street still does not comprehend, is that risk resides in gross positions, not net. A simple example suffices to illustrate.

Goldman Sachs might enter a $1 billion swap contract with Citibank where it agrees to pay an overnight interest rate based on a U.S. dollar deposit in London, and receive from Citibank a fixed rate of interest at a spread to a five-year Treasury note. This *fixed/floating swap* means the bank initially profits based on the difference between the overnight rate it pays and the fixed rate it receives. For Goldman, the swap is roughly equivalent to buying $1 billion of five-year notes and financing the position overnight in the repo market. But there's no note involved, just a contract calling for two-way payments on a $1 billion *notional amount*.

Now Goldman enters into another $1 billion swap contract, this time with Bank of America, in which Goldman receives the overnight floating rate and pays a fixed rate based on a two-year Treasury note.

Putting the two trades together, Goldman is receiving (from Bank of America) and paying (to Citibank) the overnight rate. Those cash flows net out close to zero. Goldman is also synthetically long $1 billion of five-year Treasury notes, and short $1 billion of two-year Treasury notes. Those notional positions net out close to zero (depending on agreed spreads). Both swap trades are off-balance-sheet, invisible to outsiders.

The market risk in Goldman's position boils down to the spread between the fixed rate Goldman pays and the fixed rate it receives. The spread between two-year notes and five-year notes is historically low. As a result, Goldman is required to hold very little capital against this risk. Wall Street banks use a formula called value at risk, or VaR, mentioned earlier, which implies Goldman has almost no risk. Under accounting and regulatory rules applied to swaps, the notes disappear, the accounting disappears, and almost all market risk disappears. It's all good.

Yet it's not all good. In the real world, when Citibank and Bank of America do these trades with Goldman, they turn around and do trades in the opposite direction to hedge the risk to Goldman. Counterparties to those trades with Citi and Bank of America, which could be JPMorgan or UBS, then do more trades in a mammoth, ever-widening circle of low-risk trading.

What happens if Goldman goes bankrupt? Suddenly, Citibank's

$1 billion hedged position is gross long, because the offsetting short position to Goldman has disappeared. Citi must go into the marketplace and sell $1 billion of five-year notes to rebalance its books. Bank of America is in the opposite situation; it immediately buys $1 billion of two-year notes to offset the net short position that emerged when Goldman disappeared from the synthetic long.

It would be welcome if Citibank and Bank of America had enough information to find each other and replicate the swaps that Goldman defaulted. They can't do this easily because neither has access to Goldman's books, and the market is opaque. New clearinghouses mitigate this risk for simple swaps. Still, clearinghouses do not cover more exotic swaps where liquidity is always problematic. Also, clearinghouses merely shift replacement risk from banks to the clearinghouse itself. What keeps a clearinghouse solvent when multiple markets and banks are collapsing?

This example is realistic, albeit simplified. The difficulties of replacing trades of a bankrupt counterparty when notional amounts are in the tens of trillions of dollars, represented by thousands of contracts covering underlying instruments in stocks, bonds, commodities, and currencies, spread across the books of scores of subsidiaries and special purpose entities in multitudinous markets around the world, are extraordinary. This is why select banks are too big to fail. A single point of failure collapses the entire system.

A crack-up has names like "Tipping Point," "Black Swan," and "Minsky Moment" given by sociologists, economists, and media. Those concepts, colorful as they may be, are not science. The dynamics of ruin are best understood using complexity theory, a hard science that offers tools to see collapse coming in advance.

The term "complexity" is often used loosely as synonymous with complication or connectedness. In dynamic systems analysis, those terms have quite different meanings. Complication poses challenges, yet does not produce those totally unexpected results associated with complexity called emergent properties. Mere connectedness does not produce complex dynamics without other elements such as diverse agents and adaptive behavior.

The few capital markets experts who grasp complexity are still in the early stages of applying the science to risk management. Emergence, as shown in the LTCM and later Lehman collapses, has a growing following, although it is still terra incognita to regulators constantly taken by surprise. Even advanced practitioners have not yet assimilated the importance of *scale*.

Scale in complex systems is synonymous with size, and refers specifically to those metrics that generate risk. The cases of LTCM in 1998, and AIG in 2008, as well as the preceding example, show that risk is embedded in derivatives' gross notional value, not net value as assumed by Wall Street and regulators. Gross notional value is a simple scaling metric (there are others). There is scant recognition that as gross notional value increases, *risk goes up in a nonlinear fashion*. Put plainly, if you double derivative gross notional value, you do not double the risk, you increase it by a *factor* which can be ten or one hundred times depending on specific system characteristics. A provisional law of the new science of complexity in capital markets is: *Derivatives risk increases exponentially as a function of scale measured by gross notional value.*

To illustrate, imagine an office desk with two empty drawers and one file on top of the desk. The drawers are labeled "A" and "B." An assistant puts the file away in one of the drawers each night. The assistant could put the file back in drawer A on one night, then in drawer B the next night. If he was keeping track, this would produce a time series of A, B. What are the possible sequences of drawers for putting away the file on two consecutive nights? The possible time series are: AA, AB, BB, and BA, a total of four combinations.

Now, let's say we increase the number of drawers from two to three and label the drawers "A," "B," and "C." How many different ways can the assistant put the file away on two consecutive nights? Possible time series are: AA, AB, AC, BA, BB, BC, CA, CB, CC, a total of nine combinations.

In this example, the number of drawers increased 50 percent (from two to three), yet the number of combinations increased 125 percent (from four to nine). The number of possible outcomes increased in a *nonlinear* manner relative to systemic scale. The relationship between the number of drawers and the number of combinations is *exponential*.

If one translates these outcomes to market risks (for example, the drawers represent the number of swap agreements, the sequences represent possible paths of contagion including bank failure), it's clear that increasing derivatives scale increases contagion risk even faster.

Complexity theorists generalize possible paths in the office desk example with the following equation:

$$P_2 = P_1 \times r \times (1 - P_1)$$

In this equation, P_1 is the file position at the end of day 1, P_2 is the file position at the end of day 2, and r is a variable derived from the dynamics of the system under study. This is a *recursive* function because the output of one iteration is the input for the next. Each output may be viewed as a part of a path of financial contagion.

For example, assume we were calculating one file position in a tall stack of shelves. An office assistant puts the file on one shelf at the end of each day according to a rule produced by the formula. The top shelf is "1" and the bottom shelf is "0." Every shelf in the stack has a fractional number between 1 and 0 that corresponds to its place in the stack. A shelf designated 0.5 is halfway up the stack between 0 and 1. A shelf designated 0.25 is one quarter of the way from the bottom of the stack. If there were 100 shelves in the stack, 0.25 corresponds to shelf 25 from the bottom.

If the file was on shelf 0.25 at the end of day 1, and we set $r = 3$, then P_2, the location at the end of day 2, is determined as follows:

$$P_2 = 0.25 \times 3 \times (1 - 0.25)$$
$$P_2 \approx 0.56$$

This means that at the end of day 2, the assistant puts the file on a shelf 56/100ths of the way up the stack between 0 and 1. If there are 100 shelves in the stack, he puts the file on shelf 56 from the bottom.

To determine where the file goes on day 3, or P_3, we take the output from day 2, or 0.56, and repeat the process. The recursive equation looks like this:

$$P_3 = 0.56 \times 3 \times (1 - 0.56)$$
$$P_3 \approx 0.74$$

At the end of day 3, the assistant puts the file on shelf 74 from the bottom.

We can repeat this process as many times as we like. That is exactly what complexity theorists do using computers. They graph results of long time series, then observe strange emergent properties in the results. Continuing the example above, the time series produces 0.25, 0.56, 0.74, 0.58. . . . The file bounces around from shelf 25 to shelf 56, and so on without repetition or a discernible pattern. This is called *chaos*. Now repeat the calculation changing the variable r slightly from 3 to 4. As before, start on shelf 25. Here's what happens when we run the equations.

The file position at the end of day 2 is given by:

$$P_2 = 0.25 \times 4 \times (1 - 0.25)$$
$$P_2 = 0.75$$

The file position at the end of day 3 is given by:

$$P_3 = 0.75 \times 4 \times (1 - 0.75)$$
$$P_3 = 0.75$$

Doing this repeatedly gives the following time series: 0.25, 0.75, 0.75, 0.75. . . . Using the new inputs, we are stuck on shelf 75. No matter how many times we run the equation, the output equals the input, and the file goes on shelf 75. It's as if the file were attracted to shelf 75. The name for this is a *fixed-point attractor*. When $r = 3$ as in the earlier example, the chaotic result is said to have a *strange attractor*, because it's hard to predict where the file ends up.

These examples show two important attributes of complex behavior. The first is that *small changes in inputs produce widely divergent outputs*. The only difference between initial inputs in the two examples above was a change in the value of r from 3 to 4. Still, $r = 4$ settled into a stable resting place at shelf 75, while $r = 3$ produced chaos. The second lesson is that *complex systems produce unexpected outcomes*. Complexity is full of surprises, what are called *emergent properties*.

The results of these and other experiments permit certain observations:

- Capital markets are complex dynamic systems.
- Complex dynamics exhibit memory or feedback, called *path dependence*.
- Risk in capital markets is an exponential function of scale.
- Small changes in initial system conditions produce divergent results.
- System output can be orderly or chaotic.

These observations are the scientific basis for what is popularly known as a black swan event. The term "black swan" is used widely to describe any surprising headline even by those who lack a theoretical understanding of the underlying dynamics. Black swan discussion tends to trivialize science with a fatalistic tinge, as if to say "stuff happens." Stuff doesn't just happen. Crises emerge because regulators don't comprehend the statistical properties of the systems they regulate.

LTCM was a textbook case in ignoring complexity theory. For example, traders at LTCM frequently constructed two-sided strategies using real government notes and synthetic notes in swap form. If the spread between the two trades converged as expected, a profit was realized and the trade was unwound. The conventional way to unwind a trade is to sell the note and terminate the swap by negotiation with the counterparty.

Counterparties charge a small fee for early swap termination. LTCM did not want to pay the fees. Instead, LTCM neutralized the first swap by entering into *another swap* with exactly opposite terms. The fixed/floating payments, margin payments, and other obligations of the two swaps were exactly offsetting, so cash flows and market risk netted to zero. Economically, this was the same as if the first swap were canceled, except LTCM did not incur a termination fee. Value at risk in the twin trades was zero according to regulators. LTCM called this technique the "wedding cake" because traders kept adding new layers to neutralize swap positions instead of terminating positions. The layers stacked up to make a $1 trillion wedding cake.

A complexity theorist looks at the same trade termination technique and sees gross notional value doubled, because there were now two swaps instead of one. This meant the risk *more than doubled*, because risk is an exponential function of scale. While partners were at the golf course or racetrack thinking risk was under control, LTCM was a ticking time bomb. In August 1998, the bomb exploded.

Aftermath

Complexity theory is not understood by regulators today, so perhaps LTCM partners can be forgiven for not understanding complexity in 1998. Yet once that collapse occurred, it might be expected that thought leaders in finance, like Alan Greenspan, Bob Rubin, and Larry Summers, would have learned lessons and tried to avoid a similar collapse in the future. They did just the opposite.

In August 1998, as the LTCM debacle unfolded, Alan Greenspan was Federal Reserve chairman, Bob Rubin was treasury secretary, and Larry Summers was Rubin's deputy, soon to be treasury secretary himself.

In February 1999, just months after the LTCM catastrophe, *Time* magazine featured Greenspan, Rubin, and Summers on its cover with the headline "THE COMMITTEE TO SAVE THE WORLD."

Far from learning the lessons of 1998, the three did everything possible to make the system riskier and more unstable. "The Committee to *Destroy* the World" would have been a more apt headline. In 2008, their combined efforts came close to doing just that.

What were the lessons of 1998? The first was that off-balance-sheet derivatives are dangerous because they are opaque. In a crisis, counterparties cannot find each other to net transactions due to this nontransparency. The second lesson was that leverage converts minute market moves into massive losses that threaten solvency. The third lesson was that banks should be kept out of derivatives businesses. Hedge funds and speculators can roll the dice, but banking is a special business based on bondholder and depositor trust. That trust should not be squandered with swaps speculation. The fourth lesson was that derivatives risk is in the gross value, not the net. When LTCM teetered on the brink of failure, banks were not worried about net exposure on their books, they were worried about their gross position with LTCM that would have to be replaced when LTCM failed. The last, and most important, lesson was that crises emerge from nowhere without warning. A 1997 currency crisis in Thailand is not immediately or obviously linked to a Greenwich hedge fund collapse the next year. Still, that is exactly what happened.

Based on these lessons, policy choices were obvious. Derivatives should be confined to exchanges where they are transparent and margined. Leverage should be limited, and on balance sheet where it can be observed. Banks should be banned from derivatives except for bona fide hedging. Value at risk should be scrapped as a metric due to obsolescence and statistical defects. Finally, capital requirements should be increased as a cushion against emergent crises that should be expected, but never are.

Greenspan, Rubin, and Summers pursued the exact opposite of those five policies. It is convenient to claim ignorance on their part. Yet they were explicitly warned at the time by the one regulator who understood what happened at LTCM. Her name is Brooksley Born, then chair of the Commodity Futures Trading Commission (CFTC).

In 1999, Born was a member of the President's Working Group, PWG, formed after the 1987 stock market crash. The PWG was a recommendation of the Brady Commission. Ironically, the principal author of the Brady Commission Report was David W. Mullins Jr., a Harvard professor at the time, later vice chairman of the Federal Reserve, and still later a partner at LTCM.

The PWG consisted of the president of the United States, Federal Reserve chairman, treasury secretary, SEC chairman, and the chairman of the Commodity Futures Trading Commission. PWG's purpose was to put banking, securities, and commodities regulators in one place to deal with crises. The 1987 crash involved complex interactions between the stock market, regulated by the SEC, and Chicago futures markets, regulated by the CFTC. The crisis then spread to the bank payments system because billion dollar margin calls were required between the New York and Chicago markets. Banks were hesitant to initiate wire transfers to Chicago futures brokers for fear that they would not receive incoming wires from New York stockbrokers. The system started to freeze up. Noncoordination among securities, futures, and bank regulators made crisis resolution difficult. The PWG was intended to prevent those problems in the future.

In 1998, the PWG included Bill Clinton, Bob Rubin, Alan Greenspan, Arthur Levitt, and Brooksley Born. Contagion caused by LTCM arose from swaps, which were regulated by Born; the SEC had almost no jurisdiction over swaps at the time. The policy response to LTCM fell to Rubin, Greenspan, and Born, with Larry Summers as Rubin's right hand.

Greenspan did not understand derivatives risk then and shows little understanding today. He held the view that swaps reduce risk. The analysis begins with an observation, largely correct, that traditional securities and banking transactions represent bundles of disparate risks. A single bank loan can be thought of as a bundle of risks including interest rate risk, credit risk, foreign exchange risk, liquidity risk, operations risk, sovereign risk, and other distinct risks bound together in the loan. Greenspan thought that derivatives allowed these risks to be unbundled. Using swaps, a lender could separate credit risk from foreign exchange risk, and transfer each distinct risk type to a specialized counterparty in the best position to bear that risk. The risk migrated from the bundled product to strong hands best able to bear specific subrisks. This made the system stronger and more resilient. Greenspan was correct in this analysis as far as it went.

What Greenspan missed was that there was no limit on the notional value of derivatives that could be created from a single unit of original risk. If a $1 billion loan was broken into ten subrisks via swaps, and traded separately so total notional value added up to $1 billion, that would vindicate Greenspan's view. In fact, dealers create $10 billion or more of swaps from $1 billion of underlying securities. Dealers create swaps that have no underlying instrument at all, just an index or formula for paying off bets with no connection to real-world debt. Swaps created from thin air add to the gross notional amount of risk and increase systemic scale and complexity. Greenspan's quaint notion of putting a risk quantum in strong hands was dominated by the fact that the quantum was infinitely elastic.

Swaps are economically identical to exchange-traded futures. Both are bets in which each party owes more or less to the other depending on future market levels. The main difference is that futures are traded on exchanges, and swaps are traded in private over-the-counter deals. Born, the futures regulator, understood swap risk and wanted to move swaps to futures exchanges where they are margined properly and traded transparently.

Greenspan, Rubin, and Summers treated Born as if she were a throwback ignorant of financial technology. Archaeologists have discovered Sumerian clay tablets from 4500 BC that record transactions in commodity futures such as forward delivery of livestock. Aristotle discussed how options were used for market manipulation in the fourth century BC. Futures markets Born regulated had changed little since 1848, when grain started trading on the Chicago Board of Trade. Born's beat seemed stuck in the past.

The modern swaps markets was innovated by Meriwether, Scholes, and others in the 1980s. Swaps grew in scope and sophistication as the twenty-first century drew near. Greenspan, Rubin, and Summers saw themselves as firmly on the right side of history in treating swaps differently from commodity futures.

Misogyny played a role. Greenspan, Rubin, and Summers were a powerful boys' club out to squash the voice of the one woman regulator. In 2005, Summers, while Harvard president, showed the same bias in notorious remarks about women's incapacity in quantitative science.

Distressingly, misogyny emerged again in 2008 when the most powerful woman regulator, Sheila Bair, chairwoman of the FDIC, was sidelined by a new boys' club of Summers, Tim Geithner, and Ben Bernanke. Bair's dead-on advice to close insolvent banks was scientific. Instead the boys' club bailed out bank cronies at taxpayer expense. Born in 1998, and Bair in 2008, both correctly analyzed response functions to financial crises. Summers demolished them with bias and bad advice both times.

Born's recommendations to PWG were limited to derivatives; unlike Bair, she was not a bank regulator. Her advice was to continue restrictions on new swap types and move most existing swaps to futures exchanges. Not only was Born's advice marginalized, the boys' club did the opposite.

In 1999, the sixty-six-year-old Glass-Steagall Act was repealed. Glass-Steagall, enacted in the Great Depression, separated the banking business from securities underwriting. One cause of the Great Depression was that banks in the 1920s originated weak loans and sold these as securities to unsuspecting retail investors. In 1933, Congress passed Glass-Steagall, which said that banks could either accept deposits and make loans, or underwrite and sell securities, *but they could not do both*. This was due to conflicts that led to bad loans dumped on customers in securitized form. Bankers promptly separated themselves into commercial banks that took deposits and made loans, and investment banks that underwrote and sold securities.

Separation worked well for sixty-six years and saved the United States from major banking crises. Individual banks such as Continental Illinois in 1984 might fail, and there were still conflicts and loan losses such as the 1980s savings and loan crisis. Still, after Glass-Steagall there was no general banking crisis of the kind seen from 1929 to 1933.

Glass-Steagall worked for exactly the reason complexity theory suggests. By breaking the banking system into two parts, Glass-Steagall made each part stronger by shrinking systemic scale, diminishing dense connections, and truncating channels through which failure of one institution jeopardizes all. It was exactly like building watertight compartments in a ship's hold. One compartment could flood, yet the entire vessel does not sink.

Glass-Steagall was repealed by an unholy alliance of Republicans and Democrats led by Senator Phil Gramm and President Bill Clinton. Reasons for repeal were not directly related to the LTCM crisis—they had been developing for years. Ratification of the otherwise illegal merger of Travelers and Citicorp, promoted by Sandy Weill, was the driving force for elimination of Glass-Steagall. Ironically, it was Weill's order to terminate spread trades at Salomon to facilitate the merger that catalyzed LTCM's demise; another example of dense networks in deep operation.

Repeal worked to increase risk in the financial system. By allowing new combinations of financial institutions, Glass-Steagall repeal increased systemic scale past the point where one big bank failure crashes the entire system. Repeal also allowed commercial banks to mimic the proprietary securities trading activity of investment banks, and the derivatives that went along with it.

On December 21, 2000, just a few weeks before he left office, Bill Clinton signed another law less well known than Glass-Steagall repeal, yet more insidious in spreading systemic risk. The Commodity Futures Modernization Act of 2000 repealed prohibitions on certain swap types, and allowed these swaps to be hidden off-exchange, and off-balance-sheet. Born was pushed out of the CFTC on June 1, 1999, replaced by a new chairman, Bill Rainer, a friend of Bill Clinton's from Arkansas, handpicked to pursue derivatives deregulation. Passage of the commodities act was a bipartisan gift to big banks pushed by Republican Phil Gramm, and Democrats Rubin and Summers.

Prior to 2000, swaps were limited to returns on stocks, bonds, interest rates, and currencies. Bets on commodities such as oil, metals, and grains were traded on regulated futures exchanges. Other commodities did not trade on futures markets, and were not permitted in swaps markets, and therefore did not trade in derivative form at all. With the 2000 repeal of swaps regulation, the door was open to completely unregulated trading in all derivatives. Companies like Enron quickly created markets in off-exchange electricity futures, and collapsed in multibillion-dollar frauds courtesy of Gramm, Rubin, and Summers.

The combined impact of Glass-Steagall repeal and swaps regulation repeal was a financial witches' brew. Repeal meant that banks could trade like hedge funds in an unlimited range of instruments. Still, one more ingredient was needed to complete the mix—leverage.

On November 17, 2003, Rubin protégé Tim Geithner was installed as head of the Federal Reserve Bank of New York. Geithner assiduously turned a blind eye as banks piled on risks. Commercial banks regulated by Geithner were allowed to own investment banks. Still, the investment bank entities were individually subject to more stringent SEC capital requirements. Getting the SEC to roll over on leverage was the banker's next mission.

The Republican Bush administration replaced the Democratic Clinton administration in 2001. Party affiliation does not matter when it comes to Washington's desire to deliver on bankers' wish lists. Bankers own Washington. Pressure to ease up on broker-dealer capital requirements was coming not just from banks, but from brokers such as Bear Stearns and Lehman not owned by banks. They wanted a level playing field so they could compete with banks in the securities business.

Simultaneously, banks wanted their own looser capital requirements. These were set by the Basel Committee of the Bank for International Settlements (BIS) in Switzerland. The first global bank capital rules were issued in 1988 under the name Basel I. Within a few years, these rules seemed too restrictive. Banks began pushing for new formulas to allow them to carry more risk on a smaller capital base. They justified this by promoting defective VaR models as a partial substitute for strict capital ratios. The resulting revisions to bank capital requirements implemented in stages between 2001 and 2004 were called Basel II. These rules allowed greater bank leverage based partly on VaR models that showed extreme leverage was safe.

It was against this background of easier bank capital requirements that the SEC moved to revise broker-dealer capital rules in 2003 and 2004. In 2003, the SEC expanded the definition of eligible collateral for leverage purposes to include certain mortgage-backed securities. In 2004, SEC expanded its oversight to include broker-dealer holding companies. This new comprehensive holding company oversight borrowed concepts from Basel II, including risk weightings based on security type. In particular, the SEC permitted higher leverage for certain mortgage-backed securities versus traditional stocks and bonds. The result of these two changes was that mortgage-backed securities were eligible collateral for leverage and minimal capital was required to support that leverage.

In 1998, LTCM collapsed under a critical mass of derivatives leverage. In 1999, Glass-Steagall was repealed. In 2000, derivatives regulation was repealed. In 2001, bank capital requirements were eased. In 2003 and 2004, broker-dealer capital requirements were eased. Throughout this entire period, the Fed kept interest rates artificially low. It was as if global regulators reacted to LTCM by working together to repeat that debacle on a larger, more dangerous scale. That's exactly what happened. In 2008, the entire risky, leveraged, interconnected house of cards collapsed.

CHAPTER 5
FORESHOCK: 2008

A financial market is riddled with feedback. . . . Such intrinsic feedback does not arise when gambling. . . . Likewise even if everyone had the perfect prediction model of the weather, the weather would still do what the weather does. All that would happen is that everyone would know exactly what to wear the next day. However, this is not true in the markets. If everyone were to be given the perfect prediction model, it would immediately stop being the perfect prediction model because of this strong feedback effect.

Neil F. Johnson, Ph.D.,
professor of physics, University of Miami

A New Crisis

From the perspective of complexity theory, the 2008 collapse was easily foreseen. A dynamically identical collapse happened in 1998. The scope of the 2008 panic was greater than in the 1998 panic. That increased scope was to be expected because systemic scale had increased in the intervening ten years. Our provisional law states: *Derivatives risk increases exponentially as a function of scale measured by gross notional value.*

Excessive leverage, nontransparency, and a densely interconnected bank network were common factors in both crises. The difference in catalysts—sovereign swap spreads in 1998, subprime mortgages in 2008—is irrelevant. What matters is the deep structure of financial risk. Differentiating causation into swaps and subprime is like chasing snowflakes while ignoring avalanche danger. Snowflakes don't kill you; avalanches do.

When I left LTCM in 1999, I was dissatisfied with the standard explanations for my former firm's collapse. Nobel Prize winners talked about the "perfect storm," the "hundred-year flood," and a "fifteen-standard-deviation event." I knew enough about statistics to realize this was the language of normally distributed risk and mean reversion—the language of random walks and efficient markets. My intuition said there was something rotten at the heart of modern financial economics.

In the years following the LTCM collapse, I studied physics, applied mathematics, network theory, behavioral economics, and complexity. After 9/11, I was recruited by the CIA to assist on a counterterrorism project involving identification of anomalies in stock markets. Today, the capabilities our team developed allow the intelligence community to foresee a terrorist attack based on insider trading by terrorist associates. Coincidentally, the analytic techniques I learned and applied at the CIA were the same ones I was using to untangle LTCM's collapse.

By 2005, I had worked out complexity theory dynamics in finance. The main complexity theory tenets were expounded by physicists years before, and applied in various scientific fields including seismology, meteorology, and biology. Still, physicists were making slow progress in finance because they were unfamiliar with capital markets in general. I had the advantage of approaching physics from a financial background, rather than approaching finance with a background in physics. My main theoretical breakthrough was to apply the concept of scale in finance, and work out scaling metrics such as the gross notional value of derivatives as a way to assess systemic risk. My early theoretical advances were compiled in an article published in the CIA's academic journal, *Studies in Intelligence,* in September 2006. That was a special issue of *Studies* timed to coincide with the fifth anniversary of 9/11. My contribution, and other contents of that issue, remain classified.

My experiences at LTCM in the 1990s, and my inquiries in the early 2000s, gave me a unique perspective on capital markets developments after 2005. The largest banks were getting larger, asset concentration in a few large banks was growing more dense, and derivatives' notional values were growing dramatically. Between June 30, 2001, and June 30, 2007, the gross notional value of all over-the-counter derivatives held by major banks as reported in a BIS survey grew from less than $100 trillion to more than $508 trillion. Over the same period, the Herfindahl index, a market concentration measure for U.S. dollar–denominated interest rate swaps, rose from 529 to 686, strong evidence that more swaps were concentrated in fewer large banks.

In a lecture series from 2003 to 2005 at Northwestern University's Kellogg School, I warned audiences a new financial catastrophe was coming, and that it would be more costly than the 1998 LTCM crisis. I was not particularly focused on subprime mortgages. Instead I focused on scaling metrics and density functions, technical terms for the size and interconnectedness of capital markets. I said the system was reaching critical mass, not metaphorically, but literally. I didn't know which neutron would dislodge other neutrons and start a chain reaction. It didn't matter. What mattered was we had once again shaped uranium into a nuclear weapon; we had once again put capital markets into a critical state.

When a chain reaction starts in a nuclear weapon, the energy release and fireball formation happen in nanoseconds. In capital markets, the dynamics are the same, but the process takes more time. Financial neutrons move not at the speed of light, but at the speed of humans engaged in adaptive behavior.

The financial fireball that emerged in September 2008 resulted from a chain reaction that began over a year earlier, the week of July 16, 2007. Two hedge funds sponsored by Bear Stearns that specialized in leveraged bets on debt derivatives collapsed into insolvency that week. Bear

Stearns tried to organize a self-rescue, but this failed. Counterparties like Merrill Lynch seized collateral that proved illiquid and nearly worthless.

On August 3, 2007, CNBC's Jim Cramer launched into a live TV tirade against Federal Reserve chairman Ben Bernanke's ignorance of the illiquidity infecting capital markets. Cramer told colleague Erin Burnett,

> I have talked to the heads of almost every one of these firms in the last seventy-two hours and he [Bernanke] has no idea what it's like out there. None! And Bill Poole [Fed official], he has no idea what it's like out there. My people have been in this game for twenty-five years and they're losing their jobs and these firms are gonna go out of business and it's nuts. They're nuts! They know nothing! . . . This is a different kinda market. And the Fed is asleep.

A few days later, on August 9, 2007, French bank BNP Paribas suspended redemptions on three funds that invested in subprime mortgage assets.

At the Federal Open Market Committee (FOMC) on June 28, 2007, just prior to the Bear Stearns fund meltdown, Ben Bernanke and the FOMC said, "The economy seems likely to continue to expand at a moderate pace over coming quarters." Shortly before, on March 28, 2007, Bernanke had said, "The impact on the broader economy and financial markets of the problems in the subprime market seems likely to be contained. In particular, mortgages to prime borrowers and fixed rate mortgages to all classes of borrowers continue to perform well, with low rates of delinquency." The contrast between official ignorance of risk and the ongoing market collapse in the spring and summer of 2007 could not have been more stark.

On August 24, 2007, more than a year before the Lehman collapse, I met with a U.S. Treasury official to warn about the potential for systemic collapse. I presented a detailed written analysis titled "Proposal to Obtain and Manage Information in Response to Capital Markets Crisis." My written proposal said, in part:

> The financial crisis of 2007 has as much to do with a shortage of information as a shortage of liquidity. This paper proposes use of executive authority under IEEPA to obtain . . . position information to be stored in a secure environment and used selectively to manage the financial crisis. . . . No fund would be told what to trade, how to leverage, how to manage risk, etc. The sole purpose is to provide adequate transparency for the proper exercise of the U.S. government's duty to maintain functioning capital markets which constitute part of the critical national security infrastructure. . . . The prime brokers and clearing banks . . . could be quickly identified and concentration risk in the regulated sector could be ascertained.
>
> The past 30 years have witnessed the disintermediation of the regulated financial sector by the less regulated and non-regulated sectors. . . . Every step in this evolution . . . has involved a diminution in transparency and an increase in risk. . . . When derivatives technology drives an exponential increase in the quantum of risk, the risk-increasing effects of scaling and complexity in a non-linear critical system dominate the risk-reducing effects. . . .
>
> A problem cannot be resolved unless the dimensions of the problem are known to some extent. This proposal does not involve active regulation, bail outs or top down solutions. It is a relatively modest step in the direction of information transparency . . . highly useful to officials charged with maintaining stable markets during times of panic and duress.

My meeting with the Treasury official began cordially. After initial pleasantries, I got to the point. "This crisis is just beginning. The instability has been building for some time. The system has absorbed a few shocks already." Here I was referring to the October 10, 2005, revelation of accounting fraud and later bankruptcy of Refco, then the world's largest futures broker, and the September 2006 collapse of Amaranth, a hedge fund that lost $6 billion in one week. At the time, those events seemed prompt-critical to me, yet they weren't. In both cases there was delayed criticality; markets absorbed the shocks and rebounded. Not every snowflake causes an avalanche.

After observing events from July through August 2007, I was convinced that this crisis dynamic really was unstoppable and would spread widely. Treasury needed to know and act soon.

"You should issue an order requiring all banks and hedge funds to report their derivatives positions to you, in detail, with counterparty names, underlying instruments, payment flows, and termination dates. The information should be in standardized machine-readable form delivered one week from the date the order goes out. Anyone who can't deliver should go to the top of your problem list. Once you get the information, hire IBM Global Services to process it for you in a secure environment so there's no leakage. Build a matrix and find out who owes what to whom. Rank the biggest risk concentrations and focus your attention on those names."

The Treasury official listened politely, and paused before answering. "We can't do that."

"Why not?" I expected him to recite a legal impediment. I was certain Treasury had all the authority it needed if it chose to use it.

"This Treasury and White House are free market oriented. We don't believe in interfering or telling people what to do."

I answered, "You're not telling them what to do. They can trade whatever they want. You're not interfering with anyone's operations. You're just getting information. This will end up in your lap eventually; you're entitled to know what you're dealing with. It's just information."

"It's not how we do things. It won't fly." This was pure Bush administration free market philosophy, without analysis or reflection. Free market approaches do not work for banks because banks are subsidized, insured, regulated, and implicitly guaranteed. Modern banks are the opposite of free market institutions, so different approaches are needed. This seemed lost on the Bush Treasury.

When the meeting was over. I thanked the official for his time. At least I had the meeting and warned someone inside Treasury. The warning went nowhere.

As I walked past the steps of the main Treasury building on Hamilton Place that hot summer day, I glanced at the White House next door and thought, "They're not ready for this. They think these are unconnected market blips. They have no idea what's coming."

Treasury Secretary Hank Paulson spent September 2007 chasing a chimera called Super-SIV, a special purpose vehicle sponsored by the government to strip asset-backed securities from the bank balance sheets. Banks spent years creating special investment vehicles called SIVs to hide risks and avoid capital charges on consumer debt from credit cards and auto loans. Now frightened investors were forcing that debt back onto bank balance sheets by refusing to roll over credit to the SIVs. Paulson's idea was to pool the bad assets of major banks into one Super-SIV that could be refinanced with implicit government support. The idea flopped and was quietly killed. On December 21, 2007, the major banks that had expressed interest in the Super-SIV issued a statement that said the facility "was not needed at this time." This statement confirmed that the banks were as blind to the dangers as Treasury.

On October 5, 2007, the Dow Jones Industrial Average reached a new high of 14,066.01, a nearly 10 percent rally from the August 15 low of 12,861.47. Markets were giving an all-clear signal.

Behind the scenes, mortgage losses were piling up and liquidity was evaporating. Banks would report their 2007 losses in January 2008. Treasury feared that impaired bank capital would spook investors and reignite the panic that emerged in the summer. Paulson quietly arranged for a backdoor bank bailout using sovereign wealth funds and foreign banks as fresh capital sources. On November 26, 2007, Citigroup announced the sale of 4.9 percent of its equity for $7.5 billion to the Abu Dhabi Investment Authority. On December 19, 2007, Morgan Stanley announced the sale of $5 billion of equity to the China Investment Corporation. On December 25, 2007, Temasek, a sovereign wealth fund of Singapore, announced it was buying $4.4 billion of stock in Merrill Lynch with an option to buy more. This deal flurry and other similar deals were designed to put on a brave face and convince investors that all was well in the U.S. banking sector. In fact, U.S. banks were rotten to the core, and sovereign wealth funds were played for suckers by Paulson and the bankers. Within a year, tens of billions of sovereign wealth fund money, held in trust for everyday citizens in emerging markets, would go up in smoke. Still, in the short run it was mission accomplished for the Bush administration. Markets entered 2008 with renewed confidence that the crisis was past.

The deceptive calm in the winter of 2008 bore an eerie resemblance to the winter of 1998. The latter crisis also started the summer before and appeared solved by winter, only to reemerge by spring. The 2008 crisis repeated this pattern almost ten years to the day.

In March 2008, the crisis became visible again with Bear Stearns's collapse over the course of a few days, March 12 to 16. On Wednesday, March 12, Bear Stearns CEO Alan Schwartz told CNBC, "We have no problems with our liquidity and overnight funding. . . . Bear Stearns's balance sheet, liquidity and capital remain strong . . . and the situation, with time, will stabilize." Three days later, Bear was broke and its business was absorbed by JPMorgan. The worst positions were buried off-balance-sheet at the Federal Reserve. Only days before, SEC chairman Christopher Cox said he had confidence in capital cushions at major U.S. investment banks.

Again, investors breathed easy, believing banks and regulators had the situation under control. The Dow Jones Industrial Average rallied from 11,893.69 on March 7, 2008, to 13,058.20 on May 2, an impressive 9.8 percent gain. Investors and regulators did not see the underlying critical state dynamics. Each crisis was seen as discrete and manageable. No one connected the dots to see it was all one crisis, emerging in different times and places, yet one general collapse.

By July, the illiquidity wave caught up with Fannie Mae and Freddie Mac, the government-sponsored mortgage agencies, and two of the largest financial institutions in the world. Fannie and Freddie were darlings of Washington politicos, who used them for decades as a source of campaign funds and multimillion-dollar sinecures doled out to political cronies for loyal service to Democratic and Republican administrations. Fannie and Freddie were as corrupt and mismanaged as the banks with which they competed.

On July 24, 2008, Congress passed the Housing and Economic Recovery Act of 2008, which gave Treasury authority to use taxpayer money to prop up Fannie and Freddie. Once again, the everyday citizen bailed out the elites including stockholders, bondholders, and wealthy executives of the twin entities. President Bush signed the bailout legislation on July 31, 2008. Political cronies who personally made hundreds of millions of dollars in prior decades did not contribute to the bailout. That money was theirs to keep.

Like a cock crowing for the third time, the stock market staged a third rally to signal the crisis was over. The Dow Jones Industrial Average rose from a low of 11,055.19 on July 14, at the height of the Fannie and Freddie angst, to 11,782.35 on August 11. This relief rally was weaker than the two before, only a 6 percent gain. Still, it signaled confidence in the solutions repeatedly offered up by government officials. It also signaled that investors, regulators, and bankers had no idea what lay ahead.

I had been informally advising John McCain's presidential campaign on economics in the late summer of 2008. On August 16, just one month before the Lehman blow-up, I provided the McCain campaign with this written advice using complexity theory–based models. The advice was sent as an email with the subject line "Storm Warning." The text reads:

> Here's a quick take on the financial crisis:
> I've said since last summer that it has a funny tempo. We have these periodic spikes in fear and each time we seem to be looking

into the abyss. Then some magic wand comes along and things seemed solved, markets calm down and people get a little optimistic again (but still wary because of recent experience).

The tempo seems to be every 3–4 months; not exactly every 90 days but something like that.

We had a panic in Aug–Sept 2007 which was mitigated by Paulson's "Super-SIV" idea. Oct–Nov were then calm.

We had a panic in Dec 07 which was mitigated by Sovereign Wealth Fund bailouts and new Fed lending facilities. Jan–Feb 08 were then calm.

We had a panic in Mar 08 which was mitigated by the Bear Stearns bailout and further Fed facilities. Apr–Jun were then calm.

We had a panic in Jul 08 which was mitigated by the Fannie/Freddie housing legislation. Aug has been calm (and I expect Sept will be too). . . .

Every time things calm down, markets feel the worst is over and a sense of complacency appears. But it's never over. . . .

We can expect another "panic" spike in October 08; very possibly late October when companies report third quarter earnings. This will be about 2 weeks before election day and right after the last debate. Congress will be out of session so there's no chance for a quick legislative fix. The Fed has used up its bag of tricks and Paulson's credibility has been hurt because so many of his ideas have gone nowhere. . . .

From the candidate's perspective, two thoughts:

A. **Don't let complacency on the financial crisis set in. Stay alert for another storm before election day.**

B. Be prepared with some leadership-type statements; the candidate should have the economic . . . declaration in his pocket ready to go; time may be short for improvisation and panics are rarely the best time to think clearly. (Emphasis added.)

On Monday, August 25, 2008, I was invited by a senior adviser to the McCain campaign to formally participate on a campaign conference call scheduled for August 27 with McCain's economics advisory team. I dialed in on schedule; the mood was fairly relaxed. The economists felt that there really wasn't much to do on the economic front other than stick to their pro-growth message of lower taxes and less regulation.

McCain was running as a foreign policy hawk, not as an economic policy maven. He wanted to confront the Democratic candidate, Barack Obama, on the Iraq issue. McCain's policy was to build on the military success of the Bush surge. Obama wanted to end the engagement and pull out of Iraq. The McCain team was relieved after the Fannie and Freddie bailout. Their view was that the financial crisis was over. This meant the candidate could concentrate on his foreign policy message.

After waiting for an opportunity to interject, I said to the McCain team, "Hey, this financial crisis is not over. You're not going to make it to election day without an earthquake." There was total silence on the call. I continued, "We've had blowups every few months since this started. Each one is bigger than the one before and they're not over; you need to get ready for the next one; it's all people will care about."

With the McCain economics team listening, I continued. "Here's what you need to do. Write a speech now; make it a four-point plan. It doesn't even matter what the points are, just do it. Maybe put in something about a derivatives clearinghouse and transparency. When the panic hits put your guy on the steps of the Treasury and have him read the plan to the media. The American people will be near panic; they'll find his speech reassuring. It will put the candidate over the top."

McCain's call leader said, "Thanks, Jim, but we don't see this as a problem. The crisis is over; we need to stick to our growth message." The call wrapped up after that. It was my first and last turn as a campaign adviser. I was not invited back.

The crisis did come to a head on "Lehman Weekend," September 13–14, 2008. Lehman Brothers filed for bankruptcy on September 15.

That day, the Dow Jones Industrial Average fell more than 500 points, a 4.4 percent plunge. The results were disastrous for McCain. He knew little about economics, yet his campaign needed to act. McCain seemed distracted and confused. On September 24, 2008, McCain shocked Republicans when he suspended his campaign to return to Washington to deal with the crisis. McCain insisted on a meeting with President Bush to discuss a response. With only six weeks to election day, the Bush crisis team could not appear to favor one candidate over the other. Bush invited both McCain and Obama to the West Wing Cabinet Room on September 25 for a crisis consultation. The Obama team did not know more than McCain about crisis dynamics. Still, they were smart enough to keep cool, say little, and project calm. McCain appeared nervous, ashen, and close to panic himself. With markets in free fall, the American people noticed the difference.

Since the 2008 election, conventional wisdom is that McCain's undoing was Sarah Palin's selection as his running mate, an event pressed into popular imagination in the 2012 HBO movie *Game Change*. This fits an inside-the-Beltway view of Palin as a policy lightweight and an albatross around McCain's neck. Yet data do not support this narrative. The day before Lehman's bankruptcy, McCain led Obama 47.4 percent to 45.3 percent in the RealClearPolitics average tracking poll. Two days after Lehman, the candidates were tied at 45.7 percent each. The next day, Obama pulled ahead, 47.1 percent to 45.2 percent. Obama never trailed in the polls again. The tipping point to Obama's victory was not Palin, it was Lehman.

My warnings to the Bush Treasury in 2007, and the McCain campaign in 2008, about the coming collapse failed. Bush and McCain were not alone in their inability to comprehend insights offered by complexity theory. Policymakers from Paulson to Bernanke, and CEOs from Merrill Lynch's John Thain to Lehman's Dick Fuld, were as dazed.

On September 29, 2008, ten years to the day after the LTCM bailout, Congress rejected the Paulson-Bernanke TARP bailout bill designed to use taxpayer money to prop up big banks. The next day, the Dow Jones

Industrial Average fell 777 points, an 8 percent plunge, the largest one-day point drop ever.

Two days later, on October 2, *The Washington Post* published my op-ed "A Mountain, Overlooked: How Risk Models Failed Wall St. and Washington." This was my first public effort to use complexity theory to explain the ongoing financial collapse. In the op-ed I wrote:

> Since the 1990s, risk management on Wall Street has been dominated by a model called "value at risk" (VaR). VaR attributes risk factors to every security and aggregates these factors across an entire portfolio, identifying those risks that cancel out. What's left is "net" risk that is then considered in light of historical patterns. The model predicts with 99 percent probability that institutions cannot lose more than a certain amount of money. Institutions compare this "worst case" with their actual capital and, if the amount of capital is greater, sleep soundly at night. Regulators, knowing that the institutions used these models, also slept soundly.
>
> Lurking behind the models, however, was a colossal conceptual error: the belief that risk is randomly distributed and that each event has no bearing on the next event in a sequence. . . . Such systems are represented in the bell curve, which makes clear that events of the type we have witnessed lately are so statistically improbable as to be practically impossible. This is why markets are taken by surprise when they occur.
>
> But what if markets are not like coin tosses? . . . What if new events are profoundly affected by what went before?
>
> Both natural and man-made systems are full of the kind of complexity in which minute changes at the start result in divergent and unpredictable outcomes . . . that . . . cannot be modeled with even the most powerful computers. Capital markets are an example of such complex dynamic systems.

The Washington Post takes an extremely rigorous approach to guest op-eds. My contribution on complexity theory coming at the height of the crisis was published only after a series of conference calls with Vincent Reinhart, a former monetary economist for the Federal Open Market Committee and expert on market bubbles. Reinhart was acting as a referee for the *Post*'s editorial board. I discussed my theories with him from a hotel room in Budapest where I was traveling at the time. It was the middle of the night there. I was able to answer his technical queries, and after a few tweaks to words and phrases, the *Post* published my piece. I'm certain the op-ed had no impact on the public policy debate at the time. Still, I welcomed the chance to go public after several failed private warnings.

The next day, October 3, 2008, Congress passed the TARP legislation. President Bush signed it into law within hours. Market participants, journalists, and everyday Americans were shocked at how the system spun out of control in a matter of weeks from Lehman, to AIG, to TARP. Now new rumors said more bailouts were needed. TARP helped to truncate the free fall in capital markets. Yet the problems were just beginning in the real economy. The United States entered the worst recession since the Great Depression. Unemployment peaked at over 10 percent. The Dow Jones Industrial Average crashed from 10,831.07 on October 1, 2008, to 6,547.05 on March 9, 2009—a stunning 40 percent plunge on top of the losses that had already occurred since the October 2007 peak.

As was the case in 1998, policymakers ignored crisis lessons and did the opposite of what was needed to prevent a future collapse. Policy blunders began immediately with the use of the newly approved TARP funds. Paulson and Bernanke sold this to the Congress as a fund to buy bad assets from banks and then sell them gradually to recoup costs for taxpayers' benefit. This tactic made sense; a version of this was used effectively to clean up the 1980s savings and loan crisis. Another benefit was that bad assets were removed from the banks. With clean balance sheets banks could resume lending to small-and-medium-size enterprises that are the most dynamic and create the most jobs.

Instead of implementing his promises to Congress, Paulson gave the money to the banks and allowed them to keep the bad assets in the hope that they recouped their losses. Recoveries did not go to the taxpayers. Paulson made sure future gains went to the bankers, including his former partners at Goldman Sachs.

The Paulson bait and switch was extended by the Obama administration in March 2009 when mark-to-market accounting was suspended. This meant banks' pretended assets were worth more than they were. With inflated values in place, banks waited patiently as the Fed pumped up asset prices with easy money until market values were closer to the phony accounting values. The last step was for banks to unload the assets slowly and lock in gains, which were diverted to the bankers and stockholders as executive bonuses and dividends. Taxpayers were treated like forced lenders who got their money back, but had no share in the upside. The fact that this fraud was perpetrated by both the Bush and Obama administrations shows that bank power transcends politics, and is a permanent condition in Washington.

Aftermath II

The White House and Congress spent a year from 2009 to 2010 drafting and enacting the Dodd-Frank Wall Street Reform and Consumer Protection Act. It was signed into law by President Obama on July 21, 2010. Dodd-Frank was more than one thousand pages long in its final form, and was scarcely read by members of Congress who voted on it. Dodd-Frank was an odd mix of genuine reform, pseudo-reform, dereliction, and nonessential matter from lobbyist wish lists.

Some Dodd-Frank provisions, including increased capital requirements for banks, and the Volcker Rule, which limited certain forms of proprietary trading, were useful if limited steps in the direction of a safer financial system. The most overhyped provision was "orderly liquidation" authority. In theory, this was a roadmap to wind down failing too-big-to-fail banks without the chaos of the 2008 Lehman collapse and ad hoc bank bailouts. In practice, orderly liquidation is another Washington confection that will break the minute it is tested under real panic conditions. Regulators will resort to cronyism and improvisation as they always do.

Dereliction of congressional duty is evident in the two-hundred-plus rule-writing projects required by Dodd-Frank. Congress identified important matters not covered by the statute, then delegated rule-making authority to agencies. From 2011 onward, this rule making became a feeding frenzy for bank lobbyists out to gut the intent of Congress. In the end, there was no more left of legislative intent than there was flesh on the marlin in *The Old Man and the Sea*. Nonessential matter in Dodd-Frank included creation of an overbearing new agency called the Consumer Financial Protection Bureau. To date, "The Bureau" has forced more than $11 billion of settlements from financial institutions and has made consumer credit less available, which hurts the recovery. How Bureau enforcement prevents a new banking panic remains a mystery.

Dodd-Frank did address the systemic risk issue directly by creating two other agencies: the Financial Stability Oversight Council (FSOC) and the Office of Financial Research (OFR).

FSOC is a new embodiment of the old President's Working Group, which squashed Brooksley Born's derivatives warnings in 1998. The FSOC includes the treasury secretary, Fed chairman, and heads of the SEC, CFTC, FDIC, and several other financial regulators. Dodd-Frank formalizes FSOC's power and centralizes that power in the Treasury. FSOC is intended to coordinate an emergency response to a future systemic crisis.

The Office of Financial Research is a new think tank set up inside Treasury to enable financial regulators to keep up with Wall Street whiz kids in derivatives risk measurement. The OFR is the analytic arm of the FSOC. In principle, FSOC decisions on systemic risk and policy responses to panic will be informed by OFR analysis. The two agencies are intended to work closely together.

In early 2013, I was invited to give a private briefing to FSOC and

OFR officials at the Treasury in Washington. The briefing took place on Friday, April 12. The Treasury official who organized the briefing was interested in learning more about complexity theory and its use in identifying systemic risk in capital markets. I was encouraged by the invitation. Perhaps glasnost had arrived in Washington a quarter century after it hit the old Soviet Union.

I prepared a white paper on my main risk management models and sent it to Treasury in advance. In Washington, I met with nine officials from the FSOC and OFR and launched into my presentation. The meeting lasted about two hours, a generous allotment of time by the Treasury officials. I was grateful for the opportunity.

Still, as the presentation continued, I gained the impression that despite their attentiveness, Treasury was not interested in next steps. The officials seemed to be "checking the box" with regard to hearing new ideas, yet not internalizing the implications.

At one point, I interrupted my presentation flow, turned to the senior Treasury Department official present, and said, "I don't envy your job. New ideas don't seem to matter. There's not much you can do because the banks own this town."

I expected an indignant response to my sympathetic, yet provocative remark. Instead, the official looked at me and said, "You're right," a candid admission that risk management took second place to bank profits.

Later in the presentation, I asked the senior OFR official what models they used to assess systemic risk. I knew they were not using complexity theory, and still used value at risk. I wanted to know whether refinements or advances to VaR had been adopted. The official said, "Well, we're really just doing implementation of the Dodd-Frank regulations. We leave systemic risk management to the Fed."

This admission was more disconcerting than the prior remark about bank power. I knew how flawed the Fed models were from conversations with senior Fed officials and research staff. I hoped for better from OFR. Yet Washington was serving up more of the same—bigger banks, more derivatives, more interconnectedness. OFR was taking its risk management cues from the Fed. It was the blind leading the blind.

In the past thirty years, global capital markets reached critical mass and headed toward complete collapse four times. The first was October 19, 1987, Black Monday, when U.S. stock markets fell over 20 percent in one day. The second was December 20, 1994, the Tequila Crisis, when Mexico devalued the peso 15 percent in one day. The third was August 17, 1998, when Russia devalued the ruble and defaulted on its debt, leading to the LTCM collapse. The fourth was June 20, 2007, when two Bear Stearns hedge funds collapsed after a failed rescue attempt leading to the Lehman crisis the following year. Capital markets are in what physicists call a supercritical state, which means one critical event can trigger a chain reaction and catastrophic end result. A simple extrapolation from this thirty-year time line reveals the next critical event is overdue.

There were other major market events over this period, including the popping of the Japanese asset bubble in 1990, and the dot-com bubble in 2000. Those bubble events resulted in huge losses for investors, yet did not have global systemic implications. The reaction to the Brexit vote by the United Kingdom to leave the European Union on June 23, 2016, had the potential to go critical, and may yet. For the time being, Brexit was contained by central bank promises the same way a nuclear reactor operator prevents a meltdown by inserting control rods into a radioactive core.

The 1987, 1994, 1998, and 2007 catalysts all went supercritical. The crisis chain reactions were truncated only with massive central bank and other policy interventions.

I lived through all four crises in different capacities as a banker, hedge fund executive, and analyst. I did not see the first three crises coming. They just happened, or so it seemed at the time, and I did my best to manage through them. Based on those experiences, especially 1998, I did the research and developed the models needed to properly understand the statistical properties of risk. Looking back at 1987, 1994, and 1998, I can see those crises didn't "just happen," but were a foresee-able result of critical state dynamics. Using the proper models, the 2007 crisis was foreseeable by 2005, as I warned at the time.

Using these same models and looking ahead, the contour is trou-bling. Once again the system is blinking red.

CHAPTER 6
EARTHQUAKE: 2018

No single incident can really be imagined to have brought about the end of the Bronze Age; rather, the end must have come as the consequence of a complex series of events that reverberated throughout the interconnected kingdoms and empires of the Aegean and Eastern Mediterranean and eventually led to a collapse of the entire system. . . .

Eric H. Cline

1177 B.C.: The Year Civilization Collapsed

If the crowded, interconnected, urbanized and nuclear-armed world we have created does stagger into a new dark age, it will surely be the most terrible of all.

Ian Morris

"The Dawn of a New Dark Age," July 2016

Man Without a Face

"Not yet" was Jon Faust's reply when I asked if the Federal Reserve saw a bubble like the ones that burst catastrophically in 1998 and 2008. His answer was distressing. It showed that the Fed had learned little from prior episodes. If the Fed cannot see the new bubble about to burst, then it will not stop it from bursting.

Faust is a Fed insider handpicked by Chairman Ben Bernanke in 2012 to serve as special adviser to the board of governors. The term "insider" is often used loosely to describe those who might only be tangentially involved, and not in the inner circle of the institution they are purportedly inside. This loose usage does not apply to Jon Faust. As for his role at the Federal Reserve, "insider's insider" is a more apt description.

Faust's Fed tenure from January 2012 to August 2014 included the transition from Bernanke to Janet Yellen as Fed chair. His role was broad-based, but focused on communications. This did not mean public relations or press liaison. The communications role meant Faust was consigliere and chief wordsmith with respect to forward guidance.

Forward guidance is a central bank's main monetary tool in a world of zero or low rates. The Fed uses forward guidance to manipulate market expectations. Manipulation allows the Fed to tighten or ease policy without changing rates. Instead the Fed changes expectations *about* rates. This is done with words in speeches, statements, minutes, and press leaks. Those words are forward guidance, and Faust wrote the words.

Although not a board member, Faust was arguably the third most powerful figure at the Fed after the chairman and William C. Dudley, president of the Federal Reserve Bank of New York. The fact that he was unknown outside the Fed only enhanced the power of his hidden hand, used to move markets with a few choice words. In spy novel parlance, Faust was the "man without a face."

Wordsmithing forward guidance is not done from the sidelines. Providing precise phrases for use in public disclosures required intimate knowledge of FOMC inner workings, and the private views of Bernanke and Yellen. Faust sat in the Fed's ornate, high-ceilinged boardroom at almost every FOMC meeting during his time there, which included the

Fed's largest program of money printing called QE3, Bernanke's threat to reduce money printing in a May 2013 speech, and the actual reduction in money printing beginning in December 2013. Between FOMC meetings, Faust was in Bernanke's and Yellen's offices for the brainstorming sessions as words and phrases were tried out for potential impact on markets. When I later spoke to Bernanke about Faust's role, he told me, "Yes, Jon's office was just across the hall from mine." Concerning forward guidance, Faust was the Fed's brain.

Faust is a member in good standing of the Keynesian-monetarist academic coterie. He received his Ph.D. in 1988 from the University of California, Berkeley. Janet Yellen was a professor at Berkeley before she became a senior Fed official. Faust's thesis adviser, the Nobel Prize–winning economist George Akerlof, is married to Yellen. Faust worked at the Fed in various capacities from 1981 to 2006, ultimately becoming assistant director in the international finance division. Suffice to say, Faust was no stranger to the Fed, Bernanke, or Yellen when he got a call to advise the board in 2012.

On January 20, 2015, not long after he left the Fed, Jon and I had dinner at The National, a popular New York steakhouse, in a private dining room on the second floor. The National's décor is typical for the cuisine—dark wood, brass trim, white tablecloths, and dim lighting. I had known Jon for years. Still, this was our first chance to meet in person since Bernanke tapped him in 2012. We sat at right angles, a foot apart. Our conversation continued for two hours over salmon, crème brûlée, and good wine; Jon drank red, and I my usual sauvignon blanc.

In addition to keeping up with speeches and writings by FOMC members, I spoke occasionally with Fed governors and reserve bank presidents, so I had some reference points on Faust's FOMC colleagues. That made the conversation livelier because we could share impressions on personalities in addition to policy.

I was especially interested in Jeremy Stein. Stein was a governor and FOMC member from May 2012 to May 2014, dates that overlapped with Jon's time at the Fed. Stein struck me as the only governor with a technical grasp of how the Fed's zero interest rate policy was creating hidden dangers and bubble dynamics. Some FOMC members at the time, including Dallas Fed president Richard Fisher, were outspoken about the need to raise rates and the dangers of not doing so. Yet Fisher, and the like-minded Charles Plosser of the Philadelphia Fed, had intuitive, even populist reasons for raising rates. These reasons had in part to do with the unfairness of not giving depositors a decent return on their money while Wall Street bankers used easy money to enrich themselves with leveraged stock buybacks.

Stein was subtler. He saw inside the machine. Stein knew that asset swaps—an exchange of junk collateral for good collateral so the exchanging party could pledge good collateral in another deal—were adding hidden leverage. He understood that increased regulation was driving disintermediation—so-called shadow banking—making it worse than what collapsed in 2008. He grasped that derivatives risk was in gross notional values, not net. This was clear from his speeches and writings. Stein saw the bubble dynamics. Then he was gone. No one left on the FOMC seemed to see what Stein saw.

My question to Jon was straightforward. Stein had sounded a warning inside the Fed. His analysis was rigorous, not populist. Stein also knew that if a new bubble burst so soon after 2008, that would destroy confidence for a generation and undo the work the Fed had done since the last crisis to move the economy to a self-sustaining path. I leaned forward and asked Jon, "Does Yellen see what Stein saw? Does she believe markets are in a bubble?" Then came Faust's reply: "Not yet."

This reply was revealing. It meant the Fed was sticking to obsolete models. The idea that the Fed should not try to pop bubbles, but instead clean up the mess after they pop, has a long pedigree. Discussion of this approach goes back at least as far as the classic work of Friedman and Schwartz on the origins of the Great Depression. Friedman and Schwartz were critical of the Fed's decision to raise interest rates in 1928 to cool off a stock market bubble. By raising rates at a time when inflation was not a threat, the Fed induced a recession in 1929, which was a proximate cause of the stock market crash in October of that year. That crash is frequently cited as marking the onset of the Great Depression. Both Alan Greenspan and Ben Bernanke support the Friedman and Schwartz critique. Greenspan received praise for letting the dot-com bubble that began in 1996 pop on its own in 2000. Greenspan "cleaned up the mess" without serious economic damage or systemic contagion. Bernanke echoed Greenspan's approach to handling bubbles in extensive writings and in a landmark speech on the causes of the Great Depression given on March 2, 2004.

Yet, the Greenspan-Bernanke approach to bubbles is both a misreading of history and contradicted by more recent experience. The Fed did blunder by raising rates in 1928, but the blunder was not that they attacked a bubble, but that they failed to follow the rules of the game. The United States was on a gold standard in 1928 and saw extensive gold inflows from Europe. Under the monetary rules of the game, gold inflows required monetary ease that would cause inflation, raise export prices, and rebalance gold flows in favor of Europe. Raising rates increased gold inflows to the United States and reduced liquidity in the rest of the world. This policy was the opposite of that required under a gold standard, and was a direct contributor to the Great Depression.

What Greenspan and Bernanke miss is that there is neither a gold standard today, nor any monetary standard at all. Without a monetary anchor to gauge policy, the Fed must think harder about whether it is the *cause* of a bubble rather than a mere bystander. Decisions to raise or lower rates are not guided by gold inflows, but rather by whims, and spurious correlations between inflation and employment known as NAIRU (the non-accelerating inflation rate of unemployment) and the Phillips curve.

Experience shows that Greenspan's handling of the dot-com bubble was not so deft after all. His cleanup included keeping interest rates too low for too long, which led directly to the housing bubble and the 2008 financial collapse. Bernanke's zero interest rate policy (continued by

Yellen) from 2008 to 2015 repeated Greenspan's mistake with catastrophic potential.

The better analysis is that bubbles are not automatically dangerous. What matters is whether they are fueled by debt or not. The dot-com bubble was inflated by what Greenspan earlier called "irrational exuberance," not debt, and did relatively little harm to the macroeconomy when it burst despite investor losses. In contrast, the mortgage bubble was driven entirely by debt and derivatives and caused the greatest recession since the Great Depression. All bubbles are not alike. Stein understood this.

In understanding these bubble dynamics, leverage is a more apt metric than debt. Leverage can include derivatives in addition to traditional borrowings. This was Stein's other great insight. Bernanke and Yellen not only failed to distinguish between debt- versus non-debt-driven bubbles, but failed to see that derivatives were a form of debt. The new asset bubbles still expanding in 2016 were the bad type—driven by debt and derivatives. Yellen's obsolete hands-off approach missed this distinction.

There's nothing new about economists' inability to foresee panics. One infamous example was prominent economist Irving Fisher's observation that stock markets had reached "what looks like a permanently high plateau," made days before the October 28, 1929, stock market crash that took the market down 24 percent in two days. That crash continued as the stock market fell 80 percent from the 1929 high before bottoming out in 1932. The point is not to ridicule Fisher—he was one of the twentieth century's most brilliant economists—but rather to make the point that economists, especially those at the Fed, simply don't see bubbles.

There are models that do a good job identifying bubbles using complexity theory, causal inference, and behavioral economics, although the exact timing of collapse remains difficult to predict due to the minuteness of catalysts, and the stochastics of path dependence. Jeremy Stein and former Fed governor Rick Mishkin have made the most progress in the use of recursive functions to grasp these risks. Still, Faust's reply put a spike in my hope that this thinking was more than a novelty at the Fed. In Yellen's mind, it was business as usual. There was no bubble.

The other disturbing feature of Faust's reply was the word "yet." This carried an implication that while a bubble might be in the making, there was still time to keep it under control. The notion is that it is possible for central bankers to let the air out of a balloon slowly. Another metaphor is a thermostat. If a house is too cold, you can dial the thermostat up. If the house is too warm, you dial it down. The connotation is that controlling the economy is a linear and reversible process. All it takes is a turn of the dial.

An economy more nearly resembles a nuclear reactor than a thermostat. Reactors can also be dialed up or down. Yet that process is neither linear nor necessarily reversible. When a supercritical state is reached, a reactor core melts down. No amount of dialing can cause a melt-up. Nuclear reactors are complex systems, as are capital markets. Faust was unintentionally saying the Fed has no idea how capital markets behave.

In contrast to his comment on bubbles, Faust's remarks on quantitative easing were refreshing. He candidly acknowledged that inside the Fed, QE's effect was considered "murky." QE seemed worth doing, and was probably better than nothing, but any beneficial impact was unclear.

Bernanke admitted as much when we spoke in 2015. I heard the same in private conversations with other FOMC members. They admitted they did not know what they were doing after 2008. Bernanke told me his ideal was FDR during the Great Depression. FDR was a great improviser. His administration would pursue a policy on not much more than a hunch it might work. Some ideas did work, some failed. Others had some impact, yet were blatantly illegal and later overruled by the courts. It didn't matter. FDR's mantra was to try all possible paths out of economic distress. FDR felt that in a crisis it was better to do something than nothing. Bernanke told me he agreed with that approach.

In fact, it depends. At times, it is better to do *nothing* than to flail about. That is the essence of medicine's Hippocratic oath, which in modern English reads, "I will not be ashamed to say 'I know not.' . . . Above all, I must not play at God," and "prevention is preferable to cure." The historical record strongly suggests the Great Depression would have ended sooner but for uncertainty caused by FDR's improvisations. The prolonged depression since 2008 (defined as persistent below-trend growth) owes to uncertainty caused by Bernanke-Yellen improvisations. In a state of regime uncertainty, capital goes on strike.

Faust was equally candid about the drafting sessions for the press releases issued after each FOMC meeting. He called the process "ridiculous." Significant word changes were made for the sake of change with no intrinsic meaning attached to the words. The reader was led on a hermeneutic semiotic voyage. Bernanke once looked at two drafts of an FOMC statement; one meant to signal no policy change, and one intended to signal tightening. Bernanke looked up and asked Jon, "Which one's the bad one?" The words were arbitrary, and for show. Faust's more important job was to call Jon Hilsenrath, a reporter for *The Wall Street Journal*, to explain what the Fed *wanted* the words to mean regardless of word choices. Hilsenrath dutifully reported the intended meaning, and the market responded as expected. Michel Foucault would have been proud.

After about an hour of conversation, Faust and I pivoted from policy issues to discuss the post-2008 era in historical context. Notwithstanding my Fed critique, I allowed that the Fed at least thought it was pursuing the right strategies. Yet this raised a counterfactual: If the Fed knew then what it knows now, would it have followed the same path? The premise behind the question was simple. When the Fed launched QE2 in November 2010, it expected robust results by 2011. When it launched QE3 in September 2012, it expected robust results by 2013. The hoped-for growth had not materialized. The economy was not worse; jobs were created; yet growth was weak, well below potential. Was the whole process a box canyon, a dead end from which there was now no exit?

Faust didn't answer the question directly. Instead he mused that fifty years from now, "a new Ben Bernanke will come along, a young scholar who would look back at the 1930s and this period we're in now and compare the approaches to see what worked and what didn't. That person will have two data points." Faust's dry academic remark about data points opened another window on Fed thinking.

In addition to obsolete equilibrium models, Fed staff adhere to what are called frequentist statistical methods. The frequentist method stands in contrast to another statistical style, an inferential approach based on Bayes' theorem. Both approaches, frequentist and Bayesian, wrestle with cause and effect to make forecasts. Like many dichotomous debates, there has been some synthesis in recent years; users of each approach can see something salutary in the other. But battle lines are still drawn.

Frequentists assert that statistically valid conclusions can be drawn only when large data sets with long time series are available; the larger and longer, the better. These large data sets are sorted and analyzed through baselines, regressions, and correlations to hypothesize causality and spot anomalies. That output forms a foundation for robust predictions of future behavior. One particular technique used in economics is the Monte Carlo simulation. Computers are used to spin a simulated roulette wheel or roll digital dice millions of times with output plotted into degree distributions so specific outcome frequencies can be observed and forecast with confidence. The more data, and more frequent the observation, the more confident the statistician is in her forecast—thus the name "frequentist."

Bayesians work with far less data, not because they want to, but because sometimes one must. If you need to solve a life-or-death problem, and have only one data point, Bayes' theorem helps you find an answer. Bayesians solve problems when data sets are small, even nonexistent. They do so by making an assumption, called a prior, and use the prior to form a hypothesis. The prior is based on factors including history, common sense, intuition, and what scant data might exist. The prior is assigned some probability of being true based on the best available evidence. In the absence of any data, the prior is assigned a fifty-fifty probability, the best approximation of uncertainty.

The Bayesian reasons backward from subsequent observations to test the prior hypothesis. Each subsequent event is evaluated for the separate probability that it would or would not occur if the hypothesis is true. Then the prior is updated to increase or decrease its probability of being correct. Over time the prior can become quite strong, with a 90 percent probability of being correct; or it can become weak, in which case it is discarded. The good Bayesian keeps an open mind about the impact of subsequent observations on the original hypothesis. Frequentists are horrified at the guesswork in developing the prior and assigning probabilities in the absence of data. They view the method as nonscientific, only slightly better than voodoo.

Bayesians rebut frequentists with pragmatism—what if you don't have a lot of data, yet the problem can't wait? What if U-boats have cut off Britain's food supply, and your mission is to crack the Nazi Enigma code and break the U-boat blockade? By the time frequentists had enough data to solve the problem, the United Kingdom would have been starved into surrender. This is why Bayesian approaches are widely used in military and intelligence operations. Those operators face existential questions that cannot wait for more data.

Faust's remark was frequentist to the bone. In effect, he said the Bernanke-Yellen policies from 2007 to 2015 had only one data point to process—the Great Depression. Bernanke ranks as a monetary scholar of the Great Depression just behind Milton Friedman and Anna Schwartz, giants of that field. Fifty years from now, presumably in the midst of another economic misadventure, a future policymaker would have two depressions to study, 1929 and 2008, and could perhaps compare and contrast policy responses as if answering a question on a college final exam. In fairness to Faust, Bernanke expressed the same view when I spoke to him. The former chairman ruminated that it was too soon to tell if his policies had been successful. It would take future scholarship, decades hence, to render that judgment.

My assessment of the Bernanke-Faust frequentist mind-set was that at the rate of one data point per century, we'd be well on the way to understanding linkages between monetary policy and depressions by the year 2525. What I took Faust to mean was that when crisis struck in 2008, Bernanke had only one frame of reference, and did the best he could. Interestingly, Janet Yellen's academic outpost between her stints as a central banker was the University of California at Berkeley, the intellectual ground zero of frequentist statistical science for the past century. Yellen was even more data driven and model based than Bernanke.

The world's misfortune was that the Fed had no firm grasp of Bayesian technique. Capital markets were condemned to a succession of calamities while academics-turned-central-bankers waited decades for more data to convince them of their failures.

Faust and I ended the evening at the aptly named Bull and Bear bar in the Waldorf Astoria hotel about a block from the restaurant. We sipped straight Scotch, an aged batch selected with care by our friend Dave "Davos" Nolan, the hedge fund billionaire, and shared with another dinner companion, world-class biologist Beverly Wendland. Davos, Beverly, and I toasted Jon's recent return to academia—what I called his "escape from the Fed."

Unfortunately there is no escape for the global economy.

The Power of Gold

Simply seeing market collapse, even through a complexity theory lens, is unsatisfying to investors who don't care *why* things end, but want to know *when*. Greed plays a part. Investors may concur that capital markets will crash, yet they're along for the ride until they do. In effect, investors say, "I know stocks are a bubble, but the gains are too good to resist. Call me the day before the crash; I'll sell everything, move to cash, buy gold, and keep my profits. Here's my number."

The proper reply to this penchant is that no one will know the hour or the day. The lacuna is not from lack of analysis; it's just good science.

Complexity's essence is that invisible changes in initial conditions produce radically different systemic outcomes. Market processes are nonlinear and practically nondeterministic. There may be a cause-and-effect relationship between catalyst and collapse. Still, it is too small to observe and the timing is difficult to forecast. Predicting market crashes is like predicting earthquakes. One may be certain the event will occur, and can estimate its magnitude, yet one will never know exactly when.

Laboratory science, in particular sand pile experiments (similar to a snowflake-avalanche dynamic) and computer simulations using cellular automata, reveal degree distributions of extreme events. Still, a million experiments will not let you predict which particular grain of sand causes a certain sand pile to collapse.

Systemic instability, not an individual catalyst, destroys your wealth. Anxious investors should not focus on snowflakes, they should stay alert for an avalanche. Nonetheless, the search for snowflakes is seductive.

The most sensational snowflake may be a publicized failure to deliver physical gold by a prominent bank. This will shock markets the way mortgage fund defaults did in 2007. A gold-buying panic, super-spike in gold prices, and ripple effects in other markets are predictable outcomes of such a failure.

Gold is the world's least understood asset class. Confusion arises because gold is traded like a commodity, yet gold is not a commodity, it is money. Countries with tens of thousands of tons of gold in their vaults are happy to obscure this distinction. Central banks know gold is money; they just don't want you to know.

Still, the presence of 35,000 tons of gold in government vaults, about 15 percent of all the gold mined in history, testifies to gold's monetary role despite official denials. Even the IMF, which officially demonetized gold in 1974, holds 2,800 tons. Switzerland's Bank for International Settlements, known as the central bank for central banks, holds 108 tons for its own account. Central banks and finance ministries do not hold copper, aluminum, or steel supplies, yet they hold gold. The only explanation for central bank gold hoards is the obvious one—gold is money.

Still, the central bank preference for fiat forms of money such as dollars and euros necessitates a pretense about gold. The reason is that central banks share a monopoly on fiat. There is no central bank monopoly on gold—yet.

One result of the confusion on gold's nature is schizophrenic trading. At times gold trades as a commodity and responds to inflation, deflation, and shifts in real interest rates like any other commodity. COMEX proprietary gold traders are happy to sell front-month futures contracts, and buy the back-month at a profit after adjusting for storage and carry costs, a condition called contango. Institutional gold buyers such as SAFE, a secretive Chinese sovereign wealth fund, like low prices because their gold acquisition programs are not complete. Some gold holders wait in vain for traders in gold futures to notify the COMEX that they are demanding physical delivery. There is not enough physical gold to satisfy that demand; the gold futures exchange would quickly break down if they did. Still, why should traders demand delivery? Banks and brokers make good money from current practices. There is no immediate reason for small traders or mega-institutions to break up these profitable gold price dynamics.

Gold will break out toward its intrinsic monetary value of $10,000 per ounce, versus the current commodity value of $1,400 per ounce, not because traders revolt, but because the transmission mechanism between physical and derivatives gold markets will break. The divergence between the perceived commodity value of gold and gold's real monetary value will reconcile in money's favor. Signs of this are visible.

One sign occurred in November 2014, when gold's price diverged sharply from the Thomson Reuters Continuous Commodity Index. Gold is one index component and closely tracked the index for years. That's not surprising; an index component should track the index of which it's a part. Then in November 2014, the index accelerated to the downside, while gold broke out to the upside. This divergence persisted through 2016. November 2014 marks the point at which the perception of gold as money began to dominate the perception of gold as a commodity.

Other signs are less visible, yet more intriguing. On July 18, 2014, I dined at an exclusive private club in New York with a friend, one of the most seasoned gold bullion dealers in the world. What my friend told me was shocking, yet not inconsistent with similar accounts I heard in Hong Kong and Zurich.

Little is learned about gold sitting at screens watching quotations. Gold is physical, not ephemeral. The experts in physical gold include dealers, miners, refiners, and secure logistics operators of private vaults, armored cars, and chartered jets that move gold around the world. My custom is to meet with these physical gold mavens when I can.

The club dining room was windowless and dimly lit, with typical old-school mahogany paneling and thick moldings. The walls were tightly packed with paintings, mostly nudes that gave it a bohemian feel. The club was the perfect place to discuss gold, true old-school money. We did so over oysters, soft-shelled crabs, and vintage Champagne.

My dealer friend was eyewitness to a strange sequence in 2009 involving HSBC, a too-big-to-fail bank, and one of the largest gold dealers in the world. HSBC controls a gold vault on West Thirty-ninth Street in Manhattan, near the New York Public Library. The vault's exterior is nondescript, scarcely noticed by thousands who walk by each day. There are three loading bays on Thirty-ninth Street where armored cars pull up to deposit or receive gold bullion. One bay has a double-axled armored car often standing by to shuttle gold to a larger Brink's gold vault at JFK Airport in Queens. From JFK, the gold is shipped around the world to destinations like Switzerland and Shanghai.

Behind the bay doors is a gold counting room. Dealers with small deliveries can arrive on foot with coins or bars in courier satchels. The counting room is draped in bulletproof glass. This allows dealers in one part of the counting room to observe activity around them. My friend was in the counting room to deposit 100 ounces of coins. He observed a much larger delivery of 400-ounce bullion bars being off-loaded in the adjacent bay. He quipped to the counting room clerk, "Hey, I'll trade you these coins for those gold bars over there." The clerk lowered his gaze and said, sotto voce, "You don't want to do that; these coins are more valuable," implying that the bars were "salted" or partly fake.

Shortly after this strange incident, HSBC abruptly announced it was ending its gold storage business for all but the largest customers. Small and midsize accounts were asked to leave and take their coins with them. Many support staff were fired, including the clerk who warned my friend about the fake gold. The woman who headed the physical deposit operations for more than twenty years, Stephanie Schiffman, died prematurely in her sleep.

The story didn't stop there. Not much later, China identified a shipment of salted gold bars, fakes coated in gold, received from HSBC. The bank was an intermediary in the trade. The origin of the fake bars was not disclosed to China. The Chinese demanded a make-good delivery, which HSBC promptly provided. The entire sequence was covered up and soon forgotten. Since 2009, China vastly expanded its mining and refining capabilities and is now less dependent on Western supplies. China also protects itself from bank fakes by insisting that old 400-ounce bars purchased from Western sources be re-refined in Switzerland into new one-kilo bars of higher purity. There is no point in delivering fake bars to a refinery because the fraud is discovered immediately when the gold is melted. Fake 400-ounce bars are left in the West.

Trading in gold derivatives is supported with a shrinking store of physical gold. The China fakes are just one symptom of stretched conditions on the physical side. My dealer friend said supplies are dangerously tight. Orders of ten tons or more are quite difficult to fill. U.S. law requires physical gold forward sales to be settled by delivery within twenty-eight days. Otherwise such sales are reclassified as futures contracts, which are illegal unless traded on regulated futures exchanges. In current tight market conditions, this law is routinely ignored as dealers find it difficult to complete deliveries within the twenty-eight-day requirement. The U.S. government has shown no interest in enforcing the law. These illegal forward sales should be added to the reported open interest on futures exchanges to understand the inverted pyramid of gold derivatives resting on a shrinking fulcrum of physical supply.

Physical gold at the base of the inverted pyramid of paper gold trading is the floating supply. This is different from total supply. Floating supply consists of gold available for prompt delivery to support dealer activity. Total supply consists of all the physical gold in the world. Most gold is hoarded in private vaults or worn as jewelry. It is not readily available to support trading. This is an important distinction. The difference between floating supply and total supply bears directly on how a failure to deliver physical gold could cascade into a full-blown gold-buying panic.

Gold in Western central bank, IMF, and BIS vaults is part of the floating supply available for lease to the market. Once title is obtained through leasing by a bullion bank, that gold is used to make forward sales on an unallocated basis. The term "unallocated" is a euphemism. It means the buyer has gold price exposure and a paper contract, but no gold. One ton of German gold, held on deposit at the Federal Reserve Bank of New York, and leased to Goldman Sachs in London through BIS intermediation, can be used to support ten tons of forward sales to the market. Each buyer of part of those ten tons believes she owns gold. Yet there is only one ton of physical gold to support ten tons of gold sales. Even that one ton of physical gold is leased and may be withdrawn from the market by the lessor.

When central bank gold is sold to China's government and shipped to Shanghai, that gold goes into semipermanent deep storage and is unavailable for leasing. Total supply is unchanged, yet the floating supply is diminished. The same is true when countries such as the Netherlands and Germany repatriate their physical gold from the Federal Reserve Bank of New York to vaults in Amsterdam and Frankfurt. Legally, this gold could be leased by Germany or the Netherlands, yet there is no well-developed leasing market in either location. Leasing is centered in

New York and London, where commercial law is clear and legal precedent gives transacting parties a high degree of confidence in contract enforceability. So gold repatriation to Europe diminishes the floating supply.

Floating supply is also diminished as investors demand that their gold be transshipped from bank vaults at UBS or Credit Suisse to private vaults at Loomis or Brink's. Gold in a bank vault is available for leasing or multiple unallocated sales while gold in private vaults is not. Confirmation of transshipment from bank vaults to private vaults was offered to me directly from senior executives of the vault operators.

Another failure in the physical gold market is illegal substitution of allocated bars. Some buyers own their gold on a fully allocated basis, which means they have title to specific bullion bars, not just a paper claim. Standard 400-ounce good delivery gold bars are stamped with the refiner's name, the assayer's name, a specific weight (which may be slightly more or less than 400 ounces), the date the bar was poured, the purity (which is between 99.50 and 99.99 percent pure), and a unique serial number. Based on those identifying stamps each gold bar is unique. Yet pure gold is fungible; that has always been one of gold's attractions. I have heard countless stories of gold investors who demanded physical delivery only to receive bars with different dates or other markings than those on their manifests. This means the original bars were diverted and other bars delivered as substitutes. Receiving parties rarely object because gold is gold. This is true provided the substitutions are not fakes. Any substitution is evidence of scarcity.

All of these trends—depletion of COMEX warehouses, repatriation of gold to Europe, outright gold purchases by China, private nonbank gold storage, illegal substitutions, and gold counterfeiting—are accelerating. The result is a larger inverted pyramid of gold derivatives resting on a smaller floating supply of physical gold. Shortages, delays, and fraud in gold deliveries are emerging. For now, these dysfunctions are ignored by market participants who are happy to get gold even if delays are encountered.

As physical scarcity becomes more evident to insiders, a phase transition emerges. Those with title to gold, but without physical possession, start to demand possession. This trend is seen in recent gold repatriation efforts by Germany and the Netherlands. Demand for physical gold also appears in Federal Reserve Bank of New York reports on gold deposits. In 2014, gold on deposit at the Fed dropped by 177.64 tons; over half that decline occurred in a brief two-month period, October and November 2014. The movement was all one way; there were no months when gold deposits increased. This precipitous draw-down of physical gold occurred at the same time the gold price diverged from the commodity price index. The coincident draw-down and price divergence are consistent with the view that gold is money, and is in short supply.

These trends are known only to specialists and insiders. The general public and U.S. policymakers are not alert to the implications. The shortage of physical gold relative to contracts, and the nervousness of contracting parties about good delivery, have triggered a classic run on the bank—except it's a run on gold.

This dynamic resembles the state of the gold market from 1968 to 1971, when Europeans cashed in dollars for gold from Fort Knox, leading President Nixon to shut the gold window on August 15, 1971. Today there is no fixed price for gold, and the gold is not coming from Fort Knox, but rather from private custodians such as the Federal Reserve and ETF sponsors. Still, the dynamics are similar.

The environment is ripe for a highly publicized failure to deliver. When this occurs, gold owners in paper forms will want physical gold all at once. The price will spike as intermediaries scramble to buy scarce physical gold to make good on promised deliveries. Institutions previously uninterested in gold will suddenly want gold as well for their portfolios, increasing the upward price momentum. The end result is ice-nine for gold. Gold exchanges will halt trading. Contracts will be terminated and settled in dollars at the last closing price. Counterparties will lose out on future price appreciation and access to physical gold. Those who don't have gold will be unable to get it at any price.

The financial system will be fortunate if a gold-buying panic is confined to gold and does not spill over into capital markets. That seems unlikely. Financial distress is contagious. Even if a gold panic is momentarily contained, this does not mean capital markets are stable. There are other snowflakes.

The Dollar Shortage

Gold is not the only money in short supply; there is a global dollar shortage also, and it grows worse by the day. An acute phase of the dollar shortage will manifest soon as defaults, deflation, and bank failures. The reflationary policy response will include money creation, debt monetization, and ice-nine lockdowns of financial institutions and money market funds. The conflict between countervailing forces of deflation and reflation is vast, and will be highly destructive of accumulated wealth.

The suggestion of a dollar shortage may seem strange. The Federal Reserve created more than $3.3 trillion of new money between 2008 and 2015. Other central banks created comparably large amounts relative to their economies. How is there a dollar shortage with that much new money sloshing around?

The answer is that along with $3.3 trillion of new money created by the Fed, markets created more than $60 trillion of new debt, and hundreds of trillions of dollars in new derivatives. The newly created money has been leveraged over 50-to-1 through various channels. Not all the new debt and derivatives constitute "money" as the term is conventionally defined. Still, that debt represents a state in which a counterparty expects to receive her "money back" by contractual performance in the fullness of time. When such contracts default, or when the value of collateral behind such contracts is diminished, or when the prospects of contractual performance prove doubtful, a slow-motion liquidation begins. In small stages, short-term creditors decline to roll over financing facilities, banks refuse to lend to other banks, accountants require write-downs, and the global system tips into deleveraging. In the classic formulation, everyone wants her money back. Yet there isn't enough true money to give everyone's money back. That's when liquidation accelerates and the dollar shortage shows its teeth.

Evidence for this liquidation comes from several sources. A stronger dollar measured by major dollar indices from 2013 to 2016 is good evidence of global dollar demand. Acute eurodollar interbank funding problems at major Italian banks beginning in June 2016 are additional straws in the wind. Net sales of U.S. Treasury securities by China, Russia, and Saudi Arabia in the first half of 2016 were evidence of those nations' need to obtain dollars to satisfy capital outflow demands or maintain nonsustainable currency pegs.

The most intriguing piece of evidence for a dollar shortage is the tangled trio of prices in five-year TIPS, gold, and ten-year Treasury notes. TIPS stands for Treasury Inflation Protected Securities, a special type of Treasury note where the principal is indexed to inflation. This means the TIPS yield is a real yield; there is no need to add an inflation premium to a nominal yield because principal is already protected against inflation. When an investor pays a premium over par to buy a TIPS, the resulting real yield to maturity is negative because the investor receives the inflation-adjusted principal *minus* the premium paid.

From 2006 to 2016, gold and five-year TIPS (measured by yield on an inverted scale) exhibited a powerful positive correlation. This makes sense. When bond yields are negative, gold is more attractive because gold has no yield. A greater negative yield on TIPS should correlate with a higher dollar price for gold, and it does. Negative real yields, and a higher dollar price of gold, are early warning signs of inflation. Given massive money creation by central banks around the world, higher inflation expectations are reasonable.

The odd man out in the trio is the ten-year Treasury note. Principal on these notes is not inflation protected, so investors seek higher coupons or buy notes at a discount in order to gain inflation protection. The yield to maturity on a ten-year note represents some combination of credit risk (typically low) and inflation risk (variable based on economic conditions). If gold and five-year TIPS signal inflation, yields on ten-year Treasury notes should be rising, and prices falling. The opposite occurred. The yield on ten-year Treasury notes collapsed from 5.2 percent on July 6, 2007, to 1.3 percent on July 8, 2016, one of the greatest bond market rallies in history. Hedge funds and institutions lost billions shorting a presumed bond market bubble, while yields kept dropping and prices kept rising to new heights. This price action is a powerful sign of expected deflation and weak economic growth, even depression.

Gold and TIPS prices presage inflation. Ten-year Treasuries signal deflation. Which is it? To an efficient-markets economist, markets are never wrong, yet how could these markets be right if they signal opposite outcomes? The answer is that inflationary and deflationary forces coexist today in an unstable dynamic tension with the capacity to snap in either direction like a fault line in an earthquake, and produce a price shock for which most investors are ill prepared.

The nuanced way to reconcile prices of gold, TIPS, and ten-year notes is to understand this as a bizarre price triangle of fear. An investor who fears inflation buys TIPS and gold. An investor who fears deflation buys ten-year notes. Wise investors buy all three because inflation and deflation are both in play. The likely path is short-term deflation and recession due to debt, deleveraging, demographics, and technology, followed closely by inflation due to the central bank and fiscal authority policy response to deflation. Physicists find this back-and-forth behavior familiar, an example of a complex system on the edge of chaos that goes wobbly just before it spins totally out of control. Inflation must win in the end; governments require it and always find a way. Yet deflation will persist in the short run until government grasps its potency and resorts to stronger remedies such as debt monetization.

This uncertain landscape in which deflation and inflation compete in a tug-of-war is amplified by the dollar shortage in which inflationary central bank money printing and debt creation is offset by recessionary debt default. Today's dollar shortage is a replay of the 1950s dollar shortage. In the aftermath of the Second World War, U.S. industrial capacity as a percentage of global capacity and U.S. gold reserves were both at all-time highs. Meanwhile, European and Japanese productive capacity were destroyed by the war and their reserves were depleted. Europeans and Japanese simply could not buy what America offered because they lacked dollars to do so. The first part of the solution was for the United States to give the world dollars through the Marshall Plan and Korean War spending. The second part of the solution was for the United States to supply dollars by running massive trade and budget deficits. This took time, but it worked. By the late 1960s, the dollar shortage had become a dollar glut. As inflation took over, trading partners did not want dollars and redeemed dollars for gold, leading to the closing of the U.S. gold window.

The sequence from the 1950s dollar shortage to the 1960s dollar glut is a succinct illustration of Triffin's dilemma, named for Belgian economist Robert Triffin, who first articulated the theory in 1960. Triffin correctly forecast that the United States would have to run persistent trade deficits with the rest of the world in order to supply the world with sufficient dollars to finance global trade and banking. The dilemma was that if the United States ran these deficits indefinitely, the country would eventually go bankrupt. By 2016, the United States approached the point Triffin had astutely predicted sixty years earlier. This constrained its ability to continue to supply the world with dollars. Still, because the world depended on dollars, the resulting dollar shortage threatened to destabilize global capital markets. The real dilemma was that no widely agreed, widely held substitute for the dollar had yet emerged. The SDR is waiting in the wings to pick up the dollar's crown, but the transition takes time, unless accelerated by crisis.

The world is a minefield of bad debt waiting to detonate into a generalized dollar liquidity crisis. It's just a question of which landmine explodes first. More than $5.4 trillion of energy-related debt was created from 2009 to 2015, most of it in the fracking industry. The sustainability of that debt was based on oil prices at $70 per barrel or higher. With oil below $60 from late 2014 through 2016, default rates on energy debt started to soar. Equally threatening is emerging markets' corporate dollar-denominated debt, estimated by BIS at more than $9 trillion. This is not sovereign debt of the type that caused crises in Dubai in 2009 and Greece in 2011, but rather corporate debt issued by local manufacturers, and commodity producers from Russia to Brazil, Mexico, Indonesia, Turkey, and beyond.

Sovereign debt can be serviced by the issuer's hard currency reserves supplemented by IMF loans, currency swaps, and central bank purchases if needed. Corporate debt is more vulnerable. Corporate issuers might earn dollars from exports, yet many do not. The recent strong dollar means even exporting firms earn fewer dollars in relation to debt, which makes the debt more burdensome to repay. Corporations might get access to hard currency reserves from their home country central banks, but there is no assurance of that, especially if precious reserves, as in Russia, are needed to service sovereign debt.

The default ratio on this energy and emerging markets debt could be as low as 10 percent and still cause more than a trillion dollars in loan losses, with even greater losses in linked derivatives. The world is once again vulnerable to a major debt shock, as it was in 2007.

The source of this new debt shock shows central bankers are no better than generals fighting the last war. In 1998, the global crisis came from emerging markets' sovereign debt and the hedge fund LTCM. Regulators then ordered bankers to scrutinize hedge funds more closely while emerging markets built up precautionary reserve positions in dollars. The 2008 crisis came from an unexpected direction: mortgages. Regulators then tightened mortgage lending standards, increasing down payments and improving underwriting standards. Now this new crisis comes from another unexpected direction: corporate debt.

A Chinese credit crisis is also in the cards. From 2009 to 2016, more than $10 trillion of Chinese investment was wasted on white elephant infrastructure, ghost cities, and corruption. This spending was financed in part by small savers investing in Ponzi wealth management products, Chinese banks, and foreign lenders eager to participate in the spurious

Chinese growth story. This situation is being finessed by the People's Bank of China through interest rate and reserve requirement levers, while the bad debt problem grows worse. Regulators persistently solve the last problem and are blind to the next one. This is because the real problem is not the existence of bad debt, but the easy money policies that create debt in the first place. Market participants are more ingenious than central banks (although the bar is low) at finding ways to create debt and derivatives. That was Jeremy Stein's insight and dismay.

Deflation is another pernicious threat. Even as fiscal deficits decline in developed nations, debt-to-GDP ratios keep rising because nominal growth is so low. The deflation conundrum is that it permits positive real growth with negative nominal growth. An economy can decline in the dollar value of goods and services produced, while growing in real terms if each nominal dollar is worth more due to deflation. This is fine for living standards, yet is nightmarish in terms of debt sustainability because debt is always nominal. If each dollar is worth more, the debt burden goes up even as the deficit goes down. Such is the strange, through-the-looking-glass world of deflation.

Currency wars led one central bank after another to lower rates in an effort to cheapen their currencies relative to those of trading partners. For Japan, Switzerland, and the European Central Bank among others, policy rates are negative. In other sovereign debt markets bonds offer negative total returns. Negative rates offer temporary relief for slow global growth, but where will ease come from in the next panic? Central banks assumed they could normalize rates before the next panic struck. The time to normalize rates was late 2009. Now it's too late. The next crisis will come before the current easing cycle has been reversed. Central banks will be defenseless except through the use of massive new quantitative easing programs. This new money creation binge will test the outer limits of confidence in central bank money.

In addition to this list of catalysts from gold, debt, deflation, and default, there are exogenous threats that emerge in geopolitical space and spill over quickly into financial panics. These threats include conventional wars, cyberwars, assassinations, prominent suicides, power grid outages, and terror attacks.

Finally there are natural disasters such as earthquakes, volcanic eruptions, tsunamis, category five hurricanes, and deadly epidemics.

Skeptics say that wars, earthquakes, disease, and the rest have always been with us. The world managed to survive and even prosper in their wake. That is true. Still, the world has never been so in debt. Societies with low debt burdens are robust to disaster. They can mobilize capital, raise taxes, increase spending, and rebuild when the damage is done. Heavily indebted societies are more brittle. Panicked creditors demand repayment that causes distressed sales of assets, falling markets, and default. This climate of panic is not conducive to capital formation. Stretched budgets cannot be stretched further to support emergency spending. Burdened taxpayers cannot bear more taxation. Policymakers can push buttons and pull levers, but the transmission is broken. Indebted societies do not recover, they fail.

Earthquake 2018

Metaphors made of earthquakes and avalanches are useful to convey the dynamics of financial collapse, yet these dynamics are more than metaphors. The complex system dynamics and mathematical models used to describe both natural and financial disasters are substantially the same. In considering these system metaphors, allowance must be made for timescales. Nuclear explosions occur in nanoseconds. Earthquakes play out in seconds. Tsunamis unfold over hours. Hurricanes emerge and wreak their havoc over days, sometimes weeks. These timescales vary due to the system scale in which the dynamic occurs, and the tempo of reaction functions among constituent parts of the system. A financial collapse is a supernova—a momentous event that can last for years, or, in a real supernova, millennia. This is not because the event is less dynamic, but because system scale is more vast.

A currency collapse that moved in what seemed slow motion was the fall of sterling and the rise of the U.S. dollar as the dominant global reserve currency. Ratification of the Final Act of the Bretton Woods conference on December 27, 1945, is seen as a convenient date to mark the moment the dollar officially eclipsed sterling. This was based on the new world monetary order agreed at Bretton Woods in July 1944 that defined the special role of the dollar anchored to gold with other currencies tied to the dollar, and limited scope for devaluation under IMF supervision.

But the currency eclipse took place thirty years earlier, in November 1914. That was when gold flows between the United States and the United Kingdom began flowing back to the United States. Large flows to the United Kingdom began on July 29, 1914, as Britain liquidated investments for gold to finance the First World War. The United States had no choice but to ship the gold to honor its obligations under the rules of the game. This gold flow from the United States was deftly handled by Jack Morgan and his partners at J. P. Morgan & Company.

By November 1914, the liquidation phase was complete, and the market for short-term trade paper was stable. Now the balance of trade, rather than capital flows, came to dominate. The United Kingdom desperately needed U.S. exports of food, cotton, and war matériel. Once wartime insurance and shipping impediments were resolved, goods were sent from the United States in massive quantities. Under the rules of the game, the resulting balance of trade in favor of the United States had to be settled in gold. This was the beginning of massive gold accumulation by the newly formed Federal Reserve and its private bank owners.

Sterling's role from 1914 to 1944 was a façade. The fact that London remained a financial center, and sterling remained a reserve currency, had more to do with Britain's captive market in the British Empire, and the sufferance of anglophile bankers at J. P. Morgan, than with intrinsic strength. Scholar Barry Eichengreen brilliantly laid out this transition and the seesaw struggle between the dollar and sterling for the global reserve currency crown in the interwar years in his book *Golden Fetters*.

Sterling lost reserve status de facto in 1914, yet the world did not see the denouement until 1944. Thirty years is not a nanosecond. Still, sterling's collapse was an unstoppable dynamic process. Insiders at J. P. Morgan knew the score; they handled gold on a daily basis and saw the global flows. Perhaps today's dollar has *already* lost its dominant status, a fact seen by certain insiders, yet not known to investors because of the façade of empire the United States still projects. The eclipse of the dollar may not be a dramatic, earth-shattering event that waits in our future; it may already be at hand. In "The Hollow Men," T. S. Eliot wrote, "This is the way the world ends / Not with a bang but a whimper." Most cannot hear the whimper.

Future historians may look back at September 18, 2008, as the day the dollar died. The Fed furiously printed money to put out fires at Lehman, AIG, and Goldman Sachs. At the same time, China began to orchestrate massive inflows of gold, not under a gold standard, but rather stealth purchases using secret agents and intelligence tradecraft. The mirage of dollar strength continues. Still, the ground under the dollar has shifted.

While it is possible to pinpoint a climax in hindsight, that is not how financial decline appears in real time. Collapse comes in stages, over years, and includes quiet phases when an all-clear siren is sounded and investors emerge from their shelters, then are bombed again more intensely.

Complexity in a system breeds the seeds of that system's own collapse. Why did European civilization not experience a general collapse in the thousand years from the fall of Rome to the Renaissance? The answer is there was no Europe in the systemic sense. European lands were a thinly connected patchwork of small kingdoms, principalities, and Viking raiding cultures. There were wars, conquests, culture, religion, and fine art, yet there was no highly scaled European system.

Only with the rise of concentrated political entities such as France, Sweden, Russia, and England in the sixteenth century did large-scale system dynamics appear. Increased density functions led to three great systemic collapses—the Thirty Years' War, the Napoleonic Wars, and the twentieth-century world wars. Each collapse was followed by a concerted effort to stabilize the system with agreed rules of the game. The solution to the Thirty Years' War was the 1648 Peace of Westphalia, which established the modern sovereign state system and enshrined *raison d'état* as a guide to statecraft in place of religion and the divine right of kings. The resolution of the Napoleonic Wars led to the Final Act of the Congress of Vienna on June 9, 1815. The Final Act reduced French power, yet was not overly punitive toward France. The Congress of Vienna laid the foundation for modern diplomacy and the practice of the balance of power in international relations. The relatively stable, peaceful, and prosperous period after the Congress of Vienna was called the Concert of Europe.

The aftermath of the First World War did not produce a stable system as occurred in 1648 and 1815. The Treaty of Peace signed at Versailles on June 28, 1919, was politically punitive to a defeated Germany and economically unsound. The treaty contributed to hyperinflation and global depression and was a proximate cause of the Second World War. Only at the end of that war, in a series of agreements in 1944 and 1945, including Bretton Woods and the United Nations Charter, did stability reemerge in a hegemonic new world order led by the United States and the Soviet Union.

The contrast between the thousand years from AD 500 to 1500, and the five hundred years since 1500, illustrates the importance of systemic scale. Kingdoms came and went in the Middle Ages, yet there was no catastrophic breakdown. Political fragmentation served as watertight compartments on a ship, and low network density was resistant to political and economic contagion. Since 1500, increasing scale and density in Europe have led to exponentially larger breakdowns, exactly what complexity theory predicts.

The Concert of Europe collapsed in stages about sixty years after Vienna. German and Italian unification, completed in 1871, signaled a sharp increase in European network density and systemic scale. This political density was amplified by economic networks forged by invention or expansion of telephones, train travel, steamships, electricity, and other innovations. As complexity increased, more intricate and acute crises ensued. Decline of the Ottoman Empire, the 1905 Russo-Japanese War, and the 1912 Balkan Crisis were of a piece, leading to the destruction of Europe and the collapse of empires from 1914 to 1945. The First and Second World Wars are best viewed, and will be viewed by future historians, as a single, large-scale systemic collapse of Europe, Japan, China, and the British Empire. Complexity kills.

Where are we now? Financial crises have supplanted kinetic warfare at the center of complex system dynamics. Financial crises in 1998 and 2008 are the analogues to the Russian, Franco-German, and Balkan wars of 1870 to 1912. They are warnings—tremors ahead of a misfortune beyond imagining. This is not conjecture, but an expected outcome given the system dynamics. This outcome is not inevitable. Still, it is likely. To step back from the brink requires smaller banks, fewer derivatives, less leverage, and sound money, perhaps with reference to gold. None of these remedies is in prospect; a systems failure is.

CHAPTER 7
BONFIRE OF THE ELITES

The tragedy of bad economic ideas is that once they grab hold of society's imagination, it becomes nearly impossible to persuade people to abandon them. Instead, the ideas must be . . . disproved by experience.

Thomas I. Palley, economist and author
From Financial Crisis to Stagnation (2012)

Wildebeest and Lioness

A wildebeest's defense against a lioness is the herd. One wildebeest is no match for a lioness. At dawn on the Serengeti, straddling Kenya and Tanzania, a lioness walks toward a wildebeest herd, selects a target for her attack, and charges. The wildebeests respond as one, break into a panicked rout, create a cloud of dust, change direction, and, when the lioness strikes, converge in bands to kick the lioness into submission and retreat. But the lioness rarely goes away hungry. She eventually kills a wildebeest, devours the meat on the now sunlit plain, and with warm blood on her muzzle, shares it with her pride. From the wildebeests' perspective, while one loss may be unfortunate, the herd survives.

This Serengeti scene encapsulates the elite monetary mind-set. Monetary elites are the herd. They are not a shadowy underground, but rather a specific group of individuals—finance ministers, central bankers, academics, journalists, and think tank denizens. They run wealth management firms from Boston to Beijing. They advise presidents and prime ministers, and have protégés to take their place in due course.

The cast changes over time. Today the elite list includes Christine Lagarde, Mario Draghi, and Larry Summers to name a few. In times past, Jean-Claude Trichet and Dominique Strauss-Kahn were front and center. They whirl from public to private platforms in the style of Bob Rubin. They greet one another at private dinners on the sidelines at Davos or Aspen. They meet in conclaves at BIS in Basel with no record of the conversation. They control global finance and, by extension, global politics, because politics are constrained by finance. They run the world.

Today they are a herd in full flight, stalked by a lioness. The lioness is the failure of their own ideas.

Elites conduct ritual disagreements for public consumption. These squabbles are mostly for show. There is a shocking conformity of core beliefs behind these debates. Central bankers like Lael Brainard, a Democrat, and Kristin Forbes, a Republican, agree on almost every policy point. Their political party affiliations open the door to powerful appointments regardless of which party the voters elect. Policy itself is unchanged; voters are undone.

Keynesians subscribe to monetarist orthodoxy and support central banks that promote growth. Monetarists make space for Keynesian stimulus financed by fiscal policy. Keynesians and monetarists hold hands under the umbrella of a soi-disant neoliberal consensus.

The herd agrees that markets are efficient, albeit with imperfections. They agree that supply and demand produce local equilibria, and the sum of these equilibria is a general equilibrium. When equilibrium is perturbed, it can be restored through policy. The herd agrees that floating exchange rates produce price signals and market reactions that contribute to the general equilibrium. They agree that free trade, rooted in Ricardian comparative advantage, optimizes wealth creation, albeit with individual winners and losers. They agree that gold is a barbarous relic.

Among Keynesians, there is a further phony divide between saltwater and freshwater schools. Saltwater is associated with coastal schools such as Harvard and MIT. Freshwater is associated with inland schools such as the University of Chicago. Both agree market imperfections exist, yet disagree on remedies. Saltwater scholars take the view that government intervention smooths out imperfections. Freshwater scholars take the view that intervention costs outweigh the benefits of smoothing; market imperfections should be left alone. Yet they agree on larger issues of equilibrium and efficiency. Neither school has confronted complexity and irrationality, except for lip service to the latter. There are no sides in these debates, just variations on a theme.

Elites agree that a Ph.D. in economics from a short list of schools is a prerequisite for serious consideration in policy discussions, although a few brilliant lawyers, like Bob Rubin and Christine Lagarde, or bright journeymen like Tim Geithner, also make the grade. Consistent views and exclusive vetting perpetuate this elite.

The neoliberal consensus is deeply flawed. This can be demonstrated empirically. The flaws are also proved politically in the Brexit referendum and the civic flowering of Donald J. Trump. Both Brexit and Trump were first ridiculed by the herd, then provoked vituperation as their causes evolved, and finally induced shock at their unforeseen success. We are witnessing an elite crack-up.

Markets are not efficient; they are shaped by irrationality. Equilibrium is a façade that masks unstable complex dynamics. Free trade, based on Ricardo's theory of comparative advantage, does not produce optimal outcomes because it is never free; it is a house built on the quicksand of assumptions that don't reign in the real world and never will. Floating exchange rates are not stabilizing; they are an invitation to currency wars. Gold is the best form of money because it serves as an anchor for other forms. Elite shared beliefs are uniformly obsolete. Evidence of obsolescence accumulates slowly through elite policy failures. Those failures are now too numerous to deny.

If elite consensus is so flawed, why has the consensus persisted so long? In truth, it hasn't. Neo-Keynesian economics has held sway for just seventy years since its inception by MIT's Paul Samuelson in 1947. Monetarism has been intellectually dominant for about sixty years since it emerged from the University of Chicago under Milton Friedman in the 1960s. Eugene Fama's efficient markets hypothesis percolated in academic studies in the 1960s, yet only started to exert market influence in the 1970s with the options pricing model of Fischer Black, Myron Scholes, and Robert Merton. The Black-Scholes model enabled derivatives and leverage. David Ricardo's theory of comparative advantage is two hundred years old, yet was first implemented in a widespread rules-based way after 1947 in the General Agreement on Tariffs and Trade. The link between money and gold was abandoned in stages from 1971 to 1973, concurrent with the rise of floating exchange rate regimes. In short, the herd's cognitive map is relatively new.

None of these intellectual waypoints gained immediate allegiance. Each emerged in stages over the objections of a dwindling cadre of classical economists, Austrians, and heterodox dissenters. The elite consensus in full flower is only about fifty years old—the blink of an eye in the history of ideas.

Equilibrium is the Holy Grail of modern macro- and microeconomics. Equilibrium models start with the simplest concept of supply and demand—consumers will buy more of a good if the price is lower; producers will make more of a good if the price is higher. The downward-sloping demand curve intersects the upward-sloping supply curve. The intersection represents an equilibrium point at which supply equals demand at a price satisfactory to both sides.

Intersecting curves apply to supply-chain inputs and an infinite variety of finished products. The curves apply to labor and capital costs. The curves change shape based on shifting preferences. The curves may be elastic, where demand drops away at the slightest price increase, or inelastic, where buyers demand the same quantity regardless of price.

Free markets permit price signals to flash between buyers and sellers so that dislocations in supply and demand may be remedied. If consumers reduce demand for particular goods at a price, the seller can launch a 25-percent-off sale to move the merchandise. If a certain commodity is in short supply, consumers can bid up prices, encouraging farmers or fishermen to get to work producing more.

Finally, the integral of these supply-demand curves including interactions is rolled into a general equilibrium, ostensibly dominated by a few factor inputs including preferences for labor and capital. Those two factors of production—labor and capital—and preferences for each revealed as wages and interest rates—are the core of the Federal Reserve's dual mandate. The elite view is if the right Ph.D. economist is seated as Fed chair, with the dual mandate firmly in mind, and money supply as a lever to move the world, the global economy may be pushed to equilibrium and made to run like a fine Swiss watch.

To recite this line of thought is to reveal its absurdity. Almost none of it is true. Self-deception once apparent turns quickly to deception of others to maintain a façade. The elite herd hears the lioness of neonationalism and has started to run.

Economists have spent decades identifying imperfections in the free market model. Price signals are moved by market manipulation. Monopoly power is used to restrict supply and peg prices. Information asymmetries allow sellers to deprive buyers through hidden defects. This and more are freely admitted without ruffling the general equilibrium. Instead elites propose public policy remedies. Monopolies are addressed by antitrust enforcement. Asymmetric information is addressed by warranties. Such remedies are legion. Remedial costs and benefits are hotly debated. Yet the general equilibrium goes unquestioned.

The root of general equilibrium is rational behavior. Rational people save for retirement. Rational people buy more on sale. Rational people buy and hold stocks. Rational people borrow when rates are low. Rational people think ahead. This bundle of beliefs is called rational expectations theory. It is all very neat.

Rational expectations theory holds that people behave predictably in response to price signals. Markets are a medium for the signals. When systemic equilibrium is perturbed through unemployment or recession, central bankers manipulate markets to emit price signals designed to induce preferred behaviors. Once the desired behavior results, equilibrium is restored, and growth is again optimized.

In the real world, behavior is rarely rational as economists define rationality. Economic systems are not in equilibrium; they are complex, dynamic, and subject to critical state chaos and collapse. The conundrum of useful price signals issuing from manipulated prices should give theorists pause. Reliance on MIT professor Jonathan Gruber's belief in the stupidity of everyday Americans helps to reconcile this conundrum for policymakers. But that belief does not withstand scrutiny outside the faculty lounge.

Human behavior is not rational in the ways economists need it to be for their apparatus to work. Modern human irrationality (really rational if considered in an Ice Age context) has been demonstrated by sociologists Daniel Kahneman, Amos Tversky, Dan Ariely, and others over the past thirty years. People do not save enough. They buy on impulse. They react fearfully or exuberantly at different market stages. As a result, the theory of rational expectations is in shreds. Still, central bankers give the theory credence in their policy deliberations.

General equilibrium models also suffer from a fallacy of composition. Elites assume local equilibria can be aggregated into a larger equilibrium called the economy. This is like inferring the totality of human nature from a strand of DNA without ever meeting a human. Complete information on the chemical composition of a human does not allow one to infer speech, cognition, or love. These are emergent properties of the whole human. Likewise, perfect information about the shapes of an infinity of preference curves does not allow inference about the behavior of an economy.

The fatal flaw in equilibrium models is that the degree distribution of market price movements is assumed to be shaped in a bell curve, or so-called normal distribution. The difference between a bell curve system and the alternative power curve system is not just a dusty academic debate over the shapes of two curves. The curves themselves are merely graphical representations of what goes on in each system. The bell curve represents an equilibrium system with a mean-reverting nature. The power curve represents a complex system with an open-ended capacity for extreme events. Empirical data reveal that market prices and extreme events are distributed along a power curve. The normal distribution is a fantasy.

Apple and the Cat

General equilibrium, rational expectations, and efficient markets are not the only fallen pillars of the elite edifice. Free trade is another myth, and a costly one. The modern theoretical case against ostensibly free trade is newer than the critique of efficient markets, with even less support among elite economists. Acquaintance with this critique is needed to understand why elites are defensive, and why the herd's sense of dread is spreading.

The theoretical foundation for free trade is found in the theory of comparative advantage articulated by David Ricardo in *The Principles of Political Economy and Taxation* (1817). It is no dishonor to Ricardo that his theory fails in conditions of globalization. His ideas were brilliant for their time, and advanced the then-young science of economics toward its classical phase.

The same can be said of Sir Isaac Newton, whose ideas on celestial mechanics were surpassed by Albert Einstein's relativity. Newton is counted among our greatest geniuses; Einstein thought so himself. Yet one cannot probe distant galaxies with Newtonian mechanics, nor can one run a twenty-first-century economy on Ricardian principles. You need Einstein to probe galaxies, and you need new trade theories not to wreck the U.S. economy in a globalized age.

What is Ricardo's theory and what are its fatal flaws? The theory of comparative advantage rests on the term "comparative." Before Ricardo, there was a theory of *absolute* advantage. If two nations are trading partners, and one produces goods more efficiently than the other, it favors both nations for the less efficient producer to buy from the more efficient. The importer gets cheaper goods, and the exporter gets a market. Both are better off. It might be possible for Iceland to grow blueberries, but that is hardly efficient. It makes more sense for Iceland to import blueberries from Chile, which has ideal growing conditions. Chile has an *absolute* advantage in growing blueberries, so Chile wins markets for its produce.

Ricardo took this idea further. He said that even if a country does *not* have an absolute advantage in certain products, that is, even if it is a less efficient producer, it can still be an efficient exporter if it has a *comparative* advantage relative to other goods produced by two trading partners. This somewhat counterintuitive idea is explained succinctly by economist Ian Fletcher:

> The whole theory [of comparative advantage] can be cracked open with one simple question:
> *Why don't pro football players mow their own lawns?*
> . . . The average footballer can almost certainly mow his lawn more efficiently than the average professional lawn mower. . . . Because the footballer is more efficient in economic language he has absolute advantage at mowing lawns. Yet nobody finds it strange that he would "import" lawn-mowing services from a less efficient "producer." Why? Obviously, because he has *better things to do with his time.* The theory of comparative advantage says that it is advantageous for America to import some goods simply in order to free up our workforce to produce more-valuable goods instead. We, as a nation, have "better things to do with our time" than produce these less valuable goods. . . . As a result, it is sometimes advantageous for us to import goods from less efficient nations.

In other words, it makes sense for the United States to import cars from Korea even if the United States is a *more efficient car producer,* if this frees up U.S. labor and capital to pursue nanotechnology where the comparative advantage is even greater than it is in cars.

This theory rests on a concept of efficiency. If one cannot measure efficiency, and compare measurements across borders, then the theory cannot reliably be applied. Efficiency derives from the utilization of factors of production. These factors are labor and capital. Labor comes in varied forms—skilled, unskilled, intellectual, and physical. Capital comes in diverse forms including finance, patents, trade secrets, know-how, and natural resources. A producer who applies factors of production to create output at least cost is the most efficient. Absolute efficiency produces absolute advantage, and relative efficiency across products and sectors produces comparative advantage. Efficiency comes down to cost measurement, which presupposes a system of prices measured in money, and derived from markets.

So the theory of comparative advantage relies entirely on a dense network of factors of production, costs, prices, markets, and money to work its will. If one of these network nodes is manipulated or distorted by policy or imperfection, the theory of comparative advantage *does not work* because there is no basis for comparison. Today every one of these nodes is distorted, imperfect, or both. Comparative advantage is a castle in the air—pleasant to imagine, yet totally unreal.

Comparative advantage is the touchstone of the neoliberal consensus, the theoretical foundation for free trade, open capital accounts, and other facets of globalization. When David Ricardo, and earlier, Adam Smith, developed these free market and free trade ideas the world was on a gold standard; exchange rates were anchored to gold. Price comparisons were possible. In the absence of a gold standard or fixed exchange rates, how is the comparison to be made? In theory, floating fiat exchange rates allow comparisons and easy adjustment to terms of trade. What about interest rate manipulation, currency wars, dirty floats, and the rest? Do terms of trade reflect bona fide comparative advantage or manipulated advantage? If the latter, what is the case for free trade?

One distortion embraced by elites is floating exchange rates, a flawed idea foisted on the world by Milton Friedman in the 1970s. If a builder hired you to construct a house using a one-foot ruler, then told you on day two that a foot was thirteen inches, and on day three that a foot was ten inches, and so on, the resulting house would be unsound and in danger of collapse. That's how comparative advantage works under floating exchange rates. Currency hedges are generally unavailable more than one year forward; too short a time for capital commitments that have five- to ten-year horizons.

Floating exchange rates enrich currency traders and speculators, but add costs to commerce and impede capital flows. Exchange rates are ripe for manipulation. Champions of putative free trade based on comparative advantage need to consider the fixed exchange rate regime that prevailed from 1944 to 1971, a golden age of growth and higher real incomes. The elite herd favors free trade *and* floating exchange rates, a recipe for losing U.S. jobs to foreign manipulation.

The next deficiency in the free trade case is mobility of factors of production. Ricardo posited that factors of production were rooted in a home country. Markets work out comparative costs as a basis for trade. Today factors of production, especially capital, are not rooted, they're mobile. Consider the case where China has more efficient labor (due to low costs), and the United States has more efficient capital (due to a deep, liquid financial system). If factors of production were immobile, the United States might have a comparative advantage in manufacturing even with more costly labor due to its lower capital costs. If cheap U.S. capital moves to China, and combines with cheap Chinese labor, then China gains both comparative and absolute advantage. This is not a hypothetical example; it is the quintessence of globalization. Ricardo's theory fails in a world of mobile factors.

Another flaw in Ricardo involves intertemporal flux: the difference between *static* comparative advantage and *dynamic* comparative advantage. A country that does not have comparative advantage at the start of a decade may use protectionism to nurture infant industries and gain comparative advantage by decade's end. Unfair trade practices are used by one country to undermine a trading partner's comparative advantage. The cheater can join the free trade club after its advantage is secured.

A classic use of this method is the United States, which used protectionism from 1776 to 1944 to build the greatest industrial juggernaut the world had ever seen. Since the 1970s, the United States has been on the receiving end of protectionism from Japan, Korea, Taiwan, and China. Today the high-value jobs of the future are created in Asia. This is not due to an *initial* comparative advantage in Asia, but rather a *created* comparative advantage through the use of protectionism and currency manipulation.

Other defects in the theory of comparative advantage involve what are called *externalities*. These are hidden costs that do not enter into direct cost comparisons. China seems more efficient at mining than the United States because China dumps cyanide (used to extract metal from ore) into rivers. Should China be rewarded in terms of trade if the costs of cyanide poisoning are not included in the price of metal exports?

The greatest deficiency in the theory of comparative advantage is that it fails unless *everyone* plays by the rules. The thrust of the Bretton Woods General Agreement on Tariffs and Trade (1947) and its successor, the World Trade Organization (1995), was to force adherence to free trade by the signatories. Exceptions for agricultural subsidies, and cheating by China, leave the world far from the ideal. U.S. free trade policy is best understood as a poker game where the United States is the only participant not seeing the other players' cards.

China's trade policy today resembles U.K. policy in the eighteenth century, and U.S. policy in the nineteenth century. These prior policies involved protectionism, theft of intellectual property, and accumulation of gold. These mercantilist policies worked well for the United Kingdom and the United States. Great Britain was the dominant industrial and trading power until repeal of protectionist Corn Laws in 1846. It then began a seventy-year decline that culminated in near national bankruptcy in 1914. The United States was the dominant industrial and trading power until Bretton Woods in 1944. It began a seventy-year decline, culminating in crisis in 2008.

Decline is not the same as collapse. The United Kingdom enjoyed prosperity in the 1860s, as the United States enjoyed prosperity in the 1960s, after both embraced free trade. This prosperity is best seen as a seed-corn banquet. Both countries were living off the momentum of earlier mercantilism. When that momentum is not renewed it runs out.

Elite neoliberal free traders are relaxed about U.S. job losses because their mind-set lets them imagine jobs being created elsewhere in the economy where the United States retains comparative advantage. The United States leads the world in higher education and high tech. Yet total jobs in both fields are paltry compared with lost manufacturing jobs in recent decades. Even if one accepts that there will be winners and losers in a global trading system, what happens when the number of winners is few, and the losers are many? The answer is lower labor force participation, lower productivity, stagnant wage gains, and greater income inequality—exactly what the United States has experienced since the 1990s ascent of NAFTA and the WTO.

Even if jobs won and lost from trade are comparable in numbers (they're not), all jobs are not created equal. Certain jobs persist yet go nowhere, and do not drive growth. A barista may have a steady job at decent wages, but that's all. The barista will always work behind the counter, and nothing else will come of it because her exertions leave limited scope to apply new technology. Lego-style assembly jobs are not, without exogenous effects, a source of additional jobs.

Conversely, an entrepreneur using an improved manufacturing process creates new jobs directly, spins off intellectual property, and catalyzes upstream and downstream job growth in supply and distribution chains. High-value-added manufacturing jobs that support continual supply-chain improvements in materials, machine tools, and processes are the jobs America should support through policy. Dead-end jobs without positive externalities may safely be left to trading partners.

These free trade dysfunctions were recognized long ago. Joseph A. Schumpeter, in his 1942 classic, *Capitalism, Socialism and Democracy*, wrote, "Traditional theory . . . has since the time of Marshall and Edgeworth been discovering an increasing number of exceptions to the old propositions about perfect competition and . . . free trade, that have shaken that unqualified belief in its virtues cherished by the generation which flourished between Ricardo and Marshall. . . ."

Schumpeter wrote this in an analysis of how large scale enterprises produce positive externalities that offset the perceived problems of bigness. Schumpeter's point was that the entrepreneur is not as concerned about static competition as the dynamic forces he called "creative destruction." The latter drives innovation. Modern analysts make the same point about the benefits of smart protectionist policy. American business is not really competing with foreigners, it's competing with the future, and losing.

The issue is not that Ricardian theory is wrong; it's that the theory relies on assumptions that don't conform to the real world, and is therefore useless as a guide to policy. If comparative advantage is a chimera, and if putative free trade is a rigged game, why do elites insist upon it?

Elite support for so-called free trade is due to the fact that elites share a global perspective at odds with the best interests of the United States. Policies that produce world growth at U.S. expense are endorsed. Policies that benefit the United States while slowing world growth are rejected. Today globalization's triumph over nationalism is energizing a nationalist revival as nations reassess their individual interests.

Certain global corporations profit enormously from the current flawed system. To illustrate this, consider two companies on opposite sides of the mercantilist divide—Apple Inc., the manufacturer of beloved iPhones, and Caterpillar Corporation, "Cat," the largest heavy equipment manufacturer in the world.

Apple exported capital to China, where the capital combined with cheap Chinese labor to produce both absolute and comparative advantage in the manufacture of iPhones. China facilitates this by maintaining a cheap currency, which increases the purchasing power of U.S. consumers relative to Chinese unit labor costs. The United States is by far the largest, richest consumer market in the world. China gains intellectual property, jobs, and hard currency reserves. Apple reaps enormous profits and defers U.S. taxes. Apple thrives, yet creates few jobs in the United States.

Caterpillar manufactures heavy equipment mainly in the United States and sells mainly abroad. Cat must overcome a full array of foreign mercantilist policies including protectionism, nontariff barriers, and cheap currencies. Mercantilism makes Japanese and Korean heavy equipment relatively more attractive to buyers in emerging markets. However, Cat creates high-paying, high-value-added jobs in its U.S. plants.

The divergent dynamics of Apple and Cat bear directly on economic debates about currency wars and the deflationary impact of the strong dollar. Economist Thomas I. Palley summarizes this divergence:

> When U.S. companies produced domestically and looked to export, a weaker dollar was in their commercial interest, and they lobbied against dollar overvaluation. However, under the new model, U.S. corporations looked to produce offshore and import into the United States. This reversed their commercial interest, making them proponents of a strong dollar. This is because a strong dollar reduces the dollar costs of foreign production, raising the profit margins on their foreign production sold in the United States at U.S. prices.

This summary shows the irrelevance of comparative advantage. A small group of global corporations with mobile capital, hair-trigger ability to relocate plants, and political muscle to move exchange rates in the absence of a gold standard make a mockery of free trade. These companies create their own advantages and write their own rules. Manipulations are not limited to U.S.-based global companies. They are practiced with even more success by German, Japanese, and Chinese behemoths.

This comparison of the divergent interests of Apple and Cat demonstrates why free trade is a mirage. Mobile capital, technology transfer, protectionism, and manipulation of exchange rates are used to offset the comparative advantage America might once have had. When the transfer of input factors is complete, comparative advantage is lost forever. The United States is left with dead-end jobs or no jobs at all.

U.S. trade policy is mainly about opening doors for Cat abroad. Instead policy should be aimed at bringing Apple jobs back home. More of Apple's value chain needs to reside in the United States. Those who claim this is inefficient under Ricardian theories should ask the following: If U.S. workers cannot get better jobs, and are hobbled by high debts, who will buy what global companies make? The United States should aggressively use tariffs and trade barriers to promote jobs that catalyze growth—exactly as Alexander Hamilton proposed in his *Report on Manufactures* presented to Congress in 1791.

The United States would benefit from an immediate 30 percent import duty on all goods from all sources. This could be made revenue neutral by pairing the tariff with a 10 percent cut in payroll taxes. An imported iPhone would be more expensive (unless Apple chose to reduce profit margins by lowering prices). But the payroll tax savings would help consumers pay for the phones, if that is their preference. The expected outcome is that Apple would relocate good jobs to the United States, where it could reap the combined benefits of lower tariffs and lower payroll taxes. The impact of this policy goes beyond Apple and iPhones to include all high-value-added imports.

The handmaiden of elite dominance is misinformed public opinion resulting from pro-trade propaganda by voices from the Council on Foreign Relations to *The New York Times*. This herd's party line is that free trade is good and tariffs are bad. This is what reporters were taught in undergraduate economics classes ten or twenty years ago.

Elite opinion carriers disdain those who question free trade dogma. These pseudo-experts tell you Smoot-Hawley tariffs caused the Great Depression, an implausible view because the depression began earlier and was caused by Federal Reserve monetary policy blunders. The United States had average tariffs of 44.6 percent before Smoot-Hawley, and 53.2 percent after—not an extreme increase. Ian Fletcher points out that tariff increases in 1861, 1864, 1890, and 1922 did *not* produce depressions, while recessions occurred in 1873 and 1893 *without* tariff increases. The case for causality between tariffs and recessions is somewhere between weak and nonexistent. This comes as a surprise to most pundits.

A new U.S. tariff will leave certain dead-end assembly and agricultural jobs with our trading partners, yet create more high-value-added jobs in the United States. A tariff impedes the efforts of U.S. trading partners to capture the high-value-added jobs for themselves with their own battery of trade barriers, intellectual property theft, and local content requirements. America, the world's largest consumer economy, needs this type of structural change to raise potential growth. The result is higher productivity and higher real wages, important steps toward debt sustainability.

There is a case for open markets and low tariffs, but it is a special case, not a general case, and the case is political, not economic. When your economy is intact, yet your trading partners are in ruins, exactly the relationship between the United States and Europe after the Second World War, it makes sense to provide open markets and cheap finance to the ruined party to restart the game. Free trade in the form of customs unions also makes good sense among nations with a history of warfare and destruction—exactly the case inside Europe at the same time.

A rare convergence of a special case to restart world trade with an imperative to prevent another war in the late 1940s made the Bretton Woods institutions not only useful, but necessary. Those special circumstances do not apply to China, India, and the rest of the world today. The United States is no longer helping its partners, it is hurting itself.

Empire of Debt

The elite worldview rests on the intellectual pillars of equilibrium models, monetarism, Keynesianism, floating exchange rates, free trade, globalization, and fiat money. Meanwhile, the real world is best understood through the lens of complexity theory, conditional probability, behavioral psychology, currency wars, neomercantilism, and gold. Cognitive dissonance between the elite worldview and real-world economics is taking its toll on elite self-confidence and control. The elites now divide into two types: those who are confused by lost credibility, and those who are quietly panicked because they understand their intellectual failure and its consequences.

The principal rebuttal to this critique of the elite consensus is the demonstrable global growth and prosperity since the end of the Second World War. The 1950s and 1960s witnessed exceptionally strong growth in the United States, Canada, Western Europe, and Japan, with low unemployment and little inflation. Of course, this growth emerged from a low baseline given the devastation caused by the war. There was ample space for utilization of factor inputs, especially abundant human capital, and finance capital supplied by the United States.

However, prevailing conditions in this period of initial prosperity do not conform to conditions today. The 1950s and 1960s were defined by fixed exchange rates, a gold standard, balanced budgets, tariffs, and trade preferences. All of these conditions are antithetical to the elite formula today.

The 1970s and 1980s were a transitional period for the postwar Bretton Woods institutions. Gold was abandoned as a monetary standard. Floating exchange rates emerged in the mid-1970s. Still, the demise of the gold standard was muted by the rise of a new dollar standard during the Reagan administration. King Dollar was finessed by Treasury Secretary James Baker through the Plaza Accord in 1985, and the Louvre Accord in 1987, which yielded broad agreement among major economies on acceptable exchange rates. King Dollar was not a fixed rate regime, but it was the next best thing, bolstered by Paul Volcker's success at achieving low inflation after the near-hyperinflationary episode of 1977 to 1981. Efforts at monetary convergence in Europe, albeit uneven and marked by occasional ruptures, served as a rough substitute for the gold standard.

The 1970s and 1980s were also a heyday of neo-Keynesianism and monetarism. Keynesianism justified persistent budget deficits, while monetarism disparaged fixed exchange rates and insisted that control of the fiat money stock produces maximum sustainable real growth without inflation. An intellectual battle between Hayek and Friedman on the one hand, and John Maynard Keynes on the other, was mooted, but both schools were now embedded in academia. What they shared was a thirst for government control; the only difference was whether control came from fiscal or monetary authorities. The neoliberal consensus favored both.

The ascent of globalized elites occurred after 1989, the dawn of a second age of globalization, a distant echo of the first age of globalization from 1870 to 1914. In 1989, the cold war ended, the Berlin Wall fell, and the Washington Consensus was announced in a seminal article by John Williamson, an English economist working in Washington, D.C. Williamson's article summarized views that had been evolving since the 1970s. He condensed these views into a playbook for a newly globalized world. Williams called for free trade, open capital accounts, direct foreign investment, and protection of intellectual property. He also called for fiscal discipline, yet in practice this was reserved for emerging markets, and not followed by developed economies themselves. The Washington Consensus was enforced ruthlessly throughout the 1990s by the IMF, urged on by Bob Rubin's U.S. Treasury.

The 1990s were a zenith for ostensibly free trade. NAFTA, CAFTA, and other multilateral trade agreements were imposed. Elites bathed in the longest peacetime expansion in U.S. history, from 1991 to 2000, from the end of the Bush 41 administration through almost all of the

Clinton years. Russia reached for capitalism, China emerged from a chaotic century, and Asian Tigers were on the prowl. This performance seemed to validate the elite worldview.

Beneath the surface, rot set in. Corruption was institutionalized in Russia and China, income inequality soared, and the low-hanging fruit of factor utilization in emerging markets was quickly gone. In historical terms, the economic success of the 1990s can be seen in the same way as the apparent success of free trade for the United Kingdom in the late nineteenth century, and the United States in the mid-twentieth. Success was not the fruit of new policies so much as the harvesting of gains created by prior protection. There was growth, but it was not sustainable. Beyond that, the superficial and nonsustainable success of the elite consensus in the 1990s and early 2000s can be explained in a single word: debt.

The explosive growth of debt—personal, corporate, and sovereign—over the course of the 1990s and early twenty-first century is unprecedented. In the 1990s, debt growth was driven by consumer credit, home equity loans, and corporate debt. From 2000 to 2007 the mix shifted toward developed economy sovereign debt and subprime mortgages. After 2007, growth in developed economy sovereign debt continued while student loans and emerging markets debt grew exponentially.

Since 2009, emerging markets dollar-denominated corporate debt expanded by $9 *trillion*. Total securities issued by energy exploration and development firms, much of it below investment grade, exceed $5 *trillion*. Growth in all forms of debt exceeded $60 *trillion* with no end in sight.

A standard gauge of debt sustainability is the debt-to-GDP ratio. From 2000 to 2013, the global debt-to-GDP ratio, excluding financial firms, rose from 163 percent to 212 percent. In the same period, the developed economy debt-to-GDP ratio rose from 310 percent to 385 percent. These trends show no pause or deleveraging as a result of the 2008 financial crisis. While private debt levels declined somewhat after 2008, growth in government debt more than made up the difference and kept total debt elevated. Total government debt in developed economies rose from 80 percent of GDP at the start of 2009 to 110 percent of GDP by 2014. Emerging markets debt, driven largely by China, excluding financial firms, went from 125 percent of GDP at the start of 2009 to 140 percent by 2014. The debt-to-GDP ratio for China alone, excluding financial firms, was over 200 percent by 2014.

In a definitive 2014 study (the "Geneva Report"), the influential International Center for Monetary and Banking Studies based in Geneva summarized the situation as follows:

> The world is still leveraging up . . . the debt ratio is still rising to all-time highs. . . . Until 2008, the leveraging up was being led by developed markets, but since then emerging economics (especially China) have been the driving force. . . . The level of overall leverage in Japan is off the charts. . . .
>
> Contrary to widely held beliefs, six years on from the beginning of the financial crisis in advanced economies, the global economy is not yet on a deleveraging path. Indeed, according to our assessment, the ratio of global total debt, excluding financials, over GDP . . . has kept increasing at an unabated pace and breaking new highs. . . .

These debt levels, while unprecedented, might be sustainable if there were global growth sufficient to support them. There is not. The stagnation of global growth in the past fifteen years is another facet of the failure of the elite consensus.

Researchers for the Geneva Report compiled a developed economy GDP index set at 100 for 2008 to compare actual growth since the crisis with potential growth based on pre-crisis trends. By 2014, potential growth reached a level of 111, yet *actual* growth struggled to reach 102. This difference between potential growth and actual growth is called the output gap. In a normal economic recovery, the economy briefly grows above potential (due to slack capacity and above-trend factor utilization), and the output gap disappears. That has not happened in this recovery;

the output gap is persistent and growing. Lost output is bad enough if individual well-being and living standards were the only issues at stake. Lost output combined with excessive debt is toxic. The Geneva Report describes this dangerous mix as follows:

> The ongoing vicious circle of leverage and policy attempts to deleverage, on the one hand, and the slower nominal growth on the other, set the basis for either a slow, painful process of deleveraging or for another crisis. . . . In our view, this makes the world still vulnerable to a further round in the sequence of financial crises that have occurred over the past two decades.

The report shouts alarm at the virulent cycle of high debt and slow growth:

> An important obstacle to recovery from a financial crisis consists of the vicious loop between growth and leverage . . . since paying down high debt levels deters activity, with the slowdown in GDP dynamics making the deleveraging process more painful in turn.

A useful taxonomy of crises divides collapse and recovery cycles into three types. A Type 1 crisis involves a drop in the level of actual output. If followed by an above-trend or V-shaped recovery, the output gap is made up and trend growth resumes. Economic effects of a Type 1 crisis are painful, yet temporary. Sweden in the early 1990s is an example.

A Type 2 crisis involves a drop in the level of *potential* output. In this situation, initial output losses may be small, but an output gap is created relative to the former trend and expands over time. The long-term costs in Type 2 crises are enormous. Japan since 1990 is cited as an example of a Type 2 crisis.

A Type 3 crisis involves a drop in the level of actual output *and* potential output. In this situation, initial output losses are large, are never recovered, and the output gap grows over time. This is the worst of all worlds with large losses, no recovery, and continued weak growth.

According to the data shown in the Geneva Report, advanced economies led by the United States are in a Type 3 crisis. The reason this diagnosis did not appear sooner was due to the use of leverage to mask policy failures. The Geneva Report concludes:

> The observed acceleration in growth from the late 1990s to 2007 was supported by the build-up in global debt . . . and at the same time encouraged the increase in leverage in many economies that fed the asset-price and balance-sheet expansion. This expansion phase ultimately came to an end in the financial crisis of 2008–9.

The elite dream of globalization and shared prosperity was a mirage fueled by debt. The mirage dissipated in 2008. While the mirage is gone, the debt remains. The paths out of debt are dangerous at best, catastrophic at worst. The safest path involves structural reforms to overturn the elite consensus and return to neomercantilist policies to create jobs and growth inside the United States. The most dangerous path involves more of the same—more debt, more leverage, more derivatives—in a quixotic quest for self-sustaining growth that will not appear.

As this realization sinks in, the elite herd instinct is heightened. Central bank balance sheets are distended to actuate inflation to provide nominal if not real growth to deal with debt. Still, deflation stalks the herd like a lioness on the savannah. Elites realize money printing may produce not *price* inflation, but *asset* inflation, and form new bubbles that could burst and destroy confidence for two generations. The ice-nine solution is standing by if that happens. For now elites push on with reflation like a forlorn platoon neck-deep in the Big Muddy.

Cul-de-sac

The elite neoliberal consensus rests on rhetoric about free markets and free trade limned by economists from Adam Smith and David Ricardo to Milton Friedman. Yet free markets and free trade are flawed in theory, nonexistent in practice.

Notionally, the free market paradigm resembles the popular board game Monopoly, invented in the Great Depression. In Monopoly, each player begins in the same space with the same amount of money, governed by the same rules. As in real life, luck plays a role in the dice toss, yet over time luck evens out. There are differences in players' skills; that is the point of the game. Savvy players know the orange properties starting with St. James Place are good to own because they are close to Jail; other players land near them with disproportionate frequency. In theory, markets reward this kind of skill.

What if the rules are ignored? Imagine a Monopoly game where after a few turns one player suddenly declares her money is worth twice as much as every other player's and casually reaches into the bank to grab a stack of $500 bills. The game would descend into chaos; free market elements would be lost. This is exactly what happens in the course of central bank monetary policy, currency wars, and trade manipulation. The free market model is overturned.

For the United States and the world, the solution is not to whine about unfairness or chase a chimera, but to adopt policies to ensure growth and jobs in the United States and explore ways for *cooperative* partners to share that prosperity, while they pursue their own paths. Noncooperative partners should be left to their own devices.

Viewed from the longer perspective of debt expansion since the 1990s, the financial collapse in 2008 was symptomatic of a more malign condition. Public policy used credit expansion and asset bubbles to substitute for sustainable growth. Workers did not share in the higher returns to capital from globalization. The resulting income inequality is more than a moral issue. Income inequality hurts consumption, and by extension investment, leaving net exports (and associated currency wars) and government spending (and associated debt) as the only growth engines.

Deflation is the elite's deepest secret fear. Alan Greenspan's much-criticized too-low-for-too-long interest rate policy from 2002 to 2005 was an effort to fend off deflation that appeared in 2001. Deflation was deferred, not destroyed. Greenspan's policies delayed deflation at the expense of asset bubbles, which burst beginning in 2007. Then the deflation, which never really went away, reemerged. The Federal Reserve, a one-trick pony, repeated the Greenspan blunder with Bernanke and Yellen's zero interest rate policy from 2008 to 2015. The result is larger asset bubbles today. At no point have policymakers dealt with the underlying causes of deflation, which arise from demographics, technology, deleveraging, and neomercantilism from Mexico to Malaysia.

One rejoinder in favor of free trade and open markets is that the United States is strong enough to absorb the costs of a rigged system while the world is enriched by job creation in other countries. If the world is better off, and if the United States is slightly less better off than it might otherwise be, that's a small price to pay for a richer, more peaceful planet.

Apart from the condescension toward unemployed working-class Americans embedded in this globalist view, is it even true? Or does average global growth mask grotesque income inequality where workers may be slightly better off, but the bulk of gains are siphoned by corrupt oligarchs busily buying condos from Vancouver to Mayfair for $50 million apiece or more?

If U.S. public policy focused on supporting high-value-added manufacturing at home, income gains would be spread more widely because America does not have an "oligarch problem" to the same extent as Asia, Africa, and Latin America. U.S. workers with higher real incomes could afford to buy more imported goods alongside domestic ones. U.S. trading partners would specialize in less desirable jobs while U.S. workers would have access to better ones.

The political problem in the United States is that Democrats and Republicans march in lockstep on the issue of free trade. Some voices dissent, yet the free trade paradigm embodied in NAFTA, the new Trans-Pacific Partnership (TPP), and the Transatlantic Trade and Investment Partnership (TTIP) agreements transcends partisanship. NAFTA was negotiated by Bush 41 and signed by Bill Clinton. The Trans-Pacific Partnership was proposed by President Obama and supported by Republican leaders. When the two parties join hands it's more groupthink than an end to gridlock.

A sensible solution to this political stasis begins by abolishing the corporate income tax, raising the minimum wage, and empowering workers through a version of the German codetermination law that places worker representatives on corporate boards. The left would howl about corporate tax cuts, the right would condemn codetermination, and both would be seen for the ideologues they are. Smart policy— helping capital *and* helping workers—is the way forward for the United States.

Elite fear grows with the realization that the world is not in a cyclical recovery, but a secular depression. As defined by Keynes, a depression is:

> A chronic condition of sub-normal activity for a considerable period without any marked tendency either towards recovery or towards complete collapse.

Keynes's view was refined by the Geneva Report, which describes a Type 3 crisis as one in which output drops dramatically and does not bounce back sharply, but plots a permanently lower trend. In the words of the Geneva Report:

> What occurred after 2007 was a debt crisis rather than a recession: the 5% output loss until Q1 2009 was persistent . . . and the loss actually widened relative to what could be considered as the trend prevailing until 2007, as growth slowed significantly.

Depression cannot be cured, only ameliorated, by monetary policy. The solution to depression is structural change. The Great Depression ended only with massive debt-financed investment and mobilization of labor to fight the Second World War.

The endgame has emerged. Debt is compounding faster than growth. Monetary policy is impotent except to blow bubbles and buy time. Structural change is impeded by political dysfunction. Substitution of sovereign debt for private debt has run its course; now the sovereigns themselves are stretched.

Debt, deflation, demographics, and depression are demolishing elite dreams of free trade, free markets, and free capital flows. Elites hope for the turn of a friendly card, but the deck is stacked by decades of denial about income inequality and lost jobs. Some elites are abandoning ship, taking their winnings and buying condos, private jets, even islands, storing bullion and fine art in private vaults. Other elites continue down the cul-de-sac of globalization even as their confusion grows.

CHAPTER 8

CAPITALISM, FASCISM, AND DEMOCRACY

There is little reason to believe that . . . socialism will mean the advent of the civilization of which orthodox socialists dream. It is much more likely to present fascist features. That would be a strange answer to Marx's prayer. But history sometimes indulges in jokes of questionable taste.

Joseph A. Schumpeter
Capitalism, Socialism and Democracy **(1942)**

Show me the man and I'll find you the crime.

Lavrentiy Beria,
chief of the Secret Police (NKVD) under Stalin

Schumpeter Reconsidered

Joseph Schumpeter's name conjures the phrase "creative destruction," his best-known intellectual contribution, one of the most powerful economic insights of the twentieth century, with important implications today.

Schumpeter's concept was that capitalism is a dynamic force more potent than the enterprises that rise and fall within it. Capitalist progress demands capitalists' failure. This was succinctly stated by Schumpeter in his 1942 masterpiece, *Capitalism, Socialism and Democracy:*

> Capitalism . . . never can be stationary. . . . The fundamental impulse that sets and keeps the capitalist engine in motion comes from the new consumers' goods, the new methods of production or transportation, the new markets, the new forms of industrial organization that capitalist enterprise creates.
>
> The opening up of new markets . . . incessantly revolutionizes the economic structure from within, incessantly destroying the old one, incessantly creating a new one. This process of Creative Destruction is the essential fact about capitalism.

As with many original observations, what seems obvious in hindsight was revolutionary when it was offered. The fact that capitalism is a dynamic, wealth-creating force was long recognized, starting with Adam Smith in 1776, and by the nineteenth-century classical economists. What was new in Schumpeter's creative destruction was not the *creative* force, but the *destructive* force, the idea that capital must be destroyed to unlock resources for new capitalist endeavors.

Schumpeter wrote at a critical juncture between the end of the Great Depression and the start of the Second World War. Capitalism was on trial and socialism was in vogue, including in the United States, where it had failed to take root during previous socialist cycles in the late nineteenth and early twentieth centuries. The Franklin Delano Roosevelt administration, 1933–45, was filled with socialist reformers and endeavors from the massive Tennessee Valley Authority power project to agricultural communes like the federal farm camp at Marysville, California.

Capitalism, widely seen as a failed system during the Great Depression, was associated with big business in the form of corporations such as RCA, General Motors, Standard Oil of New Jersey, U.S. Steel, and other behemoths. Competition was no longer capitalism's defining characteristic; monopoly was.

Schumpeter was unfazed by the monopoly charge thrown at capitalism. He admired big business and supported monopoly-type practices. In his view, big business offered consumers wider variety, broad distribution networks, and lower prices. He wrote,

> In analyzing . . . business strategy . . . the investigating economist or government agent sees price policies that seem to him predatory and restrictions of output. . . . He does not see that restrictions of this type are, in the conditions of the perennial gale, incidents . . . of a long-run process of expansion which they protect rather than impede.
>
> Largest-scale plans could in many cases not materialize at all if it were not known from the outset that competition will be discouraged by heavy capital requirements or lack of experience, or that means are available to discourage or checkmate it so as to gain the time and space for further developments.

It is not difficult to reconcile this seeming contradiction between Schumpeter as champion of creative destruction and as supporter of monopoly big business. Schumpeter's great intuition was that businesses do not compete against one another, they compete against the *future*. It is the unforeseen, unexpected enterprise of the future that destroys monoliths, not today's competition or antitrust enforcement. Schumpeter, writing in 1942, anticipated Uber's disruption of taxi monopolies and Matt Drudge's demolition of daily newspapers. No business, however large, is safe. What keeps a monopolist up at night is not the competition; it's the future.

Schumpeter's legacy became captive to his devotees—a common fate of iconoclasts. The creative destruction meme is now commonplace (although it may be more urgent than those who recite the cliché realize). What strikes one about Schumpeter is that his creative destruction sketch is a vignette. It takes up five pages in a standard 430-page edition of *Capitalism, Socialism and Democracy*—barely 1 percent of the book. The remainder, on historical processes, and the inevitability of socialism, is more important for comprehending the economic path we traverse today.

Joseph A. Schumpeter was born in 1883 in Moravia, then in the Austro-Hungarian Empire, today the Czech Republic. He earned a Ph.D. from the University of Vienna in 1906 under the direction of Eugen von Böhm-Bawerk, a devoted follower of Carl Menger and early exponent of the Austrian school of economics.

Schumpeter was professor of economics at Harvard University from 1932 until his death in 1950. He led a colorful private life, and may be the only twentieth-century economist who was also a duelist. In the words of his biographer, Thomas McCraw, "He often said that he aspired to be the world's greatest economist, lover and horseman. Then came the punch line: things were not working out with the horses."

Despite study in Vienna and guidance by Böhm-Bawerk, Schumpeter did not adhere to the Austrian school. He followed an earlier Historical school of economics developed in Germany in the nineteenth century. This school blends history, politics, and social science to achieve a more veracious view of economics. It rejects mathematical models for the most part because models are specific to time and place, temporary reflections of economic conditions. In contrast, history provides a broader perspective and more accurately reveals the impetus for human action. Above all, the Historical school emphasizes reality over abstraction.

What unites Historical school members are not their conclusions, which vary widely (to the point of contradiction), but rather their inductive method, which relies on close consideration of long-term processes and impressions drawn from that consideration. Earlier adherents to the Historical school include Walter Bagehot, Max Weber, and Karl Marx. Schumpeter is the last pure representative of this school, although Hyman Minsky, Alan Greenspan, and Nobelist Robert Solow were all strongly influenced by him. The Historical school's inductive method and use of history have today been brushed aside by neo-Keynesian equations and an Austrian insistence on money agency.

Yet Schumpeter's insights into capital formation through entrepreneurship, and its disruptive impact on prevalent business models—creative destruction—seem in sync with the age of Amazon and Netflix. This revival comes at a time when Austrian money theories are stymied by velocity's volatility, and neo-Keynesian models prove unprepared for a new liquidity trap. It is past time to take Schumpeter off the shelf and give historical method its due.

Consideration of Schumpeter today comes mostly from those interested in microeconomics—the theory of the firm, and the individual. A Schumpeterian renascence needs to consider his macroeconomic perspective, including his illumination of global growth dynamics. Schumpeter's long-wave historical perspective seems the right antidote to Karl Popper's slow, steady piecemeal social engineering. Schumpeter's method serves as an antagonist to the sixty-year slog of the SDR from ad hoc remedy to world money. Schumpeter lets us see these processes in historical settings and prophesy their paths.

Schumpeter's reputational eclipse in the late twentieth century was partly due to his prediction that socialism would supplant capitalism. In this, Schumpeter agreed with Karl Marx, although he was relentless at finding flaws in Marxian theory. Specifically, Schumpeter said Marx's theory of revolution was nonsense; he quipped that revolutions benefit no one but revolutionaries.

What Schumpeter admired about Marx was not his exact predictions, but Marx's method, which considered the rise and fall of social classes over centuries. Using Marx's method Schumpeter saw the slow, steady rise of socialism, existing—for a time—side by side with capitalism, and operating comfortably within a democratic framework.

Seeing capitalist success first in the 1960s in Europe and Japan, then in the 1980s Thatcher-Reagan revolution, then China's ascendance in the 1990s under Deng Xiaoping's mantra, "To be rich is glorious," it seems hard to credit Schumpeter's socialist thesis. The triumph of free market capitalism is so deeply entrenched from Seattle to Shanghai that Schumpeter's glimpse of socialism's irresistibility seems misguided.

Still, Schumpeter was right.

For Schumpeter, socialism was not a dictatorship of the proletariat, but an economic system directed by the state, operated by elites he called "Planners," for the presumed benefit of workers. The winners in this vision were the Planners and workers. The losers were the bourgeoisie—what we call the middle class.

Schumpeter was prophetic. Today's U.S. middle class has been hollowed out, and income inequality has reached extreme levels not seen since the 1920s, and before that, the 1890s. Society devolved largely into elites and workers as Schumpeter expected.

In the United States, median household income measured in constant 2014 dollars peaked at $57,843 in 1999. By 2014, the comparable figure was $53,657, a stunning *decline* of over 7 percent in fifteen years. The American household is growing poorer by the day. However, the decline was not evenly distributed. Median household income in Washington, D.C. *increased* almost 25 percent in the same fifteen-year period. While the nation stagnates, residents of the capital city grow richer. This contrast shows the elites' success at siphoning wealth from everyday Americans through taxes, regulations, and parasitic agencies.

A McKinsey Global Institute study released in July 2016 titled "Poorer than Their Parents?" documented that trends in income inequality are not confined to the United States. These trends are found globally in developed economies from Western Europe to Australia. The report says:

> The debate over rising inequality in advanced economies has focused on income and wealth gains going disproportionately to top earners. In this research, we look at an aspect that has received less attention: households in developed economies whose incomes have not advanced when compared to their peers in the past. Examining this issue in three separate ways, we found a very substantial increase in the number of such households.

Between 65 and 70 percent of households in 25 advanced economies, the equivalent of 540 million to 580 million people, were in segments of the income distribution whose real market incomes—their wages and income from capital—were flat or had fallen in 2014 compared with 2005. This compared with less than 2 percent, or fewer than ten million people, who experienced this phenomenon between 1993 and 2005. Government transfers and lower tax rates reduced the effect on disposable incomes: 20 to 25 percent of households were in segments of the income distribution whose disposable income was flat or down between 2005 and 2014, compared with less than 2 percent in 1993–2005.

In other words, middle-class incomes are stagnant even as the rich get richer. Socialism in the form of government transfer payments mitigated some, but not all, of the impact. This is exactly what Schumpeter predicted—socialism's rise, not by revolution, but rather by stealth, using capitalist wealth to buy off the working class while crushing the bourgeoisie.

The McKinsey study highlights this point about socialist income transfers,

Today's younger generation is at risk of ending up poorer than their parents. Most population segments experienced flat or falling incomes in the 2002–12 decade but young, less-educated workers were hardest hit. . . .

Government policy and labor-market practices helped determine the extent of flat or falling incomes. In Sweden, for example, where the government intervened to preserve jobs, market incomes fell or were flat for only 20 percent, while disposable income advanced for almost everyone. In the United States, government taxes and transfers turned a decline in market incomes for 81 percent of income segments into an increase in disposable income for nearly all households.

Flat or falling incomes for the majority of the population could reduce demand growth and increase the need for social spending. Social consequences are also possible. . . .

Longer-run demographic and labor trends will continue to weigh on income advancement. Even if economies resume their historical high-growth trajectory, we project that 30 to 40 percent of income segments may not experience market income gains in the next decade if labor-market shifts such as workplace automation accelerate. If the slow-growth conditions of 2005–12 persist, as much as 70 to 80 percent of income segments in advanced economies may experience flat or falling market incomes to 2025.

Schumpeter saw that it was nonsense to pay workers $40,000 per year and then have the state collect $10,000 in taxes. It is more efficient for the state to pay the worker $30,000. The net to the worker is the same, and an inefficient pretense of private salaries and public taxation is eliminated. Schumpeter's suggestion has found new life in policy proposals for a Basic Guaranteed Income championed in various forms by Bernie Sanders on the left and Charles Murray on the right. The expansion of food stamps, disability payments, Obamacare, Medicare, and the earned income credit are all forms of government income maintenance, evidence of a movement toward true socialism.

Schumpeter said democracy was not an ideology in which the will of the people was fulfilled. Instead it was a process by which elites competed for leadership roles. Once an election is over, voters are ignored and winning elites carry out preconceived plans. The United States and other democracies hold elections, yet benefits and bureaucracies balloon, regardless of electoral outcomes.

Then there is China, the world's second largest economy, officially Communist, yet using a state capitalist model that Schumpeter called socialist. Schumpeter made it clear that socialism works perfectly well with or without democratic institutions. In consonance with Schumpeter's understanding of democracy as a channel by which planners take turns, what matters economically is not voting, but planning. All the world's major economies today are planned either by central committees or by central banks.

Capitalist heroes of Silicon Valley are *entrepreneurial* in the way Schumpeter understood entrepreneurship before computers were invented. Yet Schumpeter did not equate entrepreneurship with capitalism. He expected that entrepreneurs would always play a role except in the most repressive conditions. He saw no contradiction between entrepreneurship and socialism because a successful entrepreneur slides easily into the elite class alongside the politician and planner.

The modern entrepreneur's drive to outsource or automate production has decimated the middle class, provided workers with inexpensive amusements, and allocated vast riches to elites. It is the middle class, what Schumpeter and Marx called the bourgeoisie, that disappears, not entrepreneurs.

Schumpeter diagnosed capitalism's decline with uncanny accuracy. He saw decline not as an event that occurs overnight, but rather as a process that unfolds in stages leading to inadequate aggregate demand, what he called "stagnationism." In 1946, Schumpeter wrote, "Success in conducting a business enterprise depends . . . much more on the ability to deal with labor leaders, politicians and public officials than it does on business ability in the proper sense of the term. . . . The businessman who is incessantly thrown out of his stride . . . by having to be 'up before' this or that board has no steam left for dealing with his technological and commercial problems." And Schumpeter perfectly anticipated the modern Federal Reserve when he wrote that "the business organism cannot function according to design when its most important 'parameters of action'—wages, prices, interest—are transferred to the political sphere and there dealt with . . . according to the ideas of some planners."

Schumpeter summarized the endgame for capitalism in his prognosis for the late twentieth century:

Labor unrest, price regulation, vexatious administration and irrational taxation are quite adequate to produce results for income and employment that will look exactly like a verification of the stagna-tionist theory and may indeed produce situations in which public deficit spending imposes itself. We may even witness . . . conditions in which people will be reluctant to carry out their investment decisions. . . . Whatever it is, it will be a dominant factor in the social situation not only in the United States but also in the world. But only for the next half century or so. The long-run diagnosis . . . [viz. the decline of capitalism and rise of socialism] will not be affected.

Schumpeter was not an ideologue, much less an apologist for social-ism. He was a clear-eyed analyst of economics as a historical process. He had no preference for socialism; he simply said it would inevitably re-place capitalism. It has to a great extent, although most have not no-ticed. In Schumpeter's view, the final step in capitalism's displacement by socialism is government control of capital. Ice-nine implementation in the next financial crisis will achieve that.

Schumpeter left a chilling coda to his work on socialism. He identi-fied the slippery slope by which socialism blends into fascism once plan-ning is entrenched, business and government are intertwined, and political parties are homogenous. He saw that fascism is more the left's creature than the right's. His description of Russia, ruled by Stalin when he wrote, applies squarely seventy years later: "The trouble with Russia is not that she is socialist but that she is Russia . . . essentially a militarist autocracy which, because it rules by means of a single and strictly disci-plined party and does not admit freedom of the press, partakes of one of the defining characteristics of Fascism and exploits the masses in the Marxist sense."

Finally, Schumpeter foresaw a war weariness prevalent in America today: "When violently excited by propaganda the country may enter upon or accept an activist course of interference beyond the seas. But it soon tires of it, and tired it is now. . . . Let Russia swallow one or two more countries, what of it?"

It is too much to call Schumpeter a complexity theorist—he died ten years before complexity was discovered as a branch of physics. Yet his view of historical processes fits well with the extended time frames for which complexity theory holds the most explanatory power. Complexity provides models for comprehension of the slow, steady buildup of dense networks that suddenly, catastrophically collapse. Seismic faults, forests, and financial markets are all dynamic arrays in which systems may appear stable until a sudden earthquake, conflagration, or crash destroys everything. Complexity theorists know that apparent stability is a mask for rising tension.

The rise and fall of civilizations is the grandest example of complexity theory applied to human affairs. Schumpeter's consideration of capitalism's rise and fall, while not specific to one civilization, is the kind of study to which complexity theory lends valuable tools. Schumpeter eschewed Keynesian models because of the artifice in holding most variables constant while monotonically isolating one as the "cause" of the phenomena under study. Today a twenty-first-century mélange of a Schumpeterian long view and massive computing power—unavailable to Schumpeter—allows for a rapid expansion of recursive functions and simulation of human action via cellular automata. Schumpeter would surely look benignly on such efforts as a reasonable simulacrum of his deep historical processes.

Society stands on Schumpeter's shoulders with new tools of complexity theory to look over a ridgeline at the rise of socialism and fascism, one and the same.

The New Praetorians

In ancient Rome, the Praetorian Guard were an elite military unit that provided personal protection to emperors. Their evolution is a cautionary tale.

Praetorians originally guarded the commander's dwelling while on campaign. The name "praetorian" is derived from *praetor,* a Roman general; his tent was called the praetorium. In the late Roman Republic, Julius Caesar used such a guard. Over time, the Praetorian Guard grew larger. It included the best-equipped, most elite troops, handpicked by the commander.

The presence of a personal guard in the field was not problematic. Conflicts arose when the commander returned to Rome after a victorious military campaign. The Roman Republic prohibited a troop presence inside Rome itself. Julius Caesar intentionally disregarded this taboo. Caesar brought his guard with him as he crossed the Rubicon on his way to Rome in 49 BC. Caesar remarked, *"alea iacta est"*—the die is cast.

Caesar entered Rome with his personal guard in January 49 BC. This act of insurrection led swiftly to civil war, Caesar's assassination, the fall of the Roman Republic, and the emergence of the Roman Empire under Augustus. It was Augustus who formally established the Praetorian Guard based on the earlier tradition of personal bodyguards. Its size was set at nine thousand men, about division strength in a modern army. Augustus stationed most of the guard just outside Rome in deference to tradition, but kept some forces on active duty inside the city—in effect, history's first police force.

In the early centuries AD, the Praetorian Guard's role evolved from guarding emperors to selecting them. They assassinated emperors on their own initiative or at the behest of elites including cabals of senators. Praetorians installed new emperors, sometimes of their choosing, sometimes based on bribes from ambitious office seekers. Praetorian symbolism survives today as red festooned Roman helmets on the badges of Air Force honor guards of U.S. presidents.

Yet the Praetorian Guard legacy is more than symbolic. The United States has evolved rapidly from a republic to a country in which the military and militarized police acting on orders from the Department of Justice under White House political direction, aided by high-tech surveillance and big data relationship awareness programs, target citizens based on political or social beliefs. The ideal American Republic is no more than a comfortable myth today; new praetorians are here now, inside city walls, in the service of elites. Most citizens are unaware of this because they willingly toe the line. Other innocent citizens *are* aware of the new praetorians because they are on the receiving end of a nightstick, strip search, Taser shock, no-knock raid, warrantless search, or selective prosecution.

The depth of new praetorian penetration of the republic is not widely perceived because its effects are highly selective. There is no widespread social unrest, and so no widespread repression. Actions are local, such as SWAT teams blowing off children's faces with flash-bang grenades, and targeted political prosecutions of figures such as Dinesh D'Souza and David Petraeus. It will take a social breakdown to bring the new praetorians out in force. It will take financial collapse, ice-nine freezes, hyperinflation, and confiscation. It will take money riots.

This dystopian preview rests on four pillars—*criminalization* of everyday behavior, *politicization* of justice, *militarization* of police, and *digitization* of surveillance. The elite quest for power is not new, it is part of human nature. What is new is that means now exist to achieve the ends.

Criminalization of the quotidian is captured by Harvey Silverglate, author of *Three Felonies a Day: How the Feds Target the Innocent*:

> An average, busy professional gets up in the morning, gets the kids to school, goes to work, uses the telephone or e-mail, has meetings, works on a prospectus or bank loan, goes home, puts the kids to bed, has dinner, reads the newspaper, goes to sleep, and has no idea that, in the course of that day, he or she has very likely committed three felonies. Three felonies that some ambitious, creative prosecutor can pick out from that day's activities and put into an indictment.

This is not speculation by Silverglate, but rather the consequence of a vast expansion of federal criminal law in recent decades. Citizens seem relaxed about *criminalization* due to either ignorance or a naïve view that they are not criminals. From the 1776 Declaration of Independence until recently, the scope of federal criminal law was constrained, consistent with limited powers of Congress specified by the Constitution. Until the 1920s, federal criminal law concerned itself mainly with treason, counterfeiting, insurrection, and military justice, all well within the proper scope of federal government.

Beginning in the 1920s, federal criminal law expanded in reaction to interstate flight from bank robberies and kidnappings, tax law codification after the Sixteenth Amendment, tax evasion, and prohibition of alcohol. A predecessor of the FBI was formed in 1908 as the Bureau of Investigation, and assumed a more aggressive role in 1924 upon the appointment of a new director, J. Edgar Hoover. Director Hoover launched the age of the "Public Enemy," targeting the colorful criminals John Dillinger, "Machine Gun" Kelly, and Al Capone. Hoover gave his agents the shoot-to-kill order that resulted in bank robber Dillinger's death in 1934. It was under Hoover that the FBI began aggressive wiretapping use.

The late 1930s and 1940s saw further enlargement of federal criminal law under the Supreme Court's expansive Commerce Clause construction. This judicial strain emerged in *West Coast Hotel v. Parrish* (1937), a 5–4 decision, and *United States v. Darby Lumber Co.* (1941), which respectively allowed state regulation of private contract, and federal regulation of commerce based on a minimal state interest. Once state regulation of commerce was allowed, criminal enforcement tools followed quickly. Hoover's FBI, now more powerful than ever, compiled names of targets to be taken into custody in American concentration camps in 1942, euphemistically called "relocation" at the time.

By the 1970s, federal intrusion into land use, employment practices, health care, banking, investment, education, transportation, mining, manufacturing, energy, and other spheres was ubiquitous. Every civil regulatory scheme had a complementary criminal enforcement club behind it. Once core criminal laws were amplified with conspiracy, reporting, and false statements statutes, the web was complete. Silverglate's estimate of three felonies a day is no exaggeration.

Why would prosecutors target everyday citizens? The answer is the *politicization* of justice. The Nixon-Reagan-Clinton war on drugs, the George W. Bush war on terror, and the Obama war on his ideological enemy the Tea Party illustrate how the application of law was no longer confined to the administration of justice and maintenance of public order. The criminal code is now a bludgeon in the hands of political commissars.

The Nixon, Reagan, and Clinton administrations all devoted substantial police, military, and prosecutorial resources to eradication of marijuana crops and attacks on medical marijuana use based on political calculations about being tough on crime. In fact, the marijuana business operated like a traditional black market to supply consumer wants banned by the government. There was no threat to national security or civil order from marijuana. Today the drug's use is widely accepted and legal in some jurisdictions. Marijuana use is a legitimate topic of policy debate. Nixon, Reagan, and Clinton were not interested in debate; they were interested in votes.

Wars require *militarization*. The war on drugs is no exception. Use of the U.S. military for domestic law enforcement must be authorized by the military chain of command, including the president. Local authorities are prohibited from directing the U.S. military to do police duty pursuant to the 1878 Posse Comitatus Act.

If mayors could not deputize the military, they would militarize police. From the creation of SWAT teams in Los Angeles in the 1960s through the 1977 passage of the National Defense Authorization Security Act and its infamous 1033 Program, until today the U.S. military has supplied local police with body armor, night-vision goggles, automatic weapons, grenade launchers, armored vehicles, flash-bang grenades, and other equipment designed for warfare. SWAT teams train on military bases. Veterans returned from wars in Vietnam, Kuwait, Afghanistan, and Iraq swelled the ranks of local police. Between 1980 and 2001, the number of paramilitary-style police raids annually in the United States increased from approximately 3,000 to 45,000.

Author Radley Balko in his book *Rise of the Warrior Cop* vividly describes innocent Americans' sheer terror in the face of military-style police raids. One account by Balko involved Herbert Giglotto and his wife, Evelyn, an innocent couple living in the small town of Collinsville, Illinois:

> At a little after 9:30 PM . . . the Giglottos woke to a crash. . . .
>
> "I got out of bed; I took about three steps, looked down the hall and [saw] armed men running up the hall dressed like hippies with pistols, yelling and screeching." Giglotto turned to his wife, who was still in bed, and said, "God, honey, we're dead."
>
> "That's right, you motherfucker!" one of the men screamed. The men—fifteen of them—then stormed the bedroom. One of them threw Giglotto to the bed, bound his hands behind his back, and put a gun to his head.
>
> "Move and you're dead," the man said. He then motioned in the direction of Evelyn Giglotto. "Who is that bitch lying there?"
>
> "That's my wife."
>
> . . .
>
> "You're going to die if you don't tell us where the drugs are."
>
> Giglotto pled with the man, "Please, please before you shoot us, check my wallet for my identification. Because I know you're at the wrong place."
>
> Seconds later, someone shouted from the stairs, "We've made a mistake!"
>
> The men unbound the Giglottos and began to filter out.
>
> Herbert struggled to put on his pants to chase after them for more information. He shouted, "Why did you do that?"
>
> The man who'd just held a gun to his head answered, "Boy, you shut your mouth."

Evelyn Giglotto was most upset that the police had also thrown the couple's animals—three dogs and a cat—outside. . . . When she asked the police if her pets had been harmed, one of them replied, "Fuck your animals."

The Giglottos were lucky their pets survived. In fact, thousands of dogs owned by victims of no-knock raids, including many wrong-address raids, are killed for no reason. Balko relates one example from a 2008 wrong-address raid on the home of Kevin and Lisa Henderson in Howard County, Maryland:

> The police first met the family dog, a twelve-year old lab/rottwei-ler mix named Grunt. . . . [O]ne officer distracted the dog while another shot it point-blank in the head. When one of the couple's sons asked why they had shot the dog, one officer pointed his gun at the boy's head and said, "I'll blow your fucking head off if you keep talking."

Individual raids have now expanded into roundup-style mass raids. Balko gives the account of one eyewitness to numerous SWAT team round-ups:

> "They come on helicopters, military-style, SWAT style," . . . "In the apartments I was living in, in the projects, there were a lot of children outside playing. They don't care. They throw kids on the ground, put guns to their heads. They're kicking in doors. They just don't care."

Expansion of police power in America is not limited to SWAT teams and commando-style raids. Abuse is visible every day on city streets where so-called stop-and-frisk tactics have evolved into a revenue model for taxation of the poor through state violence.

In the poverty-plagued neighborhood of Bedford-Stuyvesant in New

York City, police routinely rough up citizens on vague suspicions and then search for weapons. Occasionally some are found. Often nothing is found. To justify a baseless assault, police handcuff the victim, throw her into a police van, conduct a strip search, and issue summonses for one of a host of offenses that amount to nothing more than standing on a sidewalk in an unsanctioned way.

From the victim's perspective, stop-and-frisk is really smash-and-strip given the brutal assaults and strip searches used. Stop-and-frisk embodies the SWAT team us-against-them mentality, on a less dramatic yet more pervasive scale.

Author Matt Taibbi, in his book *The Divide: American Injustice in the Age of the Wealth Gap*, recounts a typical case, that of Andrew Brown of Bedford-Stuyvesant:

> One day he was on his way home from his commercial driver's license class, walking less than fifty yards from his apartment entrance, when someone just grabbed him from behind. "What is it? I didn't do anything!" he shouted, and before he knew it, two plainclothes detectives, one on each side of him, were pushing him up against some scaffolding. . . .
>
> "What'd I do?" Andrew asked.
>
> "You fit the description," one of the police answered.
>
> Andrew knew it was pointless to ask *what* description. "Everybody in my neighborhood fits the description," Andrew explains. . . .
>
> So they took him to the station, processed him, strip-searched him, then gave him a summons for disorderly conduct. New York Penal Law 240.20, subsection 5: "Obstructing pedestrian traffic."
>
> In other words, he was arrested for standing on the sidewalk.

In cases like Andrew Brown's, the summons might be for $500 and the arrest blatantly unconstitutional. Still, victims are poor. They cannot afford a $500 fine; even less can they afford $1,000 for a lawyer, lost days from work, and transportation costs to attend hearings and seek justice. Many victims are marginally attached to the workforce to begin with. Disruption caused by police targeting is all it takes to cause them to lose jobs, drop out of training classes, or be cast back into the poverty traps they were trying to escape. So they pay the fine and get a criminal record in the process. This sets them back financially and diminishes future job prospects because of the police record.

In these situations, the state may never have to prove its case. Taibbi explains the economics based on a courtroom visit in Brooklyn. He begins with the fact that many defendants charged with trumped-up crimes can't make bail:

> If you get arrested for a B misdemeanor in New York City . . . you might face a punishment of fifteen to ninety days. But if you don't make bail, you'll almost automatically spend at least that long in jail waiting for trial.
>
> The state knows this, so essentially, charging a person who can't make bail with a B misdemeanor is the same as convicting the person. You file the charge, the judge sets high bail, you go back inside [the jail] and then you eventually plead to time served, because, well, why not? You've already done the time.
>
> The only difference is you've got a conviction now. . . .

Given bail costs, and time awaiting trial, victims plead guilty rather than fight false charges. Taibbi continues:

> You're paying the fine not for what you did, mind you, but simply out of recognition that you'd be paying a lot more if the state decided to be difficult and proceed with its messed-up case.
>
> This is the essence of Justice by Attrition. It's like a poker game where after arrest, the accused sits down at the table with

one chip. But the other player, the state, has a stack of chips fifty feet high. Will you play, or will you fold?

Most everybody folds.

These economics might not evoke sympathy if the defendants were part of a tidal wave of violent crime, but they're not. Allegations in many cases are not only nonviolent, they are not even serious. A man smoking a cigarette outside his building at night is charged with "obstruction of a sidewalk" even if no one else is around. A woman wearing a tight dress is charged with "loitering for the purpose of engaging in a prostitution offense." There is no obstruction or prostitution in many cases, just poor people minding their own business in their own neighborhoods when police come trolling for victims to meet city arrest quotas and revenue targets.

These police methods are effectively a tax on being poor to help city budgets. This was revealed in late December 2014 when New York City police temporarily stopped these tactics to protest the murder of officers Rafael Ramos and Wenjian Liu, shot while sitting in their police car by a lone gunman from Baltimore, Ismaaiyl Brinsley. New York City revenues from routine summonses plunged in the following weeks. Still, the NYPD remained vigilant against violent crime. Reporter Dara Lind explains the disparity:

> The data suggests that while enforcement is down across the board, the slowdown is mostly showing up in enforcement of minor crimes and offenses. Transit police, who police the subways, are making very few arrests. . . . It appears the division responsible for policing public housing projects has also cut its arrests dramatically. Over a third of the drop in arrests comes from decreases in those two categories alone. Major felony arrests, however, are down only 17 percent from last year. . . . One reason that the slowdown has cut down on traffic tickets and low-level summons so much more than arrests is because tickets are a major

source of city revenue . . . the city's lost millions of dollars already
due to the slowdown.

The NYPD shootings were tragic, and the job action understand-
able. Still, the revenue drop unintentionally revealed the motive for police tactics in poor neighborhoods. Stop-and-frisk victims are not violent
cop killers. They're poor people trying to get some fresh air or walk
down the street. The poor encounter police who are de facto armed tax
collectors for the state. The poor pay the price.

A more egregious example of how policing today is armed tax collection is asset forfeiture. Police seize property such as cash, cars, boats,
and homes from citizens *before* conviction. The burden of proof is on the
property owner to prove her innocence to regain possession of the
seized property. This shift in the burden of proof reverses the innocent-
until-proven-guilty tradition of U.S. law.

Purportedly the practice of asset forfeiture is intended to deprive
drug dealers of money or means of transportation that they can use to
continue their crimes while awaiting trial. Asset forfeiture morphed
into a revenue source that police use to finance SWAT teams and purchase armored vehicles to conduct still more lethal raids. Highway
patrols are now state-sanctioned highway robbers.

Asset forfeiture began with the Comprehensive Drug Abuse Prevention and Control Act of 1970, part of President Nixon's original war
on drugs. Forfeitures swelled after 1984 when Congress passed the
Comprehensive Crime Control Act. This law created an assets forfeiture
fund administered by the U.S. Department of Justice. Seized cash and
proceeds from seized property sales go into this fund. The fund is dis-
bursed according to an equitable sharing program; all participants in a
related investigation, federal, state, and local, are entitled to a share. This
has been a boon for localities with limited resources. A share of seizures
motivates police to stop innocent citizens for the sole purpose of confiscating assets.

Cheryl K. Chumley, author of *Police State U.S.A.*, describes a typical case, the 2007 arrest of Dale Agostini of Maryland:

> Agostini . . . was driving with his fiancee, their sixteen-month-old son, Amir; and an employee of Agostini's restaurant through East Texas . . . on their way to buy some new equipment for their business. Agostini carried $50,291 in the car—a large sum, but one which he said spoke volumes among restaurant equipment sellers, who would slash prices if the buyer paid in cash. . . .
>
> [A] police officer pulled them over. . . . He found the cash, accused them of money laundering, arrested the adults, and sent the infant child to protection services. Police also confiscated six cell phones, an iPod, and the car Agostini was driving. . . .
>
> Agostini was never charged with a crime. But he was finally released, along with his fiancee and employee, was given his child back, and was about to win back his cash—that last only after months of fighting in court to prove he had rightfully earned it through his restaurant business.

Agostini was one of the lucky ones. Victims of asset forfeitures often do not have the resources to establish innocent possession of seized property. They abandon it to the state.

In an award-winning series called "Stop and Seize," *The Washington Post* documented the widespread abuse of civil forfeiture to confiscate property from innocent citizens without due process and use the proceeds to finance state and city budgets and to buy new weaponry for militarized police departments. The practice is called "policing for profit." The series documents how police departments went beyond random confiscations and used intelligence operations to target civilians deemed most likely to carry cash. Targeting was not limited to drug dealers. Instead police used data mining techniques to target innocent civilians, including poor whites in addition to the usual black targets.

Asset seizure for profit has become so widespread that a private firm called the Black Asphalt Electronic Network & Notification System emerged to train police and provide technical assistance in confiscating cash and other property. Black Asphalt created a social network called the Brotherhood and sponsors annual contests for the police officer who can seize the most cash. The prizewinner is dubbed the Royal Knight. That reference to royalty is unintentionally revealing. The Royal Knight prize honors confiscatory tactics used by monarchs in the past—tactics the U.S. Constitution was intended to curtail. Black Asphalt's services were used by local police, the U.S. Department of Homeland Security, and other federal agencies.

Blurring of public and private police powers to profile and intimidate drivers is revealed in this *Washington Post* description of Desert Snow, a training firm affiliated with Black Asphalt:

> Desert Snow charges as little as $590 for an individual for its three- and four-day workshop of lectures and hands-on training in such subjects as "roadside conversational skills" and "when and how to seize currency." The firm often sets up its training in hotel conference rooms. The firm's three-day "Advanced Commercial Vehicle, Criminal & Terrorist Identification & Apprehension Workshop" cost 88 students a total of $145,000, according to a price list posted by the state of New Jersey.

Cash confiscation became so pervasive that the Washington, D.C., police department "made plans for millions of dollars in anticipated proceeds from future civil seizures of cash and property, even though federal guidelines say 'agencies may not commit' to such spending in advance, . . ." according to *The Washington Post*.

Seizure programs are justified in the name of the war on drugs or the war on terror. In fact, they are a war on citizens. Even as some of these tactics are reined in, the training, mind-set, and capacity remain ready for use when all cash is outlawed or in response to money riots.

The final arrow in the quiver of the new praetorians and their political masters is *digitization* of surveillance. Lost privacy from the explosion of cloud storage and free media from Google and Facebook is accepted. A user's intimate secrets are routinely data-mined by these companies. The fact that some privacy policies preclude disclosure to third parties does not mean companies do not use the data themselves or reveal it to the government. Google keeps a log of every website you have ever visited, regardless of whether you deleted it from your search history or not. Most Web users understand this.

What is not widely understood is the nexus of government and private Web services and the application of massive processing power and big data algorithms to target citizens in real time. Claims by Google, Apple, and Facebook that personal privacy is protected are risible. The government has ample executive powers to require these companies to make data available in response to an emergency, including financial collapse. Emergency access to private data by government agents takes minutes.

Digital facial recognition software is more reliable than outdated fingerprint techniques. Most citizens would object to being fingerprinted every time they walk outside, yet the digital equivalent happens when closed circuit video cameras capture your image at malls, banks, and supermarkets.

Video scanners are located in buildings, along highways, and on city streets. These scanners capture facial images, license plate numbers, and auto types and makes. Drivers like the convenience of E-ZPass automated toll systems, but may not realize that every tollbooth is now a digital surveillance and interdiction point.

E-ZPass surveillance uses radio frequency identification technology (RFID). Your E-ZPass tag has a transmitter that broadcasts information about you that is read by a scanner installed overhead at a tollbooth. Now governments are installing scanners and cameras on roads everywhere to collect the same information. The New York Civil Liberties Union recently discovered that New York City and State installed scanners in diverse locations to track the whereabouts of citizens. These scanners are not collecting tolls. They are the unacceptable face of the ubiquitous surveillance state.

Continuous surveillance is not confined to video cameras and E-ZPass tags. Smartphones and credit cards use an RFID variant called near field communication (NFC) to broadcast your activities to scanners. Each time you use your credit card, a digital fingerprint of your location is recorded. Your smartphone GPS signals your whereabouts between points of purchase. This information is available to government using collection standards that do not adhere to Fourth Amendment requirements of reasonableness and probable cause.

Next on the horizon is the driverless car championed by Google, Tesla, and Volkswagen among others. The driverless car is not driverless, it's just that the driver is not human. The real driver is a network of algorithms, GPS location devices, and robotics. Driverless systems are subject to government supervision. In the future, governments will deliver political opponents to detention centers by commandeering the software, locking the car doors, and conveying the car's occupant into custody.

The poor suffer stop-and-frisk. The middle class suffers asset seizures. Antiregime elites suffer selective prosecution. No one is immune because all are felons in the regulatory state, all are targets in the surveillance state. The only issue is whether your time has come.

Those who doubt that state power is used for political persecution need to consider IRS targeting of Tea Party activists by Lois Lerner after the 2010 U.S. midterm elections. Tea Party opponents who applaud these tactics should know that a different regime will target them in the fullness of time.

Money has no ideology. When ice-nine freezes commence, left and right will be equally victimized. If organized resistance to ice-nine emerges, SWAT teams will be waiting. The new praetorians may be relied upon to take orders from the government that pays them, not the people they ostensibly serve.

The New Fascism

Fascism is not in our future, it is here now.

Fascism, a dominant force in the twentieth century, remains one of the least understood and most ill-defined political "isms." This is because fascism is not ideological like communism or socialism. Fascists espouse certain views at various times, yet their views are inconsistent, and often quickly discarded. What matters to fascists is continuous action and state control of civic life. The fascist state may allow private corporations and associations to exist, provided they operate in accordance with state goals and submit to state surveillance. Deviation from state goals results in termination or incapacitation of private deviants.

The seminal definition of fascism comes from its intellectual father, Woodrow Wilson. In 1908 Wilson wrote:

> The President is at liberty, both in law and in conscience, to be as big a man as he can. His capacity will set the limit; and if Congress be overborne by him, it will be no fault of the makers of the Constitution . . . but only because the President has the nation behind him and Congress has not.

Wilson's book, *The State*, adds, "Government does now whatever experience permits or the times demand." A fascist leader who applied Wilson's writings was the Italian dictator Benito Mussolini. His motto was "Everything inside the state. Nothing outside the state." Wilson and Mussolini created the template for the run of twentieth-century fascists including Adolf Hitler, Joseph Stalin, and Franklin Delano Roosevelt.

Understanding fascism requires one to set aside distinctions like left-wing, right-wing, liberal, and conservative as applied by the media. Honest classical liberals and conservatives still exist, yet they are dying breeds. A better schema is to locate leaders on a spectrum that runs from fascism to liberty. Viewed in that light, one sees that "right-wing fascists" and "left-wing fascists" are mere fascists pursuing state action. Any ideological gloss of right and left is for show.

Insight into fascism's nonideological nature was detailed voluminously by author Jonah Goldberg in his 2008 book *Liberal Fascism*. Goldberg shows that fascist regimes may be quite unalike. Some are murderous such as those of Hitler and Stalin. Some are dictatorial such as those of Mussolini and Franco. Some operate within democratic frameworks such as those of Wilson and FDR. What unites them is a shared view that the state is the exclusive mediator of human activity, and ends justify means. Fascists call for continuous "action." Action through state power leads the fascist to dismiss both parliamentary processes and conservative restraint.

Woodrow Wilson is a case study of a democratically elected fascist. Wilson was the first U.S. president with a Ph.D., an achievement that fit well with the progressive movement of the early twentieth century. Progressives believed science and expertise could solve the problems of government and society. This age worshipped the "expert," which diminished the legislature as a source of policy. In 1913, his administration's first year, Wilson signed legislation to create the Federal Reserve System and the federal income tax, two pillars of state power ever since.

The primary platform for implementation of Wilson's program for top-down state control was the First World War. Wilson set up the War Industries Board (WIB), which effectively nationalized broad segments of the U.S. economy. WIB imposed wage and price controls and output quotas. WIB members included Wall Street financiers Bernard Baruch and Edward Stettinius Sr. of J. P. Morgan. Other members were Robert S. Lovett, head of the Union Pacific Railroad, and Hugh Frayne, head of the American Federation of Labor. Another WIB member was Eugene Meyer, who was later chairman of the Federal Reserve and president of the World Bank. The WIB was a perfect amalgam of big business, big labor, and Wall Street.

Wilson signed the Espionage Act of 1917 and the Sedition Act of

1918 to suppress free speech and squash dissent. Wilson's attorney general, A. Mitchell Palmer, conducted the infamous Palmer Raids targeting immigrants and using Red Scare fearmongering to bypass due process. Goldberg summarizes Wilson's regime:

> Woodrow Wilson was the twentieth century's first fascist dictator. This claim may sound outrageous on its face, but consider the evidence. More dissidents were arrested or jailed in a few years under Wilson than under Mussolini during the entire 1920s. . . . Wilson . . . unleashed literally hundreds of thousands of badge carrying goons on the American people and prosecuted a vicious campaign against the press. . . .

Hitler and Mussolini referred to Wilson with approval in their own writings and adopted his repressive tactics as part of Italy's fascist movement and Germany's National Socialist movement.

Wilson's progressive-fascist legacy was on hold in the Roaring Twenties during the Harding-Coolidge administrations, 1921–29. Fascism reemerged during the Hoover-Roosevelt regimes, 1929–45.

Herbert Hoover fit the mold of expert even better than Woodrow Wilson. He was a successful and wealthy mining engineer with a track record of solving hard logistical and economic problems long before he became president. Although a Republican, he worked for Wilson as head of the U.S. Food Administration, which operated by executive orders to manage food supplies during the First World War. Hoover advocated for what today are called public-private partnerships. He supported the Progressive Era practice of Taylorism, which promised improved government operations through engineering efficiencies. Hoover believed fervently that more government intervention was a solution, not a problem, a view consistent with Wilson's.

After the 1929 stock market crash and the start of the Great Depression, Hoover's interventionist tendencies became frantic. Far from being laissez-faire Republican, Hoover's policies were consistent with those later adopted by FDR including tax increases, creation of government agencies such as the Federal Home Loan Bank, and expanded price controls through the Federal Farm Board and other agencies. Hoover embraced the progressive label, the American fascist strain.

Following Hoover, FDR continued government intervention in private spheres. Like Hoover, FDR had his first federal government position in the Wilson administration, as assistant secretary of the Navy from 1913 to 1920.

FDR's interventions into private business and civic life are well known. He used executive orders under the Trading with the Enemy Act of 1917 to confiscate gold from U.S. citizens. He created a Civilian Conservation Corps, which recruited millions of men, clothed them in military-style uniforms with military ranks, moved them on troop trains, and gathered them into camps. Private electricity transmission was partially nationalized under FDR's Tennessee Valley Authority. The 1933 National Industrial Recovery Act established the National Recovery Administration (NRA), which required business to rig prices and subscribe to codes of conduct designed to eliminate competition. FDR's first term was an effort toward a totally planned economy.

Describing FDR as a fascist is not a revisionist meme; it was a widely held view in the 1930s. Writer and social critic Waldo Frank wrote in 1934, "The NRA is the beginning of American Fascism. . . . Fascism may be so gradual in the United States that most voters will not be aware of its existence. The true Fascist leaders will not be present imitators of the German Führer and Italian condottieri. . . . they will be judicious, black-frocked gentlemen; graduates of the best universities. . . ." Al Smith, the Democratic presidential candidate in 1928, compared FDR to Karl Marx and Vladimir Lenin. While Smith overstated the case, there is abundant evidence of Stalinist admirers in FDR's administrations, including influential figure Rexford Guy Tugwell, who visited Moscow in 1927, organized government-planned cities, and established American agricultural resettlement camps.

This fascist strain in American politics, planted by Wilson and nurtured by Hoover and FDR, has never gone away. It reemerged in full flower in the 1960s with Lyndon Johnson's Great Society, and again in the 1970s with Richard Nixon's wage and price controls. It exists today. Neofascism is visible in George W. Bush's No Child Left Behind law, the community organizing perspective of Barack Obama, and Hillary Clinton's "It Takes a Village" brand of politics. Despite electoral victory or loss, this tendency never fades entirely. The fact that Wilson, FDR, LBJ, and Obama were Democrats, while Hoover, Nixon, and Bush were Republicans, is ample testimony to the fact that fascism is not an ideology, it is a process of expanding the state into private realms. Fascism is above all belief in the state rather than God or the individual as a source of authority and normative conduct.

The fascist project is ratchet-like; it does not always move, but when it does it cannot be reversed. There are long periods like the 1920s and 1980s when the progressive-neofascist project makes little headway. Still, when fascism breaks through as with the New Deal, the Great Society, and Obamacare, the changes are here to stay. Each breakthrough enhances state power at liberty's expense. Dependency is increased at the expense of self-reliance. Americans barely notice.

Fascism's advance is often aided by a crisis; an application of shock doctrine. Wilson's authoritarian tendencies were empowered by the First World War. Hoover's and FDR's programs were enabled by the Great Depression. LBJ's ambitions were boosted by the twin traumas of the 1963 Kennedy assassination and 1965 Watts riots in Los Angeles. Obama's health care, Dodd-Frank, and stimulus programs were capacitated by Democratic majorities following the Panic of 2008.

Investors should anticipate that the authoritarian, neofascist project will be revived and reenergized in the next financial crisis. Ice-nine asset freezes and seizures will be the most immediate and visible aspects of this, but not the only ones. Once capital is frozen, capitalism itself is gone. A planned economy with wage and price controls, output goals, shared monopolies, guaranteed incomes, and government jobs is capitalism's natural successor.

Money Nexus

Schumpeter's prediction of capitalism's decline was not based on its failure, but rather on its success. It was precisely because capitalism is so successful at creating wealth that Schumpeter saw it sows the seeds of its own demise.

Schumpeter wrote that once the proletariat had been relieved from tedious labor, and elites were firmly in control of politics and finance, it would be possible to pursue alternatives to the capitalist system. In effect, capitalist countries could now afford a system other than capitalism; they could afford socialism.

In Schumpeter's view, socialism's rise would not be a revolution from the bottom up, it would be an evolution from the top down. The prototype for this was Otto von Bismarck, the mid-nineteenth-century Prussian chancellor, who offered health care, old age insurance, and shorter working hours to German labor. His goal was not to undermine the monarchy, but to strengthen it. Once granted social benefits, labor had no reason to seek them by revolutionary means.

Bismarck bought off dissent with social programs in order to enhance the power of his own elite cadre, which was monarchical and imperial. That process is being repeated today, with financial elites replacing royalty. The winners are workers *and* elites. The losers are free market capitalism and the bourgeoisie.

More darkly, Schumpeter's intuition was that the evolution might end not in socialism but in fascism. The two are not incompatible. Socialism is the sugarcoated, do-good Trojan horse that fascism can ride to power.

A persistent myth is that fascism represents a condominium of corporate and government power, sometimes called corporatism. A corollary is that corporate interests dominate, and government is no more than a channel to protect corporate interests. In this view, Hitler was a pawn controlled by rich German industrialists to serve their ends until his megalomania got the better of him and led to catastrophic defeat in the Second World War. In another telling, Dick Cheney was an agent of Halliburton who ensured that corporate interests were protected by the fascist Bush 43 administration.

These views are nonsense. Hitler was a murderous fascist, while American presidents, including Bush, are of the democratic "friendly fascist" kind. What both brands of fascism have in common is state dominance. Corporations are powerful, yet distinctly subordinate to the state.

In a fascist system, a Faustian bargain is struck between big business and big government. Fascists are perfectly willing to allow private companies and private property to exist. They are unwilling to allow private realms to stand in the way of state power. Hospitals and health insurers may be private enterprises, but their products, prices, and policies are controlled by Obamacare. Google, Twitter, and Apple may be private companies, but Internet access and fees are regulated by the Federal Communications Commission, an agency established in 1933 by FDR, almost sixty years before the World Wide Web was launched. Banks are private entities, but are highly regulated under Dodd-Frank, the Federal Reserve Act, and a litany of other statutes.

Initially business lobbies against new legislation. In the end, business embraces it and provides expertise to agencies it formerly opposed because these agencies damage emergent competitors more than established enterprise. Compliance costs are easier for large enterprises to bear. Aggressive enforcement adds to compliance costs with fines, penalties, and sanctions for technical violations not difficult to find because regulations are voluminous and opaque.

Since the Panic of 2008, hundreds of separate regulatory projects have been launched under Dodd-Frank. Certain risky activities were prohibited, capital requirements increased, deposit insurance premiums raised, consumer disclosures expanded, and billions of dollars of fines, penalties, and restitution extracted by government from banks.

Have banks been hobbled? No. The five largest banks in the United States are larger and control a greater percentage of all banking assets than they did in 2008. Bank profits are greater. Executive compensation is higher. JPMorgan CEO Jamie Dimon is a billionaire just for working at a bank.

In an impressive piece of regulatory jiu-jitsu, banks captured the regulatory process through lobbyists and campaign contributions and shaped regulations to their liking. The Dodd-Frank victims were not big banks but community banks that faced the regulatory burden without the benefit of too-big-to-fail status. Silent victims of Dodd-Frank were banks that never started at all, the kind of local bank formerly formed by Chamber-of-Commerce-type entrepreneurs who used their own business deposits to get the bank off the ground. Those banks are like aborted children who never saw the light of day.

The government is pleased with this resulting oligopoly. Politicians pretended to get tough on bankers, while banks played Houdini to escape shackles like a ban on derivatives. Despite this, the Treasury and Federal Reserve still hold a gun to the bankers' heads in the form of stress tests, living wills, and resolution authority. When the Fed balance sheet hits a confidence boundary from excessive money creation, banks will be reliable buyers of last resort of new Treasury debt. Banks that don't buy Treasuries will find their living wills being read at their own funerals.

Big business is a shared monopoly with barriers to entry for upstarts and government-subsidized profits. When upstarts like Uber emerge nonetheless, a remnant of Schumpeter's creative destruction, new government regulations are almost immediate. Private property has its space, but only to the extent government permits, and never to the detriment of state power.

Schumpeter viewed economics through a lens of long historical trends. He considered historical processes that played out not in terms of a single business cycle, but over decades and centuries. Schumpeter clearly foresaw the end of capitalism. He wrote, "Since capitalist enterprise, by its very achievements, tends to automatize progress, we conclude that it tends to make itself superfluous—to break to pieces under the pressure of its own success. . . . The true pacemakers of socialism were not the intellectuals or agitators who preached it but the Vanderbilts, Carnegies and Rockefellers." He presciently said that in its most advanced stages, "Capitalism, being essentially an evolutionary process, would become atrophic . . . the rate of interest would converge toward zero." Schumpeter, writing in 1942, expected the triumph of socialism by 2000.

Socialism and fascism have shared traits. Both exalt the role of the state in directing the economy and, by extension, human action. Both expand the public sphere and diminish the civic sphere to a point where there are few truly private activities or associations. Smoking, eating, drinking, lightbulbs, toilets, health care, and more all conform to government mandates.

What distinguishes socialists from fascists is the former have historically been patient and willing to work within parliamentary processes. Socialists believe time is on their side; Schumpeter agreed. Fascists by contrast are men and women of action. They prefer orders to debate. Ends justify the means.

Another distinction between socialists and fascists is found in socialist toleration for religion and family, traditional sources of authority. Religion and family guide behavior by establishing norms and imposing limits. Fascists believe the state is the *sole* source of norms and authority. Fascists inevitably collide with alternate and far older family arrangements.

Fascists thrive on action and never let a crisis go to waste. Among the best crises to advance a fascist agenda are war and financial panic. The 9/11 attacks produced the Patriot Act, which opened the door to massive surveillance of American citizens without probable cause. The 2008 financial crisis produced Dodd-Frank, which institutionalized the role of six megabanks, JPMorgan, Citibank, Bank of America, Wells Fargo, Morgan Stanley, and Goldman Sachs. American savings and investments were herded into these portals, where they are controlled by government. A few more mega-asset aggregators—MetLife, Prudential, and BlackRock—are also in the government's crosshairs. The fact that their clients' wealth is digital makes confiscation and control for reasons of state even easier.

The next financial crisis will not be merely a bigger version of the 1998 and 2008 crises. It will be qualitatively different. It will encompass multiple asset classes on a global scale. It will exhibit inflation not seen since the 1970s, insolvency not seen since the 1930s, and exchange shutdowns not seen since 1914. State power will be summoned to contain panic. Liquidity will come from the IMF as directed by the G20, including a large voice for China. Capitalism will be discredited once and for all.

The difference between twenty-first-century neofascism and 1930s fascism is that state resources are all the greater. Democratic fascists of the Wilson-Hoover-FDR type relied on orders, experts, and government agencies with broad mandates to impose state control. Nondemocratic fascists such as Mussolini relied on black-clad thugs to gain power, then ruled as dictators once installed. History shows there is never a shortage of people willing to don black shirts, march in lockstep, and do as they are told.

Today state power is vastly more pervasive. Digital surveillance, social media, data mining, and customized content are at the fingertips of those with a fascist agenda. Selective prosecution for ill-defined crimes and selective enforcement of incomprehensible tax laws are available to silence enemies of the state. When dissent spills outside state-approved boundaries, militarized police are waiting.

This prospect does not make a case for anarchism. The state is required, crimes must be punished, and laws must be enforced. The issue is civic space. How much space should the state occupy in daily life, and how much should be reserved for private citizens in pursuit of a former ideal of liberty? The fascist impulse is to crowd out liberty and mandate all human action. Private property is allowed but only if its use is subordinate to state designs. In the fascist utopia, comportment in civil society takes a village that plays by government rules.

Schumpeter died in 1950, but not before predicting the demise of capitalism, the rise of socialism, and the progression of socialism to fascism over a fifty-year frame. His historical method is the antithesis of the two-second attention span that plagues analysts today. Time has vindicated his dystopian dissection of the dynamic forces at play.

CHAPTER 9
BEHOLD A BLACK HORSE

False messiahs and false prophets will arise and will perform
signs and wonders in order to mislead. . . . In those days . . . the
sun will be darkened and the moon will not give its light. . . . But
of the day and the hour no one knows. . . . You do not know when
the time will come . . . whether in the evening, or at midnight, or
at cockcrow, or in the morning.

Mark 13:22–35

There is a high likelihood of . . . another global crisis.

"The Geneva Report 16" (2014)

Countdown Clock

Complexity theory says we will not know the time of the next financial
collapse in advance. This conclusion is not a case of throwing up one's
hands in half knowledge. It is the best science we have mixed with a dose
of humility.

Complex systems in the critical state are fragile constructs with
countless points of failure catalyzed by immeasurably small causes.
That dynamic makes systemic failure certain. Experiments show that as

complex systems grow in scale, the size of the worst possible event expands exponentially. The frequency of small-scale adverse events also increases. We simply cannot know when exactly events will occur.

Indistinctness in timing is not a failure of theory; it is the heart of the theory. Seismologists cannot precisely predict the timing of earthquakes. Then again we don't build homes on fault lines, we take precautions. And there are warnings despite the lack of certainty on timing.

The United States Geological Survey defines "foreshocks" as "earthquakes that precede larger earthquakes in the same location." Of course, "larger" is a relative term. A 3.0 M_w earthquake can be a foreshock to a 6.0 M_w earthquake that does some damage. A 6.0 M_w earthquake can be a foreshock to an 8.0 M_w earthquake, strong enough to level a city.

As with earthquakes, so with finance. We have had our foreshocks. In 1998, and again in 2008, the global financial system came within hours of complete collapse. For all that, financial shocks differ from earthquakes in one important way. Once an earthquake begins, it cannot be stopped. An earthquake stops itself once its energy has been released. In contrast, financial earthquakes can be stopped by government intervention. By this reckoning, 1998 and 2008 were 8.0 M_w earthquakes truncated at the 6.0 M_w scale. There was extensive damage both times, but the temple of finance was not leveled, and the surrounding city was soon rebuilt. But at what cost?

If the stored energy of financial instability was not released, the energy is still there. Policy intervention in 1998 and 2008, combined with added complexity in the time since, means financial energy awaiting release may have 10.0 M_w potential, greater than any quake in recorded history, enough to sever California from the continent, enough to close every bank and stock exchange in the world. Importantly, a collapse of that magnitude will overwhelm the truncation capacity of already stretched central banks. The truncation task will fall to the IMF, and even it may not have enough financial capacity. SDRs, ice-nine, and martial law are three rings around the temple. Other instruments of state power may be required.

As concerns financial quakes, if timing is opaque and magnitude clear, what about fault lines? Where will the shock occur? We know where the fault line lies. It's a financial abstraction, but it has a name. Liquidity is the fault line.

On Wednesday, October 15, 2014, an unprecedented shock occurred in the world's most important financial venue—the market for U.S. Treasury securities. That morning, from 9:33 a.m. to 9:45 a.m. ET, in what the U.S. government later called a twelve-minute "event window," the yield on ten-year Treasury notes shook like a seismograph in the great Sumatra earthquake. In the first six minutes of the event window, yields fell 16 basis points, from 2.02 percent to 1.86 percent. In the next six minutes, yields just as suddenly surged back to 1.99 percent, about 3 basis points from where they were when the event window started. Over the course of the entire trading session including the event window, yields experienced a 37-basis-point trading range, from 2.23 percent to 1.86 percent. The full trading day also involved a rebound; yields ended 6 basis points below where they closed the day before.

To put this move in perspective, one-day changes in yield of greater magnitude than the change that occurred on October 15, 2014, have been observed only three times in a sixteen-year period studied by the U.S. government, a total of about four thousand trading days. The first was a 43-basis-point change on October 8, 2008, when global central banks executed coordinated interest rate cuts at the height of the panic following the Lehman and AIG collapses. The second was a 47.5-basis-point change on March 18, 2009. That was the date the Federal Reserve announced an expansion of its money-printing program ("QE1") and included Treasury notes on the list of assets purchased. The third was a 40-basis-point swing on August 9, 2011, when the U.S. credit rating was downgraded.

These intraday yield ranges, between 37 and 47.5 basis points on four occasions, compare with an average intraday yield range of 8 basis points on the approximately four thousand trading days since October 1998. (Interestingly, the degree distribution of all ten-year Treasury note intraday yield ranges since 1998 is not a normal distribution as VaR advocates expect, but a perfect power curve—exactly what complexity theory predicts.)

The rarity of the intraday 37-basis-point flash crash in yields is troubling enough. More troubling is the observation of a 16-basis-point fall in six minutes. That move is completely unprecedented. The other three comparable events took place over the course of an entire trading day, not an event window measured in minutes.

But the most disquieting aspect is that the October 15, 2014, yield crash occurred on a day when *nothing else happened*. There was no news that day. The crash just happened. An official joint staff report from the Treasury, Fed, SEC, and CFTC summarized the events of October 15, 2014: "For such significant volatility and a large round-trip in prices to occur in so short a time *with no obvious catalyst* is unprecedented in the recent history of the Treasury market."

Flash crashes are comprehensible on days when the world is panicked (October 8, 2008), the Federal Reserve rides to the rescue (March 18, 2009), or the United States suffers a credit downgrade (August 9, 2011). Those are highly significant events. The October 15, 2014, flash crash stands alone as an earthquake that emerged unannounced from an unobservable shift of deep tectonic plates.

Other foreshocks of comparable magnitude were soon to come. On Thursday, January 15, 2015, three months to the day after the Treasury yield flash crash, the Swiss franc surged 20 percent against the euro, and a comparable amount against the dollar, in a twenty-minute event window from 9:30 a.m. to 9:50 a.m. Central European Time. In effect, there was a flash crash in the depreciating currencies, the euro and the dollar. Before the event, one euro was pegged at 1.20 francs. Within minutes, one euro was worth only one franc. Collateral damage was extensive— Swiss stocks plunged 10 percent the day the franc was revalued.

Unlike the Treasury flash crash, the Swiss franc shock was triggered by a specific event. At the open of trading that day, the Swiss National Bank announced it would abandon the €0.8325 peg to the franc the bank had maintained since 2012. The purpose of the peg was to cheapen the Swiss franc relative to other currencies to promote Swiss exports and tourism. The problem was that global capital continued to demand Swiss francs as a safe haven because of Switzerland's low inflation, strong gold reserves, and political stability. In order to maintain the peg in the face of strong demand, the Swiss National Bank printed francs to buy euros, which in turn were invested in euro-denominated bank deposits and bonds. The asset side of the Swiss National Bank balance sheet became a destination for the world's euro liabilities. The position was nonsustainable. In a single, swift move, the Swiss National Bank broke the peg and alleviated pressure to keep buying euros with printed francs.

Still, the Swiss National Bank decision was a shock. As recently as the month before revaluation, on December 18, 2014, Swiss National Bank president Thomas Jordan issued a press release saying, "The Swiss National Bank . . . reaffirms its commitment to the minimum exchange rate . . . and will continue to enforce it with the utmost determination." Four weeks later Jordan threw in the towel.

There was nothing orderly about the revaluation process. One prominent foreign exchange market participant, Kathleen Brooks, was quoted in *The Telegraph* on the day of the shock as saying, "The . . . market has basically shut down so far this morning, while it waits for the dust to settle." When the dust did settle, traders counted the cost. Banks and hedge funds that relied on the peg had lost billions of dollars.

A third foreshock followed quickly. Now the scene shifted to China. On Monday, August 10, 2015, China's central bank, the People's Bank of China, stunned global markets with a devaluation of the Chinese yuan against the U.S. dollar. At the start of business that day, one dollar equaled ¥6.21. After central bank intervention, the yuan instantaneously sank to ¥6.33, a 2 percent move. Carnage grew worse from there. On August 12, the Chinese currency fell to ¥6.39. By August 25, the currency had sunk to ¥6.41, a 3.2 percent decline from start to finish.

While the Chinese devaluation was not as large in percentage terms as the 20 percent Swiss franc revaluation, the shock must be viewed in the context of China's significance to the global economy. China and the United States are the world's two largest national economies with a combined $30 trillion in GDP comprising 40 percent of global GDP. The United States is China's largest trading partner. China is the second-largest trading partner to the United States after Canada. One cannot overstate the importance of the U.S.-China exchange rate to world trade and global capital flows. An unexpected 3 percent move in the world's most important exchange rate relationship is an earthquake.

Effects of China's shock devaluation were immediate and severe. The Dow Jones Industrial Average fell over 11 percent from 17,615.18 on August 10 just before the devaluation to 15,666.44 on August 25 when the yuan reached an interim low. This U.S. stock market correction wiped out more than $2.5 trillion in shareholder wealth. China's Shanghai Stock Exchange Composite Index had already fallen from a post-2007 high of 5,166.35 on June 12, 2015, in anticipation of devaluation. The index took another plunge from 3,928.41 on August 10 to 2,927.28 on August 26. The collapse was 43 percent from the June high, and 25 percent from the date of the shock devaluation. Lost investor wealth on China's stock exchanges exceeded $3 trillion from June to August 2015. In addition to $5.5 trillion in investor losses from U.S. and Chinese stock markets, China suffered more than $1 trillion in capital outflows from January 2015 to August 2016, mostly related to fears of currency devaluation. China's investors and debtors were in full flight to either acquire dollar assets or pay off dollar loans before the dollar grew even stronger.

Then came a fourth foreshock, even stronger than those before. On June 23, 2016, the United Kingdom voted to leave the European Union in a referendum. The popular name for British exit was "Brexit." Parties on either side of the debate chose the words "Leave" and "Remain" to reflect their respective positions on relations with the EU. Immediately prior to the vote, markets priced in a victory for Remain, sending pounds sterling to $1.50.

The reason the market was so certain Remain would win is a fascinating case study in the misapprehension of behavioral science. Polls leading up to the vote showed the race was too close to call. However, betting markets run by Ladbrokes and Betfair showed a 70 percent probability that Remain would win. A certain type of foreign exchange market participant, the young London City banker who makes markets for his firm and clients, considered betting odds a distillation of the "wisdom of crowds" and priced sterling to reflect that ostensible wisdom.

The wisdom of crowds concept was popularized in a 2004 book by that title written by James Surowiecki. The book included an overview of published behavioral research on the subject. The classic example involved guessing the number of jellybeans in a large jar. In a typical experiment, an average of mere guesses by a large number of everyday observers proved more accurate than the estimate of a single expert who might try to calculate the jar's volume divided by the estimated volume of one jellybean with allowance for the irregular space between beans. In the crowd's estimate, extreme guesses ("one" or "a million") cancel out and the average of the remaining guesses is quite close to the actual number. Hence, the wisdom of crowds. Based on a naïve understanding of this science, the City bankers decided the everyman nature of betting markets produces a better forecast than the "expert" pollsters.

Flaws in the London bankers' logic are legion. Accuracy of betting odds in predicting an election is only as good as the correlation of views between the betting pool and the voting pool. That correlation is low. Bettors self-select for those with money to lose, and those for whom betting is an acceptable pastime. Bettors pay real money to bet and are prepared to lose. Voters do not pay to vote.

One little-noticed quirk in the betting data was that the number of Leave bets was more than four times the number of Remain bets. But Remain bets were for far larger amounts. Some hotshot City bankers bet £10,000 on Remain, while a typical punt on Leave might be a fiver. Bookies are not forecasters; their job is not to lose money. When the bookies gave Remain short odds, they were not predicting the election, they were balancing the weight of money on both sides of the bet. Money is irrelevant at the ballot box; voting is free. No doubt, rich City bettors were acting out their own cognitive biases (and skewing results) because final polls showed that London was heavily for Remain while England as a whole was for Leave.

Within hours of polls closing at 10:00 p.m. GMT on June 23, a major win for Leave was apparent. The result was near panic. The pound plunged from $1.50 to $1.32 within hours, a 12 percent decline that took sterling to its lowest level in more than thirty years. Other markets also gyrated wildly. The dollar price of gold soared from $1,255 per ounce immediately before Brexit to $1,315 at the close on June 24, a gain of 4.8 percent in one day. The intraday volatility was even greater. By July 8, gold was $1,366 per ounce for a total post-Brexit two-week bounce of 8.8 percent.

One-day gains and losses of 3 percent to 20 percent, the kind discussed here, are not unusual in stocks. A well-known company's shares can drop 95 percent in a single day if the company files for bankruptcy. But our examples are *not* equity shocks. These are *money* shocks, or in the Treasury note example, shocks in the world's safest bond.

Swiss francs, euros, pounds sterling, and the U.S. dollar are all major reserve currencies. The yuan is less freely convertible, but is still the fifth most actively traded currency in the world and, as of October 1, 2016, one of five component currencies of the SDR. The U.S. Treasury ten-year note is the safest intermediate term security in the world and the benchmark for every sovereign bond market in the world. Gold is a major international reserve asset; over 70 percent of U.S. reserves are in gold. Collectively Treasuries, gold, and major reserve currencies are the bedrock of the entire international monetary system. They should be stable. *They are not.*

A reprise shows that since late 2014:

- Treasury ten-year note yields moved from 2.02 percent to 1.86 percent in six minutes. (October 15, 2014)
- The euro fell 20 percent against the Swiss franc in twenty minutes. (January 15, 2015)

- The yuan instantaneously fell 2 percent against the U.S. dollar. (August 10, 2015)
- Sterling fell 12 percent against the U.S. dollar in two hours. (June 23, 2016)
- Gold rose 4.8 percent against the U.S. dollar, and 19 percent against sterling in two hours. (June 23, 2016)

Where major currencies, bonds, and gold are involved, moves of this magnitude formerly took years. Now they take minutes or hours.

This type of volatility may be new to currency and bond traders. It is quite familiar to complexity theorists, who recognize the volatility as the kind of turbulence that can spontaneously arise in a formerly stable system just before that system spins out of control. Such instability is also familiar to seismologists tracking foreshocks on the fault lines in anticipation of the next major catastrophic earthquake. In the language of chaos theorists, the system is going wobbly.

A critic of applied complexity in capital markets could shrug at this litany of shocks. None of them meant the end of the world. Markets bounced back from every one. Treasury note yields rose as fast as they fell in 2014. The all-important euro-dollar cross rate was relatively undisturbed by the Swiss franc revaluation in 2015. The Federal Reserve mitigated the worst effects of the August 2015 yuan devaluation by delaying its planned September 2015 "liftoff" in rates until December. The Bank of England boosted sterling after Brexit by cutting interest rates on August 4, 2016. For every foreshock, central banks stood ready to truncate dynamic processes and restore a semblance of stability.

Still, it is a semblance, not real. Unreleased energy from one foreshock is stored for the next even as the tempo and magnitude of the foreshocks themselves increase. What is unarguable is that *we are watching liquidity disappear in the world's most liquid markets*. A Geiger counter is clicking madly. Global capital markets are closing in on the supercritical state from which there is no recovery.

The liquidity crises sketched above are not the only crisis catalysts.

Natural disasters, cyberwarfare, and nuclear arms in the Middle East are all on the table. Complexity theory teaches that what counts is not the proximate cause of a collapse, but the density, interactions, and systemic scale that make collapse inevitable.

The greatest danger comes from what complexity theorists call *linked complexity*. This happens when one critical state system collapses, and that collapse cascades into another system causing it to go critical and collapse too.

There is no better example of linked complexity than the Fukushima disaster in northern Japan on March 11, 2011. The first critical state systems to snap were tectonic plates under the Pacific Ocean. The initial energy release was known as the Tōhoku earthquake, which measured 9.0 M_w, the fourth most powerful earthquake recorded since 1900 when modern record keeping started. The earthquake triggered a tsunami in a second critical state system, causing waves more than one hundred feet high. The tsunami waves crashed into the Fukushima Daiichi nuclear power plant, a third critical state system, causing nuclear meltdowns in three reactors and the massive release of radioactive material. Next, news of the disaster hit the Tokyo Stock Exchange, the fourth critical state system in the chain. The Nikkei 225 Index plunged 8.25 percent, from 10,434.38 the day before the disaster to 8,605.15 on March 15, 2011, just four days after. Finally, the fifth critical system affected was the foreign exchange market. Japanese insurance companies began to sell dollars for yen in order to have enough yen liquidity to pay property and casualty claims. Initially the yen rallied from ¥81.89 to one dollar on March 11, to ¥80.59 to the dollar by March 18, a 1.6 percent move in one week—huge by currency market standards. Then came the policy truncation. Christine Lagarde, French finance minister at the time, coordinated a G7 currency intervention to weaken the yen. This was considered necessary to boost the Japanese economy after the devastation. The intervention worked. By April 8, the yen had sunk to ¥84.70 to one dollar, a 5 percent drop from the post-Fukushima high. Lagarde's finesse was another example of policy putting a lid on the Pandora's box of complex state system dynamics.

From tectonic plates, to tsunami, to reactor cores, to stock market, to foreign exchange, critical state systems cascaded into one another causing near-record catastrophes at each link in the chain. Interestingly two of the systems—tectonic plates and tsunamis—are natural, while three others—reactor cores, the stock market, and currency markets— are man-made. This illustrates how natural and synthetic complex systems interact seamlessly when agents are arrayed in the critical state.

Some combination of unforeseen emergence and linked complexity— not a black swan, but a black horse as depicted in the book of Revelation—is the most likely cause of capital markets collapse. A small default by a Malaysian borrower could cause a loss of confidence in a related Chinese enterprise, leading to capital flight from China, a rush into U.S. Treasuries, illiquidity in the Treasury market, a stronger U.S. dollar, and a tsunami of defaults in suddenly unpayable emerging markets dollar-denominated debt. In the midst of this, an advanced persistent threat squad of Kremlin-backed hackers (APT 29, code name: COZY BEAR) shuts down the New York Stock Exchange as a force multiplier to deter U.S. naval activity on the Baltic Sea. Within two days every market in the world has announced a twenty-first-century version of "HOUSE CLOSED." The precursor of such tightly linked cascading crises is the onset of the First World War in late July 1914, foreseen by the Raven of Zurich, Felix Somary. This is how eras end.

Incoherence

The international monetary system is now in a time of dynamic uncertainty. This dynamic resembles the phase from 1971 to 1981 when extremes in inflation, interest rates, commodity prices, exchange rates, and geopolitical instability pushed markets to the edge of chaos until Henry Kissinger, Paul Volcker, Ronald Reagan, James Baker, and later

Robert Rubin provided the leadership and enlisted the international co-operation needed to restabilize the former Bretton Woods gold-based system around a new dollar-based one. The task of restabilization today is no less daunting.

In 2015, I spoke privately with two of the world's most powerful central bankers on this topic. On May 27, 2015, I spoke to Ben Bernanke, former chairman of the Federal Reserve Board, in Seoul, South Korea. Two weeks later, on June 11, I spoke to John Lipsky, former head of the IMF, in New York. (Curiously, Lipsky was the only American ever to head the IMF; he stepped in as acting head upon the unplanned resignation of Dominique Strauss-Kahn until the executive board had time to replace Strauss-Kahn with Christine Lagarde. By custom, the IMF head is never an American.) Without prompting or coordination, both central bankers used exactly the same word to describe the international monetary system today. The word was "incoherent." They meant the monetary world has no anchor, no reference frame.

The June 23, 2016, post-Brexit shock is a good case study in the point Bernanke and Lipsky made. If pounds sterling moved from $1.50 to $1.32 in two hours, what really happened? Did the dollar go up, or did sterling go down? If the answer is that the dollar went *up*, then how did the dollar go *down* 4.8 percent against gold *at the same time*? If the answer is that the dollar went up *and* down depending on the unit of measurement (gold or sterling), then why privilege one form of measurement over another? Viewed this way, today's money is lost in a valuation wilderness of mirrors. This is what Bernanke and Lipsky meant by incoherence. Implicit in this is a need for a new Bretton Woods–type agreement: a reform of the international monetary system and new rules of the game.

The predicate for a new system is to move gold to China. Under the old Bretton Woods system, Europe and Japan acquired eleven thousand tons of gold from the United States between 1950 and 1970. Market impact was never an issue because the price of gold was fixed at $35 per ounce. Today, to mitigate market impact the gold must be moved by stealth, using agents such as BIS and HSBC that intermediate consistent gold flows from London vaults, through Swiss refiners, finally to deep storage in Shanghai.

In November 2015, the IMF preannounced that China would be welcomed into the elite club of currencies that comprise the IMF's special drawing right. This move was followed by an IMF study dated July 15, 2016, that called for the creation of a market-based SDR ("M-SDR") to coexist with the official SDR ("O-SDR"). As if on cue, the World Bank and the China Development Bank planned an issue of private bonds denominated in SDRs, according to a Reuters report on August 1, 2016. Other SDR bond issues were expected soon thereafter from the China-based Asian Infrastructure Investment Bank and Chinese banking giant ICBC. Finally, on October 1, 2016, the yuan formally entered the SDR basket with a 10.92 percent weight, greater than the shares accorded yen or sterling.

The transfer of gold to China, inclusion of the Chinese yuan in the SDR, and preparation for a deep, liquid market in SDRs are the makings of a new Bretton Woods, yet lacking in the transparency and accountability of the original Bretton Woods. The new system is a grand bargain, worked out in secret, conducted by stealth, and understood fully by a relative handful of global elites.

The final phase of this grand bargain is inflation to wipe out the real cost of global sovereign debt. If central banks could not cause inflation despite their best efforts, the IMF would create inflation for them with massive issuance of SDRs to be spent on global infrastructure and global welfare. The infrastructure needs, intermediated by the World Bank, would be targeted at so-called climate change, another elite hobby horse.

Now the postcrisis global elite plan is seen in full:

- Capture the banking system, 2009–10
- Redistribute gold to China, 2009–16
- Redenominate the SDR, 2015–16
- Print and distribute SDRs, 2017–18
- Destroy debt by inflation, 2018–25

Ice-nine and shock doctrine are handmaidens to this plan. A new global financial crisis arising before inflation took hold would be highly deflationary and contrary to elite goals. Ice-nine stops the crisis in its tracks, blocking asset liquidations to give the inflation plan time to work. The shock doctrine is held in reserve to pursue wish-list agendas such as climate change, and the war on cash in the midst of a crisis.

If all went well, neither would be needed, and debt elimination would proceed as planned. As always, the winners would be governments and banks. The losers would be investors, except those elites who were in on the plan or could catch glimpses and prepare accordingly.

Complexity theory makes a mockery of plans. The most likely path is the one no one sees. A systemic crisis could erupt at any time. Monetary elites will move quickly to ice-nine solutions. Still, civil society will revolt. Citizens will not accept their $300 per day from the ATMs alongside vague promises to reopen exchanges and unfreeze accounts "as soon as conditions permit." They will riot. They may burn down banks, loot supermarkets, and destroy critical infrastructure, all in an effort to secure transitory wealth. After ice-nine and money riots come neofascism, martial law, mass arrests, and government-controlled media. This is the endgame.

Palazzo Colonna

In the heart of Rome, at the foot of the Quirinal Hill, is Palazzo Colonna, a private palace owned by one family for thirty-one generations over nine hundred years. The family legacy began in the eleventh century with Pietro Colonna, who lived in the town of Colonna, south of Rome. Family members established residence on the current palazzo site around AD 1200. The palazzo took many shapes over the centuries. It evolved from a rudimentary residence to a fortress to the palace seen today. Principal construction spanned five centuries. The façades, interior apartments, and galleries date to the late Renaissance period with seventeenth- and eighteenth-century Baroque additions.

The family history is as spectacular as the palazzo itself. The poet Dante Alighieri was a palace guest while serving as ambassador from Florence to Pope Boniface VIII in 1301. In the fifteenth century, Oddone Colonna was made bishop of Rome and took the name Pope Martin V.

In tales evocative of the *Godfather* films, the Colonna family warred incessantly with the Orsini family for control of Rome in the 1400s. In 1511, Pope Julius II arranged a sit-down, and the two families pledged to observe a peace known as the "Pax Romana." In 1527, when forces of Emperor Charles V sacked Rome, the Palazzo Colonna was spared due to the family's good relations with the Habsburgs. One prominent member of the family, Marcoantonio II Colonna, was a victorious commander, alongside Andrea Doria and Don Juan of Austria, in the battle of Lepanto, which turned back the Islamic invasion of Europe in 1571. Rewards from this Christian victory added substantially to the family fortune.

In addition to vaulted ceilings, marble floors, and gilded moldings, the Palazzo houses a priceless collection of paintings and sculptures by Tintoretto, Brueghel the Elder, and other giants of the Renaissance and Baroque periods. Marcoantonio's aunt, Vittoria Colonna, was a poetess and muse to Michelangelo who also visited the Palazzo. Michelangelo repaid the friendship by including Vittoria's portrait in a scene in the Sistine Chapel.

Even in the twentieth century, the Colonna family's clout was not eclipsed—Ascanio Colonna was Italian ambassador to Washington in December 1941. He resigned his post in protest against his own government after Mussolini's declaration of war on the United States.

On a cool Roman evening in the fall of 2012, I joined a private dinner in the Palazzo with a small group of the world's wealthiest investors. My dinner companions were mainly Europeans, some Asians, and relatively few from the United States. Amid marble, gold, paintings, and palatial architecture, I mused on the meaning of old money compared with the new money crowd that congregated for cocktails near my Connecticut home. These phrases distinguish between old family fortunes like the

Rockefellers, Vanderbilts, and Whitneys, and the new fortunes of Greenwich hedge fund mavens and Silicon Valley CEOs. Implicit in this distinction is that old money has proved they know how to preserve wealth while the jury is still out on new money busy buying yachts, jets, and sharks in formaldehyde.

Still, old money in the United States is perhaps 150 years old, or slightly older for families like the Astors and Biddles. Yet in Rome I was ensconced in a nine-hundred-year-old fortune still intact. Here was a family fortune that had survived the Black Death, the Thirty Years' War, the wars of Louis XIV, the Napoleonic Wars, both world wars, the Holocaust, and the cold war.

I knew the Colonna family were not unique; there were other families like them throughout Europe who kept a low profile. These families are only too happy to be overlooked by the Forbes 400. That type of wealth and longevity could not be due merely to good luck. In nine hundred years, too many cards are turned from the deck for luck alone to be sufficient. There had to be a technique.

I turned to a striking Italian brunette to my right and asked, "How does a family keep its wealth for so long? It defies the odds. There must be a secret." She smiled and said, "Of course. It's easy. A third, a third, and a third." She paused, knowing I needed more, and continued, "You keep one third in land, one third in art, and one third in gold. Of course, you might have a family business as well, and you need some cash for necessities. But land, art, and gold are the things that last."

I took it that "necessities" included Tom Ford and Chanel. Still, the answer made perfect sense. Her advice followed the first rule of investing—diversification. Yet the answer denoted a deeper meaning, captured in her phrase "things that last." That's what I had asked her; how does a fortune *last nine hundred years*?

Art and gold make sense because both are portable; you can take them with you when the time comes to flee adversity. Interestingly, art is more valuable than gold by weight. In some future crisis, when gold has spiked to $10,000 per ounce, an especially valuable Picasso might be worth $500,000 per ounce. That's not the most aesthetic way to view Picasso, but it is a way to move massive wealth across borders with minimal risk of detection. Gold requires no defense as a store of wealth. Gold has been doing that job with continual success for five thousand years.

The land component was harder to grasp at first. History is filled with conquests, looting, and political change. Land can be lost. Nevertheless, good title to land, once established, is durable. There are thousands of Cuban refugees in the Miami vicinity who will show you deeds to properties in formerly wealthy neighborhoods of Havana they took with them when they fled the Communist takeover in 1959. Those homes have been occupied by party officials for the past fifty-seven years; some were destroyed. Yet the refugees still hold title and they, or their descendants, will return someday. As the United States and Cuba normalize relations, those titles will not be ignored.

An early seventeenth-century noble, hearing marauding armies approaching his manor, could remove his paintings from their frames, stow the canvases in a sack, put his gold in a pouch, and ride away with both in tow. Months later he could return to the manor, reclaim possession, stack his gold on a table, and hang his art on the wall. His wealth would be intact while his neighbors' wealth was perhaps destroyed.

An interesting twenty-first-century take on this millenarian portfolio is that land, art, and gold are nondigital. They cannot be wiped out by power outages, asset freezes, or cyberbrigades. They are immune from ice-nine.

Gold, in physical form, bullion bars or coins, in nonbank storage is the heart of every portfolio. Ten percent of investible assets is the right allocation. Gold has no yield (it's not supposed to—it's money), yet gold's wealth preservation and insurance properties are nonpareil. Avoid so-called rare and antique gold coins: the numismatic value is nil; they are grossly overpriced. Buy new coins or bars directly from the U.S. Mint or a reputable dealer with low commissions.

Gold is more accessible than most realize. I was once a passenger in a Las Vegas taxi. My driver, Valerie, asked why I was in town. I said I was there for an investment conference. This led to a consultation on wheels. As a former taxi driver, I know there is no more captive audience than a passenger. Valerie asked for investing advice and I made my usual reference to a 10 percent gold allocation. At one point I said to her by rote, "So, if you have a million dollars, put $100,000 in gold; if you have $100,000, put $10,000 into gold, and so on. Ten percent is the right amount."

She said, "You must be kidding, I'm fifty and have ten thousand dollars to my name; that's it." I said, "Fine. Buy one gold coin, put it in a safe place, and sit back. That's your insurance. When the time comes, the government will steal your ten thousand dollars with inflation and taxes, but you'll still have the gold." She said she would do that, but in my experience savers do not follow through.

Land is accessible to most investors. Investors may own a home—a good start. Income-producing land, either rental properties or farms, provides current income along with wealth preservation. Retirement properties in locations attractive to prospective retirees are a good buy-and-hold investment.

The most difficult asset to access is art. Investments should be confined to fine art, either paintings, drawings, collage, or sculpture. The art should be museum quality, meaning that the artist either already has some work in a museum or is considered a good candidate for acquisition by curators.

The challenge with museum-quality art is how to buy it. A multibillionaire can pay $100 million or more for a well-known Picasso painting, not an option open to most investors. Interestingly, Picasso was highly prolific, producing thousands of small paintings and sketches along with his best-known works. Some of these pieces can be purchased for $10,000 or less. They're worth a look.

The best way to invest in museum-quality fine art for $1 million or less is through a well-structured, well-curated fine art fund. Not all art funds are created equal. Some are poorly structured with misaligned incentives. Some have inherent conflicts of interest with dealers who sponsor them. But other art funds are managed conflict-free with good alignment of interest between sponsors and investors, and reasonable fees. These funds may be hard to find, but they're out there.

Of course, a one-third, one-third, one-third mix of land, art, and gold is highly stylized. That mix can never be a complete portfolio; some cash is always needed. There is also room in a model portfolio for stocks, bonds, and alternatives subject to careful selection. A family business is an asset that belongs in a separate category. From the vast industrial holdings of the Wallenberg family in Sweden to a local dry cleaner or pizza parlor proprietor, a going concern should be seen as unique and set apart, not included in an investment portfolio.

For those with expertise and uncommon connections, angel investing and early stage venture capital make sense. While risky, these investments are not blind gambles like the stock market. They are sensible risk-adjusted bets on bona fide wealth creation by entrepreneurs, inventors, and those with superior skills at executing a business plan.

High-quality bonds have a role in helping investors hit their goals. Bonds have set maturities and coupons. Investors have long-term goals like their children's education, parental care, or retirement. With high credit quality and ancillary inflation protection—gold is good for this—a ladder of bonds can be built to deliver returns timed to meet future needs. A bond ladder is true buy-and-hold investing.

Listed equities should occupy a relatively small allocation. As late as the 1960s, some state statutes prohibited fiduciaries from purchasing stocks at all. Memories of the 1929 crash were still fresh. The stock market was considered no better than the biblical den of thieves. Until the 1970s insurance and pension portfolios were about careful selection of bonds to meet future liabilities owed to beneficiaries. Not until passage of the Employee Retirement Income Security Act of 1974 (ERISA) were the floodgates opened to allow the flow of funds from fiduciary accounts into stocks. Wall Street was the not-so-hidden hand behind ERISA, 401(k)s, mutual funds, conflict waivers, and numerous extensions ever since, all designed to normalize and enlarge the scope for risky stock investments in what should be conservatively managed wealth preservation accounts. Wall Street's concern is for its commissions, not your nest egg.

Private equity funds are best avoided because of nontransparency, high fees, and misalignment of interests. Private equity deals begin as a looting expedition aimed at the prior shareholders of target companies. Then, the target companies are looted through special fees, preferred dividends, and sweetheart terms for fund managers. Putative profits are obtained with leverage, another form of looting when deals occasionally crater leaving banks with bad loans, although this is really a matter of one pirate band attacking another. (If banks fall into distress, taxpayer funds are available for bailouts, another form of looting.) Finally, private equity fund investors are looted because managers target acceptable bondlike returns that scarcely compensate for equity-type risks. All excess returns available through leverage are siphoned off by fund managers rather than directed to the investors. As a coup de grâce, fund managers claim capital gains tax treatment on what are thinly veiled management fees, so everyday taxpayers are looted again. This is why private equity fund mavens are billionaires living on latifundia-style estates near Telluride, Colorado, and Jackson Hole, Wyoming. There's no reason for you to facilitate the looting or be a victim.

Hedge funds are a challenging case. They work in theory, not in practice. Hedge funds aim to produce real risk-adjusted returns, known as alpha. This is done through market timing, long-short strategies, and arbitrage. Investors who are long stocks for the long run endure periodic crashes and prolonged bear markets to enjoy spectacular bull markets. The problem is we may not live long enough to recover severe losses, or we may be forced sellers (tuition, anyone?) at market lows. Hedge funds purport to outperform long-only portfolios. Paths to outperformance—market timing and long-short strategies—are easy to describe, yet real talent is difficult to find.

Successful market timing is a rare skill done consistently only with inside information. There is legal inside information—the kind you find yourself—but the temptation to seek illegal information is one reason many former fund managers are behind bars. Successful (and legal) market timing requires out-of-the-box analysis—always rare—and nonstandard models—even more rare. Only a handful of managers offer both, and they are not much in the public eye.

Long-short strategies based on stock fundamentals are more accessible. Some stock sectors typically outperform others. In the early stages of an expansion, riskier stocks in technology and biological sciences are good bets. In the mid-stages of an expansion, small-cap stocks play catch-up and can outperform. In the late stages of an expansion a retreat to undervalued utilities and consumer nondurable producers serves investors well. Moving from one category to the other at the right time is known as sector rotation, commonly practiced on Wall Street. A hedge fund manager can go long stocks that promise to outperform, and short those due for underperformance. In this way, managers amplify gains from sector rotation and build a market-neutral firewall against shocks. Michael Belkin is a past master at this; he has peers, but not many. The problem is long-short equity managers don't walk the walk. They crowd into flavor-of-the-month trades and are crushed when the RORO (risk-on, risk-off) wheel turns based on macro catalysts unconnected to the fundamental securities analysis the managers learned in business school.

Arbitrage is a mathematically driven long-short strategy applied to stocks, bonds, commodities, and currencies. If done properly, it works in all market conditions. Arbitrage relies on relative value. Two bonds issued by the same borrower with identical credit risk and similar maturities should theoretically trade at similar yields to maturity. Often they do not because institutions have liquidity preference for one bond over the other based on the fact that one of the bonds is more recently issued and more actively traded. Arbitrageurs can buy the bond that is "cheap," short the bond that is "rich," then sit tight and wait for prices to converge (this will happen at maturity, if not sooner), capturing a relatively risk-free spread.

Arbitrage can be applied to other categories of cheap and rich assets, although the less the similarity between the two, the greater the risk that perceived spreads do not converge as expected. To the extent two instruments in an arbitrage trade have low volatility and credit risk, the trade may be regarded as relatively risk-free and amplified with leverage to synthesize S&P volatility with a higher expected return.

The flaw in this neat theory of risk-free arbitrage is that in a panic, price spreads can widen before they converge. A leveraged player will be bled dry with margin calls on mark-to-market losses before reaching the promised land of convergence. Success at arbitrage also derives from market timing.

In fact, all alpha results from market timing, and the only consistent source of successful market timing is inside information. This was demonstrated by the Nobelist Robert C. Merton in an obscure 1981 paper, "On Market Timing and Investment Performance. I. An Equilibrium Theory of Value for Market Forecasts." Inside information comes either from theft, which is illegal, or from superior analytic ability, which is perfectly legal, yet rare.

On September 10, 2009, I testified under oath before Congress on the role of risk-management models in the 2008 financial crisis. A fellow witness was Nassim Taleb, celebrated author of *The Black Swan*. In the hearing, Taleb and I said Wall Street compensation of "heads I win, tails you lose" design was a contributing factor to the crash. We testified that bankers were grossly overpaid and incentivized to reckless behavior. One free market oriented member of Congress chastised us from his high dais and said our proposals to limit compensation would keep Wall Street from attracting "talent." Taleb's answer was priceless: *"What talent? These people destroyed ten trillion dollars of wealth."*

Taleb was right. Most traders on Wall Street are not super-talented. Decamping from an investment bank to a hedge fund does not improve a trader's talent; it just moves the compensation model in favor of the trader. Still, there are a small number of hedge funds managed by highly talented traders using global macro, long-short equity, and arbitrage strategies. They are worth their fees, yet difficult to find.

The superstructure of a robust all-weather portfolio to preserve wealth in the coming collapse and mitigate an ice-nine asset freeze looks like this:

Physical gold and silver, 10 percent (coins and bars, no numismatics)

Cash, 30 percent (some in physical notes)

Real estate, 20 percent (income producing or agricultural)

Fine art fund, 5 percent (museum quality only)

Angel and early venture capital, 10 percent (FinTech, natural resource, water)

Hedge funds, 5 percent (global macro, long-short equity, or arbitrage)

Bonds, 10 percent (high-quality sovereigns only)

Stocks, 10 percent (natural resource, mining, energy, utilities, tech only)

A family business should not be counted among investible assets. It should be held outside this portfolio. All of these assets, except cash, stocks, and bonds, can be held by direct title in physical or contractual form without reliance on banks, brokers, exchanges, or digital records. Those assets cannot be hacked. Some are illiquid. Most are immune from ice-nine lockdowns. This allocation offers protection from inflation, deflation, and panics.

Importantly, investors must be vigilant and nimble. The time will come when the cash allocation needs to be moved quickly into another category, perhaps land, gold, or art. Likewise bonds may need to be sold once inflation emerges. This is not a "set it and forget it" portfolio. Still, it's a good starting place for uncertain times.

Above all, investors should study history. There is nothing on the horizon that has not happened before, but there is much that has not happened lately. Memories are short. Psychologists have demonstrated that human behavior overweighs recent experience. Wall Street relies on this recency bias to rob investors by running the same playbook at ten-year intervals. P. T. Barnum said, "There's a sucker born every minute." The modern corollary is that suckers have short memories. Wall Street relies on this.

Reading is a fine way to study history, and travel as well. Better yet, read about a historical place, then go there. Before you structure a portfolio, pay a visit to the Eternal City. Arrange to see Palazzo Colonna from inside. As you admire the galleries and private apartments, traverse the marble floors, and gaze at gilded moldings, all still owned by the same family after nine hundred years, ask yourself how they did it.

The Colonna family remains wealthy after surviving wars, plagues, revolutions, lootings, and the ravages of time. Survival was not all about assets. The Colonnas were deeply involved in Roman politics and the Church. Friends at the Habsburg court proved helpful at crucial junctures.

Yet others had friends at court and did not survive nearly so well. The difference between mere money and dynastic wealth is profound. In Palazzo Colonna, you see the difference all around.

CONCLUSION

ON FEBRUARY 11, 2015, A BITTERLY COLD EVENING, I TOOK PART IN A formal debate before a live audience in a theater just off Broadway on Manhattan's upper west side. The debate proposition was a loaded gun: "Declinists Be Damned: Bet on America." This was intended to elicit dueling points on whether America was still ascendant or a power in decline. There were two debaters on each side of the proposition, for and against. My partner and I were against. The proposition left us literally damned before we walked onstage; not a great way to start an evening.

My debate partner was a brilliant Canadian writer and member of Parliament, Chrystia Freeland. Opposing us were Josef Joffe, editor of *Die Zeit*, the leading newsmagazine in Germany, and Peter Zeihan, a geopolitical consultant, part of a group that founded Stratfor, the private intelligence service. The moderator was John Donvan, a seasoned, sharp-witted international correspondent for ABC News.

The audience voted on the proposition before the debate. The format then called for three presentation rounds interspersed with informal dialogue and questions from Donvan. At the end, the audience voted again. A winner was decided not by majority, but by which team changed the most minds.

Joffe's argument was straightforward. Critics argued America's decline for decades, and were consistently wrong. In 1957, America panicked over the Soviet Sputnik satellite, which presaged a Communist conquest of space. In fact, Sputnik was little more than a basketball-size aluminum alloy sphere with a transmitter that went dead after a few weeks. Twelve years later America put a man on the moon, a feat not equaled by another nation. The Sputnik shock energized science education in America and led directly to advances in computers, miniaturization, and telecommunications. America should have said "thank you" to the Soviets for the Sputnik launch. In Joffe's view, America always wins in the end.

Joffe then offered a litany of other challenges to American power that failed as quickly as Sputnik. In the 1960s, John F. Kennedy was elected president on fears of a missile gap with the Soviet Union. In the 1970s, it was feared that Arab oil money would buy all the farmland in America. In the 1980s, Japan dominated to the point that the Imperial Palace grounds in Tokyo were said to be worth more than the entire state of California. In the 2000s, China was a behemoth that would leave America in the rearview mirror with its cheap labor and high savings.

Yet the Soviet, Arab, and Japanese threats evaporated, and China was failing in real time. America was number one, and remained so despite American anxieties.

Zeihan's argument was less historical, more classically geopolitical. He articulated America's demographic destiny and hardwired geographic advantages. Zeihan showed that Europe and China were doing demographic cliff dives, that their populations were aging from highly productive to least productive cohorts, a severe limitation on growth. Russia and Japan were in even worse shape; both had passed the point of aggregate reproductive capacity. Russian and Japanese population declines were irreversible; both nations were destined to fade into economic irrelevance. Of the major economies, only America had the right mix of demographics and immigration to provide enough population growth to produce economic growth as well.

Zeihan also elaborated the economic advantages of water transportation versus trucks. America had, by far, the largest and most widely

distributed navigable river system and intracoastal waterways to facilitate cheap transport for agricultural produce, energy, and manufactured
goods. Not only did the Atlantic and Pacific oceans make America invulnerable to invasion from east or west, a friendly border with Canada
and the deserts and mountains of Mexico made us equally invulnerable
to attack from north or south. No other country had such secure borders, and capital-creating capacity within those borders. Case closed.

My partner, Chrystia Freeland, offered a critique based not on technological or geopolitical prowess, but on social justice. She described
how the middle class in America has been squeezed almost out of existence. No longer did a rising tide lift all boats; instead the rich got immeasurably richer as the poor grew desperate. America was divided into
an elite who attended Ivy League schools and aspired to jobs at Wall
Street banks, and an underclass who could not read. Those left in the
middle were indebted with mortgages and student loans, and got lower
real wages as a result of globalization and the winner-take-all dynamics
of twenty-first-century competition. Political polarization emerged
from economic polarization, as night follows day. Division was seen
daily in the media, polls, and political process. Similar division and de-
cay destroyed representative systems from the Roman Republic to Wei-
mar Germany. Now division defined America.

I was the last debater at the podium. I said our opponents were
right. Joffe was correct that prior reports of America's demise had been
greatly exaggerated. Zeihan was right that America's resources and demographics gave her long-term advantages over rivals. That much was
easy to concede.

My line of attack was that a hundred years is too narrow a frame to
fathom collapse. History is abundant with sudden collapses of kingdoms, essentially complex social systems, that had stood for centuries.
Understanding American decline took a longer perspective.

A dawn observer at the battle of Hastings would have expected the
English king Harold to prevail—he had a larger force, higher ground,

and home field advantage. That view would have been reinforced by late morning. William the Conqueror's archers failed to do decisive damage. By afternoon, Harold's lines stood firm against repeated charges by William. As nightfall approached, Harold had only to hold out awhile longer. William's forces, without hope of resupply, might have retreated to leave Harold and his progeny on the English throne. Then William mustered one last charge using flanking maneuvers. The English lines suddenly broke. Harold and his closest supporters were killed. William took the throne of England. The collapse of Harold's kingdom came swiftly, unexpectedly. That is the nature of complexity.

Joffe's complacency about American success did not diminish my concerns about a sudden reverse. His small slice of history was insufficient bedrock. Joffe was focused on Harold at high noon. I weighed William at twilight.

Zeihan's case also missed the real threat to America. His history and geography were flawless. Still, no one expects amphibious landings on the Jersey shore or Mexican armored columns advancing across Arizona. America was safe from these threats, yet these were not threats that mattered. On March 1, 2016, Admiral Michael S. Rogers, director of the National Security Agency and commander of U.S. Cyber Command, said, "It's only a matter of . . . when . . . you are going to see a nation state, a group or an actor engage in destructive behavior against critical infrastructure of the United States." Zeihan's oceans won't keep America safe from missiles, satellites, and computer viruses.

Zeihan's point that America's waterborne transportation network was an enormous source of capital creation was also correct. Still, what good is capital creation if capital is wasted through inefficient and corrupt public policy? Benefits reaped from America's natural bounty are repeatedly wasted in asset bubbles and speculation enabled by Federal Reserve interest rate policies. America's wealth is diverted to a few instead of shared among many.

In pre-debate, I considered reciting the dismal litany of debt and deficits that undermine America's future. It would have been easy to list

CBO projections on U.S. debt-to-GDP ratios, the coming insolvency of Social Security, pathetic growth in the current recovery compared with robust recoveries from the 1950s to the 1990s, declining labor force participation, stagnant real wages, growing income inequality, and more. These trends are not more of the same as Joffe would have it. These trends are new and threatening.

In the event, I took a different, more theoretical approach. I did not posit a long, slow decline. My warning was about instantaneous decline, what I refer to in this book as catastrophic collapse. This type of decline made Joffe's and Zeihan's cases irrelevant. The United States might have better prospects in 2025 based on comparative trends. My point was that we would not make it that far.

Collapse could come sooner with consequences so profound that a demographic edge on Russia or Japan would not matter. The United States might have more people to pick up the pieces; the vase would still be shattered.

I took the crowd through a simplified complexity model, using the audience itself to show how a few panicked attendees could cause the entire audience to panic and flee. Fear is contagious, like a virus. My next point was to show that as a system grows in a linear way, instability of the system grows exponentially.

I showed that systemic risk has grown exponentially by concentration of bank assets, growth in derivatives, and increased density through asset swaps, leverage, and shadow banks. I challenged the audience to see how a systemic collapse was not only possible, but inevitable. It will be the greatest collapse in history because it begins at the greatest scale.

To complete the case for America in decline, I described what would ensue in the next collapse. The Federal Reserve would be unable to print money as it had in past crises because its balance sheet remains bloated. Another $4 trillion of money on top of $4 trillion already printed since 2008 could push confidence past the breaking point. Emergency liquidity would come from the IMF in the form of SDRs. An IMF rescue would entail greater control of the international monetary system by China, Russia, and Germany. This dollar hegemony denouement would illuminate American decline as decisively as Bretton Woods ended the British Empire.

When I mentioned SDRs, someone in the live audience laughed aloud. Whether this was ridicule, nerves, or the shock of recognition is impossible to say.

Having taken the audience through complexity, scale, and the consequences of collapse, I concluded my case for America in decline. I trusted the audience to realize this has all happened before, and would happen again.

Complexity theory is a guide to the future, yet there is no greater guide than the past. About fifty yards off Turkey's southern coast, near a place called Uluburun, lies one of the most important archeological discoveries ever made. Two hundred feet underwater is the wreck of a vessel reliably dated to 1300 BC with its cargo scattered around the site. The wreck was discovered by a local sponge diver, Mehmed Çakir, who reported it to officials.

Authorities arranged for expert archeologists to explore the wreck in dive expeditions starting in 1984. What divers found was a mélange of trade, culture, and economy culled from the interconnected civilizations of the Late Bronze Age. They found evidence of financial complexity 3,300 years ago that would not be unfamiliar to financiers today.

Cargo included ten tons of copper and one ton of tin that could be alloyed to make bronze weapons. Also found were precious materials such as ebony, ivory, gold, cobalt blue glass ingots, and amber. Among the weapons were swords, spears, and daggers. Foodstuffs in the cargo included figs, olives, and grapes. The most spectacular find was a gold scarab inscribed with the name of Egyptian queen Nefertiti.

What most impressed archeologists was the cargo's provenance. Copper came from Cyprus, and tin from Turkey. Amber came from the Baltic Sea area, more than two thousand miles away. The cobalt blue glass ingots were bound for Egypt where they were highly prized. Foodstuffs originated in the areas of present-day Israel and Syria. What emerged is an ancient version of today's globalized system of trade and finance.

The wrecked vessel was part of an eastern Mediterranean coastal trade that used prevailing winds—westerly along the African coast, easterly along the Turkish coast—to conduct a counterclockwise circuit through lands now known as Egypt, Syria, Cyprus, Turkey, and Greece.

The cargo revealed a wider trade network that stretched from the Baltic Sea in the north to Sudan in the south, and from the Indus River in the east to Spain in the west—more than sixteen million square miles. The wealth, sophistication, and density of this network are difficult to comprehend, even today.

Then suddenly it collapsed.

The collapse of Bronze Age civilization around 1200 BC, one century after the Uluburun wreck, came with surprising swiftness. Within fifty years, almost every major kingdom and empire crumbled.

Collapse did not affect one culture, but all—Hittites, Egyptians, Mycenaeans, Mesopotamians, and more fell into chaos. Cities burned, trade vanished, invaders arrived, and wealth was lost. Urbanites fled to villages and abandoned the complexity of city life to adopt agrarian lifestyles. A three-hundred-year dark age began that lasted until the rise of Athens and Rome.

The Bronze Age collapse and dark age 3,000 years ago resembles the better-known collapse of the Roman Empire and subsequent dark age about 1,500 years ago. What these twin collapses teach us is that civilization is not linear, it's cyclical. Society does not get endlessly richer and more sophisticated. Periodically things collapse. It is not the end of the world. It is the end of an age.

The Bronze Age and Roman collapses took place 1,500 years apart. It has been 1,500 years since the last collapse. Is another catastrophe in the works?

It is difficult to know. One can say a civilization's complexity is the cause of its own collapse. In a stratified society, elites demand more inputs to maintain their privileged position. In ancient societies, these inputs were tribute, taxes, forced labor, slavery, and the spoils of war. In postindustrial societies, these inputs are energy and money. When carbon-based energy is scarce we drill deeper and in more remote locales. We seek substitutes such as nuclear power. When money becomes scarce we print more or seek substitutes such as swaps and SDRs. Societal scale increases. Instability grows exponentially. Complexity breeds complexity.

The collapses of Bronze Age civilization and ancient Rome were not monocausal. Linkages that lift a civilization during its rise accelerate its ruin. Tax revolts in parts of an empire can incite barbarian invasions. Invasion disrupts transportation routes, which cuts off food at a terminus. Commerce along the route withers, which injures precincts far from invaders, and so on.

Historians might identify one of these factors—taxes, invasion, transportation, commerce—and point to it as the cause of civilizational ruin. In fact, all of the factors were causes because all were tightly linked in a network. Once a network is perturbed, nodes die out for seemingly exogenous reasons. Nodes actually fail because energy from the network, as trade, commerce, or money, is constricted. Disruption makes each node vulnerable to formerly weak exogenous factors that suddenly become fatal.

Civilization's lost networks were as densely connected as those today. Enormous energy, in all its forms, is needed to maintain a complex system. Those energy inputs in the form of money have been synthesized using credit and derivatives in place of money representing real wealth. The new networks are nonsustainable because synthetic money is based on confidence, and what economists call money illusion, both vulnerable to sudden shifts in perception. Today's network scale means that when collapse comes it will possess unprecedented destructive force.

Each debater had two minutes for closing arguments. Joe and Peter recapitulated their positive themes. Chrystia's care for society's left-behinds shone through. After my main argument on the likely dire consequences of complex system dynamics, I opted for a grittier example of real-world decline.

I asked the audience how many had walked to the theater that evening. I knew some had done so; the theater is in a vibrant neighborhood. I suggested that those who walked to the theater had arrived without incident. This was a good guess. New York is the safest major city in the world; crime rates have tumbled since the 1990s.

I said that if the theater were in Brooklyn, a few miles away, and the audience walked there from the Bedford-Stuyvesant neighborhood, their walk would not have been risk free. For Bed-Stuy residents, an undisturbed walk is not a foregone conclusion. There was a chance the police would assault you, smash your face against a wall, handcuff you, and force you into a police van while a quota of other innocents were rounded up. After riding around for hours, the human cargo would be dumped at a precinct for a strip search. This is called stop-and-frisk. The reality is smash-and-strip.

Stop-and-frisk sounds reasonable. In a tough neighborhood, a passerby who fits a profile is stopped and searched. If a gun is found, the person is arrested. If not, he is allowed on his way. This may be unconstitutional, yet most New Yorkers, especially an upper west side audience, turn a blind eye to extrajudicial conduct if it gets guns off the street and keeps New York safe.

As with every devil's bargain, the devil wins. Stop-and-frisk has morphed into a shakedown operation with quotas and revenue goals to help New York meet its budget. Occasionally guns are found. More often an innocent victim is handed a summons on a trumped-up charge like blocking the sidewalk, sometimes at 1:00 a.m. when sidewalks are literally empty.

The victim is required to appear in court. Public defenders are assigned. Victims routinely pay $250 fines because the costs of maintaining innocence are too great. Fines go to the city's bottom line to help it avoid going broke. The system amounts to a tax on being poor, black, an immigrant, or just in the wrong place at the wrong time.

A mile from Bed-Stuy is the headquarters of JPMorgan, one of the most corrupt enterprises in history. JPMorgan and its ilk, including Citibank, Goldman Sachs, and Bank of America, collectively paid more than $30 billion in fines, penalties, restitution, compliance costs, and disgorgement since 2009 in connection with a litany of civil and criminal claims. These claims include securities fraud and rigging markets in interest rates, foreign exchange, energy, silver, and gold. New claims keep arising.

Not one executive of these banks was charged with a crime. The U.S. Department of Justice refrained from criminal charges for fear of collateral consequences, including a run on the bank whose officer was charged. Innocent victims in Bed-Stuy suffer collateral consequences too, including lost jobs, unaffordable fines, and the stigma of a conviction. No one cares.

Injustice has always existed. The poor are always at a disadvantage to the rich when it comes to defending themselves in court. Still, what's happening today—not only in New York, but throughout America—is new. It is not mere injustice, it is institutionalized, systematic injustice supported by military-grade armor and tactics. The injustice is driven not merely by bad intent, but by a need for money. The system now feeds on itself, unable to pay its way. Inputs exceed outputs, marginal returns are negative. Wealth extraction replaced wealth creation as the way to get along. This is the endgame of a complex dynamic system past the point of no return.

Joffe and Zeihan were not wrong, yet they missed the point about American decline. The decline was not material, it was social, as Chrystia explained. I made plain that America's enemies would not attack by land or sea, but with gold and data processors. We both pointed to the enemies within—greed, self-serving elites, and incomprehension of systemic risk.

Then the debate was over. The audience voted; complacency won.

America was not in decline, at least as far as the upper west side was concerned. Chrystia and I congratulated Joe and Peter. We headed off in limos to a VIP dinner in a nearby penthouse. The elite bubble was intact, at least for the evening.

ACKNOWLEDGMENTS

This book is the third volume in a planned quartet on the future of the international monetary system and its implications for investors. That plan, and this book, would not exist without the support and encouragement of my super-agent, Melissa Flashman, and my publisher, Adrian Zackheim. Thank you, Mel and Adrian; let's keep a good thing going.

Movies are a collaborative art with hundreds of unseen hands behind every film. Books are no different. Authors get credit, yet I've never written a manuscript that was not substantially improved by good editing. I'm fortunate to have two superb editors with me every step of the way, Niki Papadopoulos, executive editor at Portfolio/Penguin, and freelance editor Will Rickards. Niki and Will take different approaches, and I benefit from both. Leah Trouwborst provided valuable editorial direction for which I am truly thankful, and Bruce Giffords managed the production editing with patience and fine professional skill.

Sometimes a writer's greatest challenge is not writing, but finding time to write. I have nothing but admiration and gratitude for the organizational talents of my business manager and media adviser, Ali Rickards. Without her ability to filter and prioritize media requests my schedule would drift like a leaf on the ocean. With her, we get things done.

One of the touchstones of this book is a recapitulation of the analytic method used by economist and banker Felix Somary as described in his memoir, *The Raven of Zurich*. I am immensely grateful to my

Viennese friends Ronni Stoeferle and Mark Valek for calling Somary's work to my attention. *The Raven of Zurich* has been out of print for more than thirty years. I doubt I would have encountered the book without the recommendation from Ronni and Mark. It has proved helpful beyond words.

I wish John Makin were with us to receive my thanks in person. Sadly he passed away just as I was completing the first draft of this book. He was a powerful influence on me as an economist, mentor, and, above all, friend. Dinners in Darien and Georgetown organized by John's brilliant spouse, Gwendolyn van Paasschen, along with our correspondence and one-on-one chats in New York, served to illuminate and help organize my own amorphous views.

John had an uncanny ability to foresee financial crises and recessions beginning with his classic 1984 book, *The Global Debt Crisis*. That book was decades ahead of its time in describing the relationship between excessive debt and failing growth. He was the first prominent economist to warn of the 2007 recession, which grew into the Panic of 2008. John was a worthy successor to Felix Somary in his ability to synthesize economics, banking, and markets. We miss him greatly.

My family keeps me grounded and mediates between the writer's need for solitude and the need for contact. All of my love and deep appreciation go to my wife, Ann, and our still growing family of Scott, Dominique, Thomas, Sam, James, Ali, Will, Abby, and the adorable pups, Ollie and Reese.

Everyone mentioned, and more unmentioned, contributed to the merits of this book. Any errors are mine alone.

NOTES

INTRODUCTION

2 **The English-language translation of Somary's memoir:** Felix Somary, *The Raven of Zurich: The Memoirs of Felix Somary* (New York: St. Martin's Press, 1986).

2 **A vivid example is a chapter:** Ibid., 40–43.

2 **"The Russian-French alliance had reacted":** Ibid., 41.

3 **"Europeans found the Chinese amusing":** Ibid., 68.

4 **"Doubtless the King too had spoken in good faith":** Ibid., 74.

7 **Churchill once sent a cable to Keynes:** Noel F. Busch, "Close-Up: Lord Keynes," *Life*, September 17, 1945, accessed August 7, 2016, https://books.google.com/books?id=t0kEAAAAMBAJ&q=%22a+cable%22&hl=en#v=snippet&q=%22a%20cable%22&f=false.

10 **For example, Kahneman's experiments show:** This example illustrates a cognitive bias Kahneman called "risk aversion." See Daniel Kahneman, *Thinking, Fast and Slow* (New York: Farrar, Straus and Giroux, 2011), 434–36.

CHAPTER 1: THIS IS THE END

15 **"Nice, nice, very nice":** Kurt Vonnegut, *Cat's Cradle* (New York: Dial Press, 2010), 3.

16 **Under Larry Fink's direction, BlackRock emerged:** Some descriptions of Larry Fink's management style and work habits in this material are from Carol J. Loomis, "BlackRock: The $4.3 Trillion Force," *Fortune*, July 7, 2014, accessed August 7, 2016, http://fortune.com/2014/07/07/blackrock-larry-fink/.

18 **"Fink . . . is a strong Democrat":** Ibid.

22 **In the 1963 dark comedic novel:** Vonnegut, *Cat's Cradle,* 44–51.

26 **The meeting's final communiqué includes reference:** See "G20 Leaders' Communiqué, Brisbane Summit, 15–16 November 2014," November 16, 2014, accessed August 7, 2016, www.mofa.go.jp/files/000059841.pdf.

26 **Behind that bland language is a separate:** See "Adequacy of Loss-Absorbing Capacity of Global Systemically Important Banks in Resolution," Financial Stability Board, November 10, 2014, accessed August 7, 2016, www.fsb.org /2014/11/adequacy-of-loss-absorbing-capacity-of-global-systemically-import ant-banks-in-resolution/.

26 **The report says bank losses:** Ibid., 5 (emphasis added).

27 **On Wednesday, July 23, 2014, the U.S. Securities and Exchange Commission:** See "SEC Adopts Money Market Fund Reforms," Harvard Law School Forum on Corporate Governance and Financial Regulation, August 16, 2014, accessed August 7, 2016, https://corpgov.law.harvard.edu/2014/08/16/sec-adopts -money-market-fund-reforms/.

29 **On December 8, 2014, *The Wall Street Journal:*** See Kirsten Grind, James Sterngold, and Juliet Chung, "Banks Urge Clients to Take Cash Elsewhere," *The Wall Street Journal,* December 7, 2014, accessed August 7, 2016, www.wsj.com /articles/banks-urge-big-customers-to-take-cash-elsewhere-or-be-slapped -with-fees-1418003852.

30 **On February 11, 2016, Federal Reserve chair Janet Yellen:** Jon Hilsenrath, "Yellen Says Fed Should Be Prepared to Use Negative Rates if Needed," *The Wall Street Journal,* February 11, 2016, accessed August 7, 2016, www.wsj .com/articles/yellen-reiterates-concerns-about-risks-to-economy-in-senate -testimony-1455203865.

30 **On February 16, 2016, former secretary of the treasury Larry Summers:** See Lawrence H. Summers, "It's Time to Kill the $100 Bill," *The Washington Post,* February 16, 2016, accessed August 7, 2016, www.washingtonpost.com /news/wonk/wp/2016/02/16/its-time-to-kill-the-100-bill/?postshare=867145 5627637815&tid=ss_tw.

30 **On August 30, 2016, Kenneth Rogoff:** Kenneth S. Rogoff, *The Curse of Cash* (Princeton, NJ: Princeton University Press, 2016).

31 **On November 10, 2014, the Financial Stability Board:** See "Adequacy of Loss-Absorbing Capacity of Global Systemically Important Banks in Resolution," Financial Stability Board, November 10, 2014.

32 **On May 3, 2016, the Federal Reserve:** "Restrictions on Qualified Financial Contracts of Systemically Important U.S. Banking Organizations and the U.S.

Operations of Systemically Important Foreign Banking Organizations; Revisions to the Definition of Qualifying Master Netting Agreement and Related Definitions—Notice of Proposed Rulemaking," Board of Governors of the Federal Reserve System, May 3, 2016, accessed August 7, 2016, www.federal reserve.gov/newsevents/press/bcreg/20160503b.htm.

32 **Yet, in an extraordinary speech on May 24, 2016, David Lipton:** David Lipton, "Can Globalization Still Deliver?" International Monetary Fund, May 24, 2016, accessed August 7, 2016, www.imf.org/en/News/Articles/2015/09/28/04/53/sp052416a.

37 **A small sign posted on the members' entrance:** For a detailed and highly readable account of the financial panic of 1914 from the perspective of London banks and the U.K. financial system, see Richard Roberts, *Saving the City: The Great Financial Crisis of 1914* (Oxford: Oxford University Press, 2013).

38 **On Monday, August 3, 1914:** For a detailed and colorful account of the closing of the New York Stock Exchange in 1914, and the rise of the Curb Market, including the source of this quotation, see William L. Silber, *When Washington Shut Down Wall Street: The Great Financial Crisis of 1914 and the Origins of America's Monetary Supremacy* (Princeton, NJ: Princeton University Press, 2007), 104–15.

38 **Research conducted by William L. Silber:** Ibid., 110–15.

41 **The conference itself was the end result:** See Benn Steil, *The Battle of Bretton Woods: John Maynard Keynes, Harry Dexter White, and the Making of a New World Order* (Princeton, NJ: Princeton University Press, 2013).

47 **It warned that markets were "euphoric":** "84th Annual Report, 2013/14," Bank for International Settlements, June 29, 2014, accessed August 7, 2016, www.bis.org/publ/arpdf/ar2014e.htm.

47 **The BIS report was followed on September 20, 2014:** "Communiqué—Meeting of G20 Finance Ministers and Central Bank Governors, Cairns, 20–21 September 2014," G20, September 21, 2014, accessed August 7, 2016, www.oecd.org/tax/transparency/automatic-exchange-of-information/implementation/communique-G20-finance-ministers-central-bank-governors-cairns.pdf.

47 **Just a few days later:** Luigi Buttiglione, Philip R. Lane, Lucrezia Reichlin, and Vincent Reinhart, "Deleveraging? What Deleveraging? Geneva Reports on the World Economy 16," International Center for Monetary and Banking Studies, September 2014, accessed August 7, 2016, http://cepr.org/content/deleveraging-what-deleveraging-16th-geneva-report-world-economy.

48 **The head of the IMF's powerful policy committee:** Transcript of the IMFC Press Conference, International Monetary Fund, October 11, 2014, accessed August 7, 2016, www.imf.org/en/news/articles/2015/09/28/04/54/tr101114a.

48 **The U.S. Treasury's Office of Financial Research:** Office of Financial Research 2014 Annual Report, United States Department of the Treasury, December 2, 2014, accessed August 7, 2016, https://financialresearch.gov/annual-reports/files/office-of-financial-research-annual-report-2014.pdf, i.

48 **Claudio Borio, head of the monetary department:** Claudio Borio, "On-the-Record Remarks," *BIS Quarterly Review,* December 2014—media briefing, December 5, 2014, accessed August 7, 2016, www.bis.org/publ/qtrpdf/r_qt1412_ontherecord.htm.

49 **The United States has been under a state of emergency:** President George W. Bush, Proclamation 7463, Declaration of National Emergency by Reason of Certain Terrorist Attacks, September 14, 2001, accessed August 7, 2016, www.gpo.gov/fdsys/pkg/WCPD-2001-09-17/pdf/WCPD-2001-09-17-Pg1310.pdf.

53 **T. S. Eliot had a vision:** T. S. Eliot, *The Waste Land* (New York: W. W. Norton & Company, Inc., 2000).

CHAPTER 2: ONE MONEY, ONE WORLD, ONE ORDER

55 **"Massive progress has been made":** Remarks of Christine Lagarde, managing director of the International Monetary Fund, at a Bloomberg Panel, World Economic Forum, Davos, Switzerland, January 22, 2015, accessed August 7, 2016, www.bloomberg.com/news/videos/2015-01-22/lagarde-cohn-summers-botin-dalio-on-bloomberg-panel.

55 **"You never want a serious crisis to go to waste":** Rahm Emanuel, as quoted in Gerald F. Seib, "In Crisis, Opportunity for Obama," *The Wall Street Journal,* November 21, 2008, accessed August 7, 2016, www.wsj.com/articles/SB1227 21278056345271.

55 **It first appeared in Fleming's 1961 novel:** Ian Fleming, *Thunderball* (Las Vegas: Thomas & Mercer, 2012).

58 **While Soros is not the unofficial chairman:** For an extended explanation of the concept of piecemeal engineering, see Karl R. Popper, *The Open Society and its Enemies: Volume 1, The Spell of Plato* (Princeton, NJ: Princeton University Press, 1971), 157–59.

63 **John Maynard Keynes, an adviser to the Treasury:** For a detailed examination of Keynes's view of the role of gold in the Panic of 1914, see Roberts, *Saving the City,* 125–28.

66 **Friedman built his academic reputation:** Milton Friedman and Anna Jacobson Schwartz, *A Monetary History of the United States, 1867–1960* (Princeton, NJ: Princeton University Press, 1993).

69 **This economic conundrum was posed by:** For more background on Triffin's dilemma, including reference to Triffin's congressional testimony and the relationship between deficits and reserve currencies, see "System in Crisis (1959–1971): Triffin's Dilemma," International Monetary Fund, accessed August 7, 2016, www.imf.org/external/np/exr/center/mm/eng/mm_sc_03.htm.

70 **"We're actually quite open to that":** Ben Smith, "Geithner 'Open' to China Proposal," *Politico,* March 25, 2009, accessed August 7, 2016, www.politico .com/blogs/ben-smith/2009/03/geithner-open-to-china-proposal-017088.

75 **The G7 use the Organisation for Economic Co-operation and Development:** For extensive information on the OECD's global tax project on base erosion and profit shifting (BEPS), see the OECD website, at "OECD, Base Erosion and Profit Shifting," accessed August 7, 2016, www.oecd.org/tax/beps/.

75 **Here's what the G7 leaders:** "G7 Ise-Shima Leaders' Declaration / G7 Ise-Shima Summit, 26–27 May 2016," G7 Ise-Shima Summit, May 27, 2016, accessed August 7, 2016, www.mofa.go.jp/files/000160266.pdf, 6–7.

79 **In particular, Piketty advanced the thesis:** French economist Thomas Piketty advanced the thesis that high tax rates have been associated with strong economic growth and equitable income distribution, while low tax rates have been associated with weaker growth and extremes of income inequality. See Thomas Piketty, *Capital in the Twenty-First Century* (Cambridge, MA: Belknap Press, 2014).

84 **Henry Kissinger offers a brilliant overview:** For an in-depth history and analysis of the Westphalian state system, other historical forms of world order, and implications for policy today, see Henry Kissinger, *World Order* (New York: Penguin Press, 2014). The historical discussion of world order in this book draws heavily on Kissinger's thesis.

85 **One such attack virus:** Michael Riley, "How Russian Hackers Stole the Nasdaq," *BloombergBusinessweek,* July 21, 2014, accessed August 7, 2016, www .bloomberg.com/news/articles/2014-07-17/how-russian-hackers-stole-the -nasdaq.

87 **In October 2015, the UN issued:** For a detailed study in the relationship between climate change and the use of public finance for global climate change infrastructure spending, see "The Financial System We Need," United Nations Environment Program, October 2015, download available, accessed August 7, 2016, www.unep.org/newscentre/Default.aspx?DocumentID=26851&ArticleID =35480, ix.

87 **UN project adviser Andrew Sheng:** Xiao Geng and Andrew Sheng, "How to Finance Global Reflation," *Project Syndicate,* April 25, 2016, accessed

August 7, 2016, www.project-syndicate.org/commentary/sdr-reserve-currency -fight-deflation-by-andrew-sheng-and-xiao-geng-2016-04.

89 **Naomi Klein's 2007 book,** *The Shock Doctrine:* Naomi Klein, *The Shock Doctrine: The Rise of Disaster Capitalism* (New York: Picador, 2007).

91 **Shock doctrine is an ideal tool:** Popper, *The Open Society and Its Enemies: Volume 1, The Spell of Plato,* 157–59.

91 **the Open Society Foundations:** Ibid.

CHAPTER 3: DESERT CITY OF THE MIND

92 **"Keynes asked me what I was advising":** Somary, *The Raven of Zurich,* 146–47.

94 **LANL is the crown jewel:** Extensive information about Los Alamos National Laboratory, including history, operations, security protocols, and a virtual tour, is available at the laboratory's website, "Los Alamos National Laboratory," accessed August 9, 2016, http://lanl.gov.

96 **In a seminal 1963 paper, Lorenz:** Edward N. Lorenz, "Deterministic Nonperiodic Flow," *Journal of the Atmospheric Sciences,* Vol. 20, January 7, 1963, accessed August 8, 2016, http://eaps4.mit.edu/research/Lorenz/Deterministic_63.pdf, 133.

99 **A starting place for:** For a comprehensive history of Bayes' theorem including numerous contemporary applications, see Sharon Bertsch McGrayne, *The Theory That Would Not Die: How Bayes' Rule Cracked the Enigma Code, Hunted Down Russian Submarines, and Emerged Triumphant from Two Centuries of Controversy* (New Haven, CT: Yale University Press, 2011).

104 **Before the G20 meeting was quite over:** Lael Brainard, "What Happened to the Great Divergence?," Board of Governors of the Federal Reserve System, February 26, 2016, accessed August 8, 2016, www.federalreserve.gov/newsevents /speech/brainard20160226a.htm.

104 **At the conclusion of the Shanghai G20:** David Keohane, "Did the G20 Agree a Currency Accord and Does It Matter?" *Financial Times: FT Alphaville,* April 12, 2016, accessed August 8, 2016, http://ftalphaville.ft.com/2016/04/12 /2159112/did-the-g20-agree-a-currency-accord-and-does-it-matter/.

104 **Also at the Shanghai G20 meeting:** "G20 Promises to Promote Economic Growth, Avoid Devaluations," Voice of America, February 27, 2016, accessed August 8, 2016, www.voanews.com/content/g20-promises-to-promote-economic -growth-avoid-devaluations/3210931.html.

104 **Federal Reserve chair Janet Yellen makes:** Janet Yellen, "The Outlook, Uncertainty, and Monetary Policy," Board of Governors of the Federal Reserve

System, March 29, 2016, accessed August 8, 2016, www.federalreserve.gov /newsevents/speech/yellen20160329a.htm.

104 **Luc Everaert, the IMF's mission chief:** Toru Fujioka, "IMF Sees No Cause for Japan to Intervene Now in FX," *Bloomberg,* April 13, 2016, accessed August 8, 2016, www.bloomberg.com/news/articles/2016-04-13/imf-sees-no-cause-for -japan-to-intervene-now-in-currency-market-imyf459k.

104 **Lagarde also says she is "quite pleased":** Christine Lagarde, "Transcript: Press Briefing of the Managing Director," International Monetary Fund, April 14, 2016, accessed August 8, 2016, www.imf.org/en/News/Articles/2015/09/28/04/54 /tr041416.

105 **An unnamed ECB official tells Reuters:** Balazs Koranyi, "ECB Not Aiming to Weaken Euro Against Dollar: Sources," *Reuters,* April 15, 2016, accessed August 8, 2016, www.reuters.com/article/us-imf-g20-currency-ecb-idUSKCN0 XC2RS.

109 **Adaptive behavior arises in many:** This discussion of adaptive behavior in complex social systems, including crowd and anticrowd behavior, is based on similar examples and related experiments presented in Neil Johnson, *Simply Complexity: A Clear Guide to Complexity Theory* (London: Oneworld, 2012), 72–85.

112 **Research conducted by physicists Neil Johnson, Pak Ming Hui, and Paul Jefferies:** Pak Ming Hui, Paul Jefferies, and Neil F. Johnson, *Financial Market Complexity: What Physics Can Tell Us About Market Behavior* (Oxford: Oxford University Press, 2003), 19–54.

113 **Neil Johnson and other physicists:** See Johnson, *Simply Complexity,* 115–24.

115 **Professor Neil Johnson puts the matter starkly:** Ibid., 117.

CHAPTER 4: FORESHOCK: 1998

118 **"I have reflected a long time":** Stanley Fischer, "General Discussion: Has Financial Development Made the World Riskier? Chair: Malcolm D. Knight," Proceedings—Economic Policy Symposium—Jackson Hole, Federal Reserve Bank of Kansas City, August 25–27, 2005, accessed August 8, 2016, www .kansascityfed.org/publicat/sympos/2005/pdf/GD5_2005.pdf, 392.

121 **LTCM's story was told in detail:** Roger Lowenstein, *When Genius Failed: The Rise and Fall of Long-Term Capital Management* (New York: Random House, 2000).

123 **A coming-out announcement for LTCM:** Saul Hansell, "John Meriwether Rides, Again, Without Salomon This Time," *The New York Times,* Septem-

ber 5, 1993, accessed August 8, 2016, www.nytimes.com/1993/09/05/business/john-meriwether-rides-again-without-salomon-this-time.html.

127 **LTCM coinvented the sovereign credit default swap market:** Gillian Tett, *Fool's Gold: The Inside Story of J. P. Morgan and How Wall St. Greed Corrupted Its Bold Dream and Created a Financial Catastrophe* (New York: Free Press, 2009).

145 **To illustrate, imagine an office desk:** The following example using file drawers is based on highly similar examples from Johnson, *Simply Complexity*, 21–24, 41–50.

150 **In February 1999, just months after:** Joshua Cooper Ramo, "The Three Musketeers," *Time,* February 15, 1999, accessed August 8, 2016, http://content.time.com/time/covers/0,16641,19990215,00.html.

CHAPTER 5: FORESHOCK: 2008

157 **"A financial market is riddled with feedback":** Johnson, *Simply Complexity*, 114.

158 **My early theoretical advances were compiled:** *Studies in Intelligence,* Vol. 50, No. 3, September 2006, *Journal of the American Intelligence Professional,* Central Intelligence Agency, CLASSIFIED EDITION, accessed August 8, 2016, www.cia.gov/library/center-for-the-study-of-intelligence/csi-publications/csi-studies/studies/vol50no3/index.html.

159 **Between June 30, 2001, and June 30, 2007:** "Statistical Release, OTC Derivatives Statistics at End-June 2013," Monetary and Economic Department, Bank for International Settlements, November 2013, accessed August 8, 2016, www.bis.org/publ/otc_hy1311.pdf, Graph 1, 6; Table A, 9.

159 **Over the same period, the Herfindahl index:** Ibid., Table 9a, 31.

160 **Cramer told colleague Erin Burnett:** The Jim Cramer interview with Erin Burnett quoted is available in video format. The quotation was transcribed from the video, accessed August 8, 2016, www.youtube.com/watch?v=rOVXh4xM-Ww.

160 **At the Federal Open Market Committee (FOMC) on June 28, 2007:** Press release, Board of Governors of the Federal Reserve System, Federal Open Market Committee, June 28, 2007, accessed August 8, 2016, www.federalreserve.gov/newsevents/press/monetary/20070618a.htm.

160 **Shortly before, on March 28, 2007:** Ben S. Bernanke, "The Economic Outlook," Statement before the Joint Economic Committee, U.S. Congress,

March 28, 2007, accessed August 8, 2016, www.federalreserve.gov/newsev
ents/testimony/bernanke20070328a.htm.

161 **I presented a detailed written analysis:** This written proposal is retained by
the author among his private papers and in digital form.

163 **On December 21, 2007, the major banks:** David Ellis and Ben Rooney,
"Banks to Abandon 'Super-SIV' Fund," *CNN Money,* December 21, 2007, accessed August 8, 2016, http://money.cnn.com/2007/12/21/news/companies
/super_siv/index.htm?postversion=2007122116.

164 **On Wednesday, March 12:** Henry Blodget, "Did Bear Sterns CEO Alan
Schwartz Lie on CNBC?," *Business Insider,* March 19, 2008, accessed August 8,
2016, www.businessinsider.com/2008/3/bear-stearns-bsc-did-ceo-alan-schwartz
-lie-on-cnbc-.

165 **The advice was sent as an email:** The original email text of this written proposal is retained by the author among his private papers and in digital form
(emphasis added).

169 **This was my first public effort:** James G. Rickards, "A Mountain, Overlooked," *The Washington Post,* October 2, 2008, accessed August 8, 2016, www
.washingtonpost.com/wp-dyn/content/article/2008/10/01/AR2008100
101149.html.

CHAPTER 6: EARTHQUAKE: 2018

176 **"No single incident can really be imagined":** Eric H. Cline, *1177 B.C.: The Year
Civilization Collapsed* (Princeton, NJ: Princeton University Press, 2014), 174.

176 **"If the crowded, interconnected, urbanized":** Ian Morris, "The Dawn of a
New Dark Age," *Stratfor,* July 13, 2016, accessed August 9, 2016, www.stratfor
.com/weekly/dawn-new-dark-age.

181 **One infamous example was prominent economist:** *The New York Times,*
October 16, 1929, accessed August 9, 2016, http://query.nytimes.com/mem
/archive/pdf?res=9806E6DF1639E03ABC4E52DFB6678382639EDE.

184 **Bayesians solve problems:** For a detailed history of the debate between frequentist and Bayesian statistical methods, see McGrayne, *The Theory That
Would Not Die.*

193 **In 2014, gold on deposit at the Fed:** International Summary Statistics, "Selected
Foreign Official Assets Held at Federal Reserve Banks (3.31)," Board of Governors of the Federal Reserve System, July 2016, accessed August 9, 2016, www
.federalreserve.gov/econresdata/releases/intlsumm/forassets20160731.htm.

193 **over half that decline:** Koos Jansen, "Federal Reserve Bank New York Lost 47t of Gold in November," BullionStar.com, December 29, 2014, accessed August 9, 2016, www.bullionstar.com/blogs/koos-jansen/federal-reserve-bank-new -york-lost-47t-of-gold-in-november/.

201 **Scholar Barry Eichengreen brilliantly laid out:** Barry Eichengreen, *Golden Fetters: The Gold Standard and the Great Depression, 1919–1939* (New York: Oxford University Press, 1995).

202 **In "The Hollow Men," T. S. Eliot:** T. S. Eliot, "The Hollow Men," 1925, All Poetry, accessed August 9, 2016, https://allpoetry.com/The-Hollow-Men.

CHAPTER 7: BONFIRE OF THE ELITES

205 **"The tragedy of bad economic ideas":** Thomas I. Palley, *From Financial Crisis to Stagnation: The Destruction of Shared Prosperity and the Role of Economics*, 1st ed. (New York: Cambridge University Press, 2012), 9.

211 **The theoretical foundation for free trade:** See David Ricardo, *The Principles of Political Economy and Taxation* (Mineola, NY: Dover Publications, 2004).

212 **This somewhat counterintuitive idea:** Ian Fletcher, *Free Trade Doesn't Work: What Should Replace It and Why*, 2nd ed. (Sheffield, MA: Coalition for a Prosperous America, 2011), 97 (emphasis in original).

217 **Joseph A. Schumpeter, in his 1942 classic:** Joseph A. Schumpeter, *Capitalism, Socialism and Democracy*, (New York: Harper Perennial, 2008), 103.

218 **Economist Thomas I. Palley summarizes:** Palley, *From Financial Crisis to Stagnation*, 46.

220 **The United States had average tariffs:** See Fletcher, *Free Trade Doesn't Work*, 135–41.

222 **In 1989, the cold war ended:** John Williamson, "What Washington Means by Policy Reform," in John Williamson (ed.), *Latin American Adjustment: How Much Has Happened?* (Washington, DC: Institute for International Economics, Conference Volume, 1989), accessed August 9, 2016, https://piie.com/commen tary/speeches-papers/what-washington-means-policy-reform.

224 **In a definitive 2014 study (the "Geneva Report"):** Buttiglione, et al., "Deleveraging? What Deleveraging?," 11.

225 **The Geneva Report describes this dangerous mix:** Ibid., 19.

225 **The report shouts alarm at:** Ibid., 22.

225 **A useful taxonomy of crises:** Ibid., Appendix 3A, 27–34.

226 **According to the data shown:** Ibid., 21.

229 **As defined by Keynes:** John Maynard Keynes, *The General Theory of Employ-ment, Interest, and Money* (New York: Harvest/Harcourt Inc., 1964), 249.

229 **In the words of the Geneva Report:** Buttiglione, et al., "Deleveraging? What Deleveraging?," 34.

CHAPTER 8: CAPITALISM, FASCISM, AND DEMOCRACY

231 **"There is little reason to believe":** Schumpeter, *Capitalism, Socialism and Democracy,* 375.

231 **"Show me the man":** As quoted in "The Criminalization of Almost Everything," *Cato Institute Policy Report,* January/February 2010, accessed August 9, 2016, www.cato.org/policy-report/januaryfebruary-2010/criminalization-almost -everything.

232 **This was succinctly stated by Schumpeter:** Schumpeter, *Capitalism, Social-ism and Democracy,* 82–83.

233 **"In analyzing . . . business strategy":** Ibid., 88–89.

234 **In the words of his biographer:** Ibid., Introduction, x.

236 **In the United States, median household income:** Justin Fox, "Where Me-dian Incomes Have Fallen the Most," Bloomberg, August 19, 2016, accessed August 25, 2016, www.bloomberg.com/view/articles/2016-08-19/where-median -incomes-have-fallen-the-most.

236 **A McKinsey Global Institute study:** Richard Dobbs, Anu Madgavkar, James Manyika, Jonathan Woetzel, Jacques Bughin, Eric Labaye, and Pranav Kashyap, "Poorer Than Their Parents? A New Perspective on Income Inequality," McK-insey Global Institute, July 2016, accessed August 9, 2016, www.mckinsey.com /global-themes/employment-and-growth/poorer-than-their-parents-a-new -perspective-on-income-inequality, Preface, viii.

237 **The McKinsey study highlights:** Ibid.

239 **"Success in conducting a business enterprise":** Schumpeter, *Capitalism, Socialism and Democracy,* 388.

239 **And Schumpeter perfectly anticipated:** Ibid., 386.

239 **Schumpeter summarized the endgame:** Ibid., 398.

240 **His description of Russia:** Ibid., 404.

240 **Finally, Schumpeter foresaw:** Ibid., 401–2.

243 **Criminalization of the quotidian:** Harvey A. Silverglate, *Three Felonies a Day: How the Feds Target the Innocent* (New York: Encounter Books, 2011).

243 **"An average, busy professional":** "The Criminalization of Almost Every-thing," *Cato Institute Policy Report,* January/February 2010.

243 **Author Radley Balko in his book:** Radley Balko, *Rise of the Warrior Cop: The Militarization of America's Police Forces* (New York: PublicAffairs, 2013).

246 **One account by Balko:** Ibid., 116–17.

247 **Balko relates one example:** Ibid., 317.

247 **Balko gives the account of one eyewitness**: Ibid., 246.

248 **Author Matt Taibbi, in his book:** Matt Taibbi, *The Divide: American Injustice in the Age of the Wealth Gap* (New York: Spiegel & Grau, 2014), 101–2.

249 **He begins with the fact that:** Ibid., 117.

249 **"You're paying the fine not for what you did":** Ibid., 118.

250 **Reporter Dara Lind explains the disparity:** Dara Lind, "The NYPD 'Slowdown' That's Cut Arrests in New York by Half, Explained," *Vox*, January 6, 2015, accessed August 9, 2016, www.vox.com/2015/1/6/7501953/nypd-mayor-arrests-union.

252 **Cheryl K. Chumley, author of *Police State U.S.A.*:** Cheryl K. Chumley, *Police State U.S.A.: How Orwell's Nightmare Is Becoming our Reality* (Washington, DC: WND Books, 2014), 70–71.

252 **In an award-winning series called:** Robert O'Harrow Jr., Steven Rich, Michael Sallah, and Gabe Silverman, "Stop and Seize," *The Washington Post*, September 6, 2014, accessed August 9, 2016, www.washingtonpost.com/sf/investigative/2014/09/06/stop-and-seize/.

253 **Blurring of public and private:** Robert O'Harrow Jr., Steven Rich, and Michael Sallah, "Police Intelligence Targets Cash," *The Washington Post*, September 7, 2014, accessed August 9, 2016, www.washingtonpost.com/sf/investigative/2014/09/07/police-intelligence-targets-cash/.

253 **Cash confiscation became so pervasive:** Robert O'Harrow Jr. and Steven Rich, "D.C. Police Plan for Future Seizure Proceeds Years in Advance in City Budget Documents," *The Washington Post*, November 15, 2014, accessed August 9, 2016, www.washingtonpost.com/investigations/dc-police-plan-for-future-seizure-proceeds-years-in-advance-in-city-budget-documents/2014/11/15/7025edd2-6b76-11e4-b053-65cea7903f2e_story.html.

256 **"The President, is at liberty":** Wilson quote found in Jonah Goldberg, *Liberal Fascism: The Secret History of the American Left from Mussolini to the Politics of Meaning* (New York: Doubleday, 2008), 86.

256 **"Government does now whatever experience permits":** Ibid.

257 **Insight into fascism's nonideological nature:** Ibid.

258 **Goldberg summarizes Wilson's regime:** Ibid., 80–81.

259 **Writer and social critic Waldo Frank:** Frank quote found in ibid, 161.

263 **Schumpeter clearly foresaw the end of capitalism:** Schumpeter, *Capitalism, Socialism and Democracy,* 134.

264 **He presciently said:** Ibid., 131.

CHAPTER 9: BEHOLD A BLACK HORSE

267 **"There is a high likelihood":** Buttiglione, et al., "Deleveraging? What Deleveraging?," 81.

270 **An official joint staff report:** Joint Staff Report, "The U.S. Treasury Market on October 15, 2014," U.S. Department of the Treasury, Board of Governors of the Federal Reserve System, Federal Reserve Bank of New York, U.S. Securities and Exchange Commission, U.S. Commodity Futures Trading Commission, July 13, 2015, accessed August 9, 2016, www.treasury.gov/press-center/press-releases/Documents/Joint_Staff_Report_Treasury_10-15-2015.pdf, 1 (emphasis added).

271 **As recently as the month before revaluation:** Press release, "Swiss National Bank Introduces Negative Interest Rates," Swiss National Bank, December 18, 2014, accessed August 9, 2016, www.snb.ch/en/mmr/reference/pre_20141218/source/pre_20141218.en.pdf.

271 **One prominent foreign exchange market participant:** Peter Spence, "Swiss Franc Surges After Scrapping Euro Ceiling," *The Telegraph,* January 15, 2015, accessed August 9, 2016, www.telegraph.co.uk/finance/currency/11347218/Swiss-franc-surges-after-scrapping-euro-peg.html.

273 **The wisdom of crowds concept:** See James Surowiecki, *The Wisdom of Crowds: Why the Many Are Smarter Than the Few and How Collective Wisdom Shapes Business, Economics, Societies, and Nations* (New York: Anchor Books, 2005).

279 **This move was followed by an IMF study:** "Staff Note for the G20: The Role of the SDR—Initial Considerations," International Monetary Fund, July 15, 2016, accessed August 9, 2016, www.imf.org/external/np/pp/eng/2016/072416.pdf.

279 **As if on cue, the World Bank:** Daniel Stanton, Frances Yoon, and Ina Zhou, "China to Lead Way with Landmark SDR Bond Offerings," *Reuters,* August 1, 2016, www.reuters.com/article/china-debt-bonds-idUSL3N1AI2L7.

288 **This was demonstrated by the Nobelist:** Robert C. Merton, "On Market Timing and Investment Performance. I. An Equilibrium Theory of Value for Market Forecasts," *The Journal of Business,* Vol. 54, No. 3, July 1981, accessed August 9, 2016, www.people.hbs.edu/rmerton/onmarkettimingpart1.pdf.

288 **On September 10, 2009, I testified:** Details of this hearing including witnesses, written statements, and a video of the testimony are available at: Committee on Science, Space & Technology, Subcommittee on Investigations and Oversight, "The Risks of Financial Modeling: VaR and the Economic Meltdown," September 10, 2009, accessed August 9, 2016, https://science.house.gov/legis lation/hearings/subcommittee-investigations-and-oversight-hearing-risks -financial-modeling-var.

CONCLUSION

291 **The debate proposition was a loaded gun:** The debate proceedings including participants, audience participation, outcome, and moderator are available at: "Declinists Be Damned: Bet on America," Intelligence[2] Debates, February 11, 2015, accessed August 9, 2016, http://intelligencesquaredus.org/debates/past -debates/item/1251-declinists-be-damned-bet-on-america.

294 **On March 1, 2016, Admiral Michael S. Rogers:** Laura Hautala, "We're Fighting an Invisible War—in Cyberspace," *CNET,* March 5, 2016, accessed August 9, 2016, www.cnet.com/news/were-fighting-an-invisible-war-in-cyberspace/.

SELECTED SOURCES

ARTICLES

De Martino, Benedetto, John P. O'Doherty, Debajyoti Ray, Peter Bossaerts, and Colin Camerer. "In the Mind of the Market: Theory of Mind Biases Value Computation during Financial Bubbles." *Neuron* Vol. 79, 1222–31, September 18, 2013.

Henriksson, Roy D., and Robert C. Merton. "On Market Timing and Investment Performance. II. Statistical Procedures for Evaluating Forecasting Skills." *The Journal of Business*, Vol. 54, No. 4, October 1981.

Lorenz, Edward N. "Deterministic Nonperiodic Flow." *Journal of the Atmospheric Sciences*, Vol. 20, January 7, 1963.

Merton, Robert C. "On Market Timing and Investment Performance. I. An Equilibrium Theory of Value for Market Forecasts." *Journal of Business*, Vol. 54, No. 3, July 1981.

Rickards, James. *Studies in Intelligence*, Vol. 50, No. 3, September 2006. *Journal of the American Intelligence Professional*, Central Intelligence Agency, CLASSIFIED EDITION.

Whitehead, Lorne A. "Domino 'Chain Reaction'." *American Journal of Physics*, Vol. 51, No. 2, February 1983.

BOOKS

Ahamed, Liaquat. *Lords of Finance: The Bankers Who Broke the World*. New York: Penguin, 2009.

———. *Money and Tough Love: On Tour with the IMF*. London: Visual Editions, 2014.

Alpert, Daniel. *The Age of Oversupply: Overcoming the Greatest Challenge to the Global Economy*. New York: Portfolio/Penguin, 2013.

Ariely, Dan. *Irrationally Yours: On Missing Socks, Pickup Lines and Other Existential Puzzles*. New York: Harper Perennial, 2015.

Bak, Per. *How Nature Works: The Science of Self-Organized Criticality*. New York: Copernicus, 1999.

Balko, Radley. *Rise of the Warrior Cop: The Militarization of America's Police Forces*. New York: PublicAffairs, 2013.

Bernanke, Ben S. *Essays on the Great Depression*. Princeton, NJ: Princeton University Press, 2000.

Böhm-Bawerk, Eugen von. *The Positive Theory of Capital*. Translated by William Smart. New York: G. E. Stechert & Co., 1930.

Bruner, Robert F., and Sean D. Carr. *The Panic of 1907: Lessons Learned from the Market's Perfect Storm*. Hoboken, NJ: John Wiley & Sons, Inc., 2007.

Calomiris, Charles W., and Stephen H. Haber. *Fragile by Design: The Political Origins of Banking Crises and Scarce Credit*. Princeton, NJ: Princeton University Press, 2014.

Casti, John. *X-Events: The Collapse of Everything*. New York: William Morrow, 2012.

Chumley, Cheryl K. *Police State U.S.A.: How Orwell's Nightmare Is Becoming Our Reality*. Washington, DC: WND Books, 2014.

Cline, Eric H. *1177 B.C.: The Year Civilization Collapsed*. Princeton, NJ: Princeton University Press, 2014.

Conway, Ed. *The Summit, Bretton Woods 1944: J. M. Keynes and the Reshaping of the Global Economy*. New York: Pegasus Books LLC, 2014.

Dam, Kenneth W. *The Rules of the Game: Reform and Evolution in the International Monetary System*. Chicago: University of Chicago Press, 1982.

DiMicco, Dan. *American Made: Why Making Things Will Return Us to Greatness*. New York: Palgrave Macmillan, 2015.

Eichengreen, Barry. *Golden Fetters: The Gold Standard and the Great Depression, 1919–1939*. New York: Oxford University Press, 1995.

——. *Hall of Mirrors: The Great Depression, the Great Recession, and the Uses—and Misuses—of History*. New York: Oxford University Press, 2015.

Eliot, T. S. *The Waste Land*. New York: W. W. Norton & Company, Inc., 2000.

Fleming, Ian. *Thunderball*. Las Vegas: Thomas & Mercer, 2012.

Fletcher, Ian. *Free Trade Doesn't Work: What Should Replace It and Why*. Sheffield, MA: Coalition for a Prosperous America, 2011.

Freeland, Chrystia. *Plutocrats: The Rise of the New Global Super-Rich and the Fall of Everyone Else*. New York: Penguin Press, 2012.

Friedman, Allan, and P. W. Singer. *Cybersecurity and Cyberwar: What Everyone Needs to Know*. New York: Oxford University Press, 2014.

Friedman, Milton, and Anna Jacobson Schwartz. *A Monetary History of the United States, 1867–1960*. Princeton, NJ: Princeton University Press, 1993.

Friedman, Thomas L. *The World Is Flat: A Brief History of the Twenty-first Century*. New York: Farrar, Straus and Giroux, 2005.

Gardner, Dan, and Philip E. Tetlock. *Superforecasting: The Art and Science of Prediction*. New York: Crown, 2015.

Gilder, George. *The Scandal of Money: Why Wall Street Recovers but the Economy Never Does*. Washington, DC: Regnery, 2016.

Goldberg, Jonah. *Liberal Fascism: The Secret History of the American Left from Mussolini to the Politics of Meaning*. New York: Doubleday, 2008.

Grant, James. *The Forgotten Depression: 1921: The Crash That Cured Itself*. New York: Simon & Schuster, 2014.

Hayek, F. A. *The Fortunes of Liberalism: Essays on Austrian Economics and the Ideal of Freedom*. Indianapolis: Liberty Fund, 1992.

———. *Good Money Part I: The New World*. Indianapolis: Liberty Fund, 1999.

———. *Good Money Part II: The Standard*. Indianapolis: Liberty Fund, 1999.

Hudson, Michael. *Killing the Host: How Financial Parasites and Debt Destroy the Global Economy*. Bergenfield, NJ: ISLET, 2015.

Hudson, Richard L., and Benoit Mandelbrot. *The (Mis)behavior of Markets: A Fractal View of Risk, Ruin, and Reward*. New York: Basic Books, 2004.

Hui, Pak Ming, Paul Jefferies, and Neil F. Johnson. *Financial Market Complexity: What Physics Can Tell Us About Market Behavior*. Oxford: Oxford University Press, 2003.

Jensen, Henrik Jeldtoft. *Self-Organized Criticality: Emergent Complex Behavior in Physical and Biological Systems*. Cambridge: Cambridge University Press, 1998.

Joffe, Josef. *The Myth of America's Decline: Politics, Economics, and a Half Century of False Prophecies*. New York: Liveright, 2015.

Johnson, Neil. *Simply Complexity: A Clear Guide to Complexity Theory*. London: Oneworld, 2012.

Kahneman, Daniel. *Thinking, Fast and Slow*. New York: Farrar, Straus and Giroux, 2011.

Keynes, John Maynard. *The General Theory of Employment, Interest, and Money*. New York: Harvest/Harcourt Inc., 1964.

———. *Monetary Reform*. New York: Harcourt, Brace and Company, 1924.

Kindleberger, Charles P. *The World in Depression 1929–1939*. Berkeley: University of California Press, 1986.

King, Mervyn. *The End of Alchemy: Money, Banking, and the Future of the Global Economy*. New York: W. W. Norton & Company, 2016.

Kissinger, Henry. *World Order*. New York: Penguin Press, 2014.

Klein, Naomi. *The Shock Doctrine: The Rise of Disaster Capitalism*. New York: Picador, 2007.

Kuhn, Thomas S. *The Structure of Scientific Revolutions*. Chicago: University of Chicago Press, 1996.

Lenin, V. I. *Imperialism: The Highest Stage of Capitalism*. Mansfield Center, CT: Martino Publishing, 2011.

Lindsay, Lawrence B. *Conspiracies of the Ruling Class: How to Break Their Grip Forever*. New York: Simon & Schuster, 2016.

Lowenstein, Roger. *When Genius Failed: The Rise and Fall of Long-Term Capital Management*. New York: Random House, 2000.

Makin, John H. *The Global Debt Crisis: America's Growing Involvement*. New York: Basic Books, 1984.

Mandelbrot, Benoit B. *The Fractal Geometry of Nature*. New York: W. H. Freeman and Company, 1983.

Martin, Felix. *Money: The Unauthorized Biography*. New York: Alfred A. Knopf, 2014.

Marx, Karl. *Selected Writings*. Edited by David McLellan. New York: Oxford University Press, 1977.

McGrayne, Sharon Bertsch. *The Theory That Would Not Die: How Bayes' Rule Cracked the Enigma Code, Hunted Down Russian Submarines, and Emerged Triumphant from Two Centuries of Controversy*. (New Haven, CT: Yale University Press, 2011).

Mian, Atif, and Amir Sufi. *House of Debt: How They (and You) Caused the Great Recession, and How We Can Prevent It from Happening Again*. Chicago: University of Chicago Press, 2014.

Milanovic, Branko. *Global Inequality: A New Approach for the Age of Globalization*. Cambridge, MA: Belknap Press, 2016.

Miller, John H., and Scott E. Page. *Complex Adaptive Systems: An Introduction to Computational Models of Social Life*. Princeton, NJ: Princeton University Press, 2007.

Minsky, Hyman P. *Stabilizing an Unstable Economy*. New York: McGraw Hill, 2008.

Mitchell, Melanie. *Complexity: A Guided Tour*. New York: Oxford University Press, 2011.

Murray, Charles. *In Our Hands: A Plan to Replace the Welfare State*. Washington, DC: AEI Press, 2016.

Noah, Timothy. *The Great Divergence: America's Growing Inequality Crisis and What We Can Do About It*. New York: Bloomsbury Press, 2012.

Palley, Thomas I. *From Financial Crisis to Stagnation: The Destruction of Shared Prosperity and the Role of Economics*, 1st edition. New York: Cambridge University Press, 2012.

Piketty, Thomas. *Capital in the Twenty-First Century*. Cambridge, MA: Belknap Press, 2014.

Popper, Karl R. *The Open Society and Its Enemies: Volume 1, The Spell of Plato*. Princeton, NJ: Princeton University Press, 1971.

———. *The Open Society and Its Enemies: Volume 2, The High Tide of Prophecy: Hegel, Marx, and the Aftermath*. Princeton, NJ: Princeton University Press, 1971.

Rappleye, Charles. *Herbert Hoover in the White House: The Ordeal of the Presidency*. New York: Simon & Schuster, 2016.

Reinhart, Carmen M., and Kenneth S. Rogoff. *This Time Is Different: Eight Centuries of Financial Folly*. Princeton, NJ: Princeton University Press, 2009.

Ricardo, David. *The Principles of Political Economy and Taxation*. Mineola, NY: Dover Publications, 2004.

Rickards, James. *Currency Wars: The Making of the Next Global Crisis*. New York: Portfolio/Penguin, 2011.

———. *The Death of Money: The Coming Collapse of the International Monetary System*. New York: Portfolio/Penguin, 2014.

Roberts, Richard. *Saving the City: The Great Financial Crisis of 1914*. Oxford: Oxford University Press, 2013.

Rodrik, Dani. *Economics Rules: The Rights and Wrongs of the Dismal Science*. New York: W. W. Norton & Company, Inc., 2015.

Rogoff, Kenneth S. *The Curse of Cash*. Princeton, NJ: Princeton University Press, 2016.

Schelling, Thomas C. *Micromotives and Macrobehavior*. New York: W. W. Norton & Company, Inc., 2006.

Schumpeter, Joseph A. *Capitalism, Socialism and Democracy*. New York: Harper Perennial, 2008.

———. *Ten Great Economists: From Marx to Keynes*. New York: Galaxy Books, 1965.

Shlaes, Amity. *The Forgotten Man: A New History of the Great Depression*. New York: Harper Perennial, 2007.

Silber, William L. *When Washington Shut Down Wall Street: The Great Financial Crisis of 1914 and the Origins of America's Monetary Supremacy*. Princeton, NJ: Princeton University Press, 2007.

Silverglate, Harvey A. *Three Felonies a Day: How the Feds Target the Innocent*. New York: Encounter Books, 2011.

Somary, Felix. *The Raven of Zurich: The Memoirs of Felix Somary*. New York: St. Martin's Press, 1986.

Sorkin, Andrew Ross. *Too Big to Fail*. New York: Penguin Books, 2010.

Spiro, David E. *The Hidden Hand of American Hegemony: Petrodollar Recycling and International Markets*. Ithaca, NY: Cornell University Press, 1999.

Steil, Benn. *The Battle of Bretton Woods: John Maynard Keynes, Harry Dexter White, and the Making of a New World Order*. Princeton, NJ: Princeton University Press, 2013.

Surowiecki, James. *The Wisdom of Crowds: Why the Many Are Smarter Than the Few and How Collective Wisdom Shapes Business, Economics, Societies, and Nations*. New York: Anchor Books, 2005.

Taibbi, Matt. *The Divide: American Injustice in the Age of the Wealth Gap*. New York: Spiegel & Grau, 2014.

Taylor, Frederick. *The Downfall of Money: Germany's Hyperinflation and the Destruction of the Middle Class*. New York: Bloomsbury Press, 2013.

Temin, Peter. *Lessons from the Great Depression*. Cambridge, MA: MIT Press, 1991.

———, and David Vines. *The Leaderless Economy: Why the World Economic System Fell Apart and How to Fix It*. Princeton, NJ: Princeton University Press, 2013.

Tett, Gillian. *Fool's Gold: The Inside Story of J. P. Morgan and How Wall St. Greed Corrupted Its Bold Dream and Created a Financial Catastrophe*. New York: Free Press, 2009.

Tuohy, Brian. *Disaster Government: National Emergencies, Continuity of Government and You*. Kenosha, WI: Mofo Press LLC, 2013.

Turner, Adair. *Between Debt and the Devil: Money, Credit, and Fixing Global Finance*. Princeton, NJ: Princeton University Press, 2016.

Viera, Edwin Jr. *Pieces of Eight: The Monetary Powers and Disabilities of the United States Constitution,* Second Revised Edition, Volume I and Volume II. Chicago: R. R. Donnelley & Sons, Inc./GoldMoney Foundation, 2011.

Vonnegut, Kurt. *Cat's Cradle*. New York: Dial Press, 2010.

Waldrop, M. Mitchell. *Complexity: The Emerging Science at the Edge of Order and Chaos*. New York: Simon & Schuster, 1992.

Wallas, Graham. *Human Nature in Politics*. Middletown, CT: The Perfect Library, reprint, 1920.

Zeihan, Peter. *The Accidental Superpower: The Next Generation of American Preeminence and the Coming Global Disorder*. New York: Twelve, 2014.

INDEX